D1058510

URBAN MORTGAGE LENDING: COMPARATIVE MARKETS AND EXPERIENCE

NATIONAL BUREAU OF ECONOMIC RESEARCH

FINANCIAL RESEARCH PROGRAM

Studies in Urban Mortgage Financing

1. Urban Mortgage Lending by Life Insurance Companies, by R. J. Saulnier
2. The Impact of Government on Real Estate Finance in the United States, by Miles L. Colean
3. Urban Real Estate Markets: Characteristics and Financing, by Ernest M. Fisher
4. History and Policies of the Home Owners' Loan Corporation, by C. Lowell Harriss
5. Commercial Bank Activities in Urban Mortgage Financing, by Carl F. Behrens
6. Urban Mortgage Lending: Comparative Markets and Experience, by J. E. Morton

Urban Mortgage Lending: Comparative Markets and Experience

BY J. E. MORTON

A STUDY BY THE
NATIONAL BUREAU OF ECONOMIC RESEARCH, NEW YORK

PUBLISHED BY
PRINCETON UNIVERSITY PRESS, PRINCETON
1956

London: Geoffrey Cumberlege, Oxford University Press

L.C. CARD 56-8372

J. E. Morton has been associated with the National Bureau of Economic Research for a number of years while professor of statistics at Cornell University, and at present is chief statistician at the National Science Foundation. He holds degrees from the Universities of Prague and Geneva.

Printed in the United States of America
by Princeton University Press, Princeton, New Jersey

Relation of the Directors to the Work and Publications of the National Bureau of Economic Research

1. The object of the National Bureau of Economic Research is to ascertain and to present to the public important economic facts and their interpretation in a scientific and impartial manner. The Board of Directors is charged with the responsibility of ensuring that the work of the National Bureau is carried on in strict conformity with this object.

2. To this end the Board of Directors shall appoint one or more Directors of Research.

3. The Director or Directors of Research shall submit to the members of the Board, or to its Executive Committee, for their formal adoption, all specific proposals concerning researches to be instituted.

4. No report shall be published until the Director or Directors of Research shall have submitted to the Board a summary drawing attention to the character of the data and their utilization in the report, the nature and treatment of the problems involved, the main conclusions, and such other information as in their opinion would serve to determine the suitability of the report for publication in accordance with the principles of the National Bureau.

5. A copy of any manuscript proposed for publication shall also be submitted to each member of the Board. For each manuscript to be so submitted a special committee shall be appointed by the President, or at his designation by the Executive Director, consisting of three Directors selected as nearly as may be one from each general division of the Board. The names of the special manuscript committee shall be stated to each Director when the summary and report described in paragraph (4) are sent to him. It shall be the duty of each member of the committee to read the manuscript. If each member of the special committee signifies his approval within thirty days, the manuscript may be published. If each member of the special committee has not signified his approval within thirty days of the transmittal of the report and manuscript, the Director of Research shall then notify each member of the Board, requesting approval or disapproval of publication, and thirty additional days shall be granted for this purpose. The manuscript shall then not be published unless at least a majority of the entire Board and a two-thirds majority of those members of the Board who shall have voted on the proposal within the time fixed for the receipt of votes on the publication proposed shall have approved.

6. No manuscript may be published, though approved by each member of the special committee, until forty-five days have elapsed from the transmittal of the summary and report. The interval is allowed for the receipt of any memorandum of dissent or reservation, together with a brief statement of his reasons, that any member may wish to express; and such memorandum of dissent or reservation shall be published with the manuscript if he so desires. Publication does not, however, imply that each member of the Board has read the manuscript, or that either members of the Board in general, or of the special committee, have passed upon its validity in every detail.

7. A copy of this resolution shall, unless otherwise determined by the Board, be printed in each copy of every National Bureau book.

(Resolution adopted October 25, 1926
and revised February 6, 1933 and February 24, 1941)

NATIONAL BUREAU OF ECONOMIC RESEARCH

FOREWORD

THE plan of Professor Morton's study of the comparative markets and experience of the major mortgage lending agencies was drawn with two principal purposes in mind. The first was to summarize the factual materials bearing on the markets and lending experience of specific institutions that have been developed in the mortgage lending studies made under the National Bureau's Urban Real Estate Finance Project; the second was to supplement these materials with information on mutual savings banks, which were not covered in the National Bureau's monographs, and on the mortgage market as a whole, in order to place the activities and experience of each of the principal lending agencies in proper perspective. Developed on this design, the study accomplishes more than a mere summary of facts pertaining to mortgage lending institutions; its cross-institutional comparisons contribute significantly to our understanding of the supply side of the mortgage market, and its review of risk studies in this field brings into sharper focus the lessons that may be learned from the mortgage investment experience of the last thirty years.

The study was made under the Financial Research Program of the National Bureau with the support of funds received from the Association of Reserve City Bankers; the Life Insurance Investment Research Committee, acting for the Life Insurance Association of America and the American Life Convention; and the Rockefeller Foundation. Many of the substantive findings which it presents are drawn from earlier monographs in the Urban Real Estate Finance series, where specific acknowledgments are made of assistance received from public and private agencies in compiling relevant information. Special mention should be made here, however, of the cooperation of the Bureau of the Census, which supplied certain preliminary tabulations from the 1950 Survey of Residential Financing. It is a pleasure to express the gratitude of the National Bureau of Economic Research for the aid received from these sources.

R. J. SAULNIER
Director, Financial Research Program

December 1954

ACKNOWLEDGMENTS

THIS volume is in essence a summary of findings of several monographs developed through the Urban Real Estate Finance Project of the Financial Research Program of the National Bureau of Economic Research. I am, therefore, very much indebted to the authors of those studies, and especially to R. J. Saulnier, not only as an author of one of the major monographs but also as the director of the project; without his candid comments and persistent encouragement this study would not have been completed. My thanks are also due to Donald S. Thompson and Ralph A. Young, under whose guidance the project was initiated, and to Leo Grebler, David Durand, Simon Kuznets, and Geoffrey H. Moore for helpful comments later.

The nature of the project makes it impossible to mention all the institutions, lending officers, and others who cooperated at many stages of the investigation. To all of them my indebtedness is great. I also wish to acknowledge my debt to the research staffs of the Board of Governors of the Federal Reserve System and the several Federal Reserve Banks for valuable suggestions; to Morris H. Hansen and William N. Hurwitz of the Bureau of the Census for their advice on some of the more intricate aspects of sample design, and to Howard G. Brunsman and Wayne F. Daugherty of the same agency for making available preliminary findings of the census Survey of Residential Financing.

Finally, I am deeply grateful to Doris P. Warner, and to Catherine P. Martin and her computing staff, for untiring and generous assistance. Mary Phelps contributed helpful editorial suggestions, and H. Irving Forman drew the charts.

J. E. MORTON
Cornell University

CONTENTS

≺ TABLES ≻

≺ CHARTS ≻

URBAN MORTGAGE LENDING: COMPARATIVE MARKETS AND EXPERIENCE

INTRODUCTION

BY R. J. SAULNIER

It is doubtful whether any financial development in the United States during the last half century is as significant in its economic effect as the change that has occurred in the structure of outstanding debt. The leading feature of this change has been an increase in the ratio of public to private debt, especially in the ratio of the federal debt to total private debt, but changes having far-reaching effects have taken place also within the private debt sector. The most important of these has been the sharp increase of nonfarm mortgage debt—the subject of the present volume. As Dr. Morton points out in the opening pages of his book, the nonfarm mortgage debt of all borrowers—corporate and noncorporate—rose from 28.1 percent of private long-term debt in 1920 to 54.7 percent in 1953; and the proportion of mortgage debt secured by one- to four-family (mainly one-family) structures rose from around 50 percent in 1925 to 70 percent in 1953.

Notable changes have also taken place on the supply side of the urban mortgage market, the most important of which has been an increase in the proportion of nonfarm mortgage credit supplied by institutional lenders—insurance companies, commercial banks, mutual savings banks, and savings and loan associations. As Dr. Morton points out in his text, the urban mortgage debt held by these lenders increased from 50 percent of the total outstanding in 1920 to nearly 80 percent in 1953. Institutional investors are not committing a larger proportion of their assets to mortgage investments than they were in the twenties, but the proportion of savings which flows through these intermediaries has increased so rapidly in recent years that they now hold an increased part of the outstanding debt. This increase in the importance of institutional investors has naturally exerted great influence on the organization and operation of the mortgage market and has appreciably raised the interest of these institutions in the mortgage as an investment medium. There can be no doubt, therefore, as to the importance and timeliness of this study.

Changes occurring at the financial level of the economy are often reflections of changes in the sphere of production, and to a considerable degree the shifts that have taken place in the composition of long-term debt are of this type. The increase in the ratio of public to private debt, for example, reflects the spectacular rise in this century of governmental activity, growing in good part out of the Great Depression and the nation's involvement in two world-wide wars; the upward surges of mortgage debt in the twenties and again in the late forties and early fifties reflect the vast homebuilding and general construction expansions which followed the termination of World Wars I and II. The growth within total urban mortgage debt of home mortgage debt also reflects basic changes in the housing and home financing markets. Between 1920 and 1940 both the proportion of owner-occupied homes mortgaged and the amount of mortgage debt on these homes relative to their value increased appreciably; the frequency of home ownership, on the other hand, was roughly unchanged over the two decades. Just the opposite changes occurred between 1940 and 1950; the frequency of mortgage debt and the ratio of debt to value either were unchanged or fell, whereas the frequency of home ownership rose sharply. Finally, the increase in the proportion of the mortgage debt held by institutional lenders can be traced to the fact that federal mortgage loan insurance and guarantee programs have given residential mortgages a higher investment quality than they previously possessed. But it is not the author's object to explore the reasons why these changes have occurred, interesting though this effort would be; the important fact is that events have conspired to give the urban mortgage, and in particular the home mortgage, more prominence as an investment medium than it has ever had before.

It was principally a recognition of these facts that led the National Bureau in 1945 to initiate its Urban Real Estate Finance Project. Dr. Morton's book summarizes those studies made under the Project that deal with the lending policies and experience of particular institutions. He has done more, however, than merely summarize the findings of separate studies: he makes cross-institutional comparisons and gives a picture of the urban mortgage investment market as a whole, carrying his account through 1953. The studies on which he draws especially are:

Urban Mortgage Lending by Life Insurance Companies
by R. J. Saulnier,
Commercial Bank Activities in Urban Mortgage Financing
by Carl F. Behrens,
History and Policies of the Home Owners' Loan Corporation
by C. Lowell Harriss,

Urban Real Estate Markets: Characteristics and Financing
by Ernest M. Fisher,

and the unpublished work of E. E. Edwards on savings and loan associations. Other monographic studies in this field have been utilized, such as John Lintner's volume on the mortgage lending activities of Massachusetts mutual savings banks, prepared in the Division of Research at the Harvard University Graduate School of Business Administration under a grant from the Mutual Savings Banks Association of Massachusetts.

The first three chapters of Dr. Morton's study focus on the supply side of the mortgage market. They elaborate on the broad shifts mentioned above and compare the amounts of mortgages held by various institutional investors. It is perhaps unnecessary to comment on this portion of the book, but it may be useful to summarize the findings, presented there and in later chapters, in which the author traces the changes that have occurred since 1920 in the characteristics of mortgage loans and shows what there is to learn from loan experience studies as to the factors that are most significant in gauging the quality of mortgage investments.

Turning to the first of these matters—the characteristics of outstanding loans—Dr. Morton summarizes data obtained through special sample surveys of the portfolios of institutional lenders as of 1946-47, and draws on the 1950 census survey of residential financing. The foremost fact to be noted here is the extent to which mortgage loans are now made under federal insurance or guarantee. In developments starting with the Federal Housing Administration program in 1934 and continuing with the Veterans' Administration program which began in 1944, the home mortgage debt and the debt secured by multifamily projects have increasingly been made in an insured or guaranteed form, until, as the author puts it, the problem of investment analysis has become less one of judging the risk quality of individual mortgages than of understanding and correctly anticipating the loan insurance and guarantee policies of the federal government. At the present time something over two-fifths of the mortgage debt on one- to four-family homes and almost as high a proportion of the debt on multifamily properties are protected by federal insurance or guarantee. It should be observed, however, that although the proportion in the one- to four-family dwelling field rose rapidly to its present level, it has tended to level out recently, suggesting that a rough balance may have been struck between the federally protected and the conventional field of home lending.

Bearing directly on the question of how far one might expect the mortgage insurance and guarantee feature to spread, and possibly indicating some limitation on its use, are the data brought out by the author on the tendency for insured and guaranteed lending to be concentrated in certain segments of the mortgage market. In general, insured and guaranteed loans are made with greatest frequency on homes, and to borrowers, in an intermediate economic position. Whether one takes the borrower's income, the value of the house, or the occupational status of the owner as a basis for comparing conventional loans with insured or guaranteed loans, the evidence shows that insured and guaranteed loans are most prevalent in the intermediate range and that conventional loans are most important at the upper and lower ends of the scale. This fact has many interesting implications, not the least of which relates to loan experience. The studies which the author discusses in his final chapter show clearly that the best experience during the trying years of the thirties was on the very types of loans that are now most frequently protected by federal loan insurance or guarantees—those secured by small, medium-priced dwellings—and that the least favorable experience was on those that are still made predominantly without such protection. This suggests that one may overestimate the risk-reducing effects of federal insurance and guarantee programs on the mortgage market as a whole and appreciably underestimate the risk elements which that market still contains.

The facts which the author uses to describe the mortgage loan portfolios of institutional lenders, and which inferentially suggest the markets which these lenders serve, were employed in the separate monographic studies to depict lending by particular agencies, but in his use of them he seeks mainly to bring out the points of difference and similarity among lenders in the kinds of loans made, and thus to reveal whatever functional specialization there is on the supply side of the urban mortgage market. As might be expected, institutional specialization is most marked in connection with the type of property underlying the transaction. Judged by the number of loans held, loans secured by one- to four-family structures, and notably by single family homes, predominate in the portfolios of institutional lenders. Nine-tenths of the number of loans held by insurance companies and commercial banks and nearly all of those held by savings and loan associations were in this category. A somewhat different picture emerges when the dollar volume of loans held is taken as the basis of comparison. By this measure, 44 percent, 64 percent, and 94 percent, respectively, of the mortgage debt held by insurance companies, commercial banks, and savings and loan associations were secured, as of 1946-47, by one- to four-family residential properties. Nearly 50 percent of the mortgage loans of mutual savings banks were secured as of the end of 1947 by one- to four-family structures. Life insurance companies, and to a lesser degree mutual savings banks and commercial banks, extend substantial amounts of their mortgage credit outside of the small home field; savings and loan associations, on the other hand, devote their resources almost exclusively to the financing of single family dwellings. In so far as there is functional specialization, therefore, it is in the nearly total limitation of the savings and loan associations to home mortgage financing, and, looked at from the borrower's viewpoint, in the fact that facilities for the financing of large residential and commercial properties are available primarily among the life insurance companies, and to a lesser extent among the mutual savings banks and commercial banks.

There are differences also among institutional mortgage lenders in the terms on which loans are made, but these are overshadowed in importance by the striking changes that have occurred in the last twenty years in the terms on which all lenders extend mortgage credit, changes that are brought out clearly for the first time in the data which the Urban Real Estate Finance Project obtained on the characteristics of loans made since 1920. Perhaps the most important of these changes has been the spread of the principle of full amortization. Savings and loan associations have always made the bulk of their mortgage loans on that basis, but only a relatively small percentage of the loans made by life insurance companies in the twenties—a quarter or less—were fully amortized. The loans made by commercial banks in the twenties were even less frequently extended on a full repayment basis. Less than 15 percent of the amount of credit secured by one- to four-family structures and less than 10 percent secured by other types of property required full repayment by maturity, and in a large proportion of the cases the loan contracts made no provision at all for amortization. The reason for this, quite obviously, was that commercial banks were compelled to make their loans with contract maturities so short that only very little repayment, if any, was feasible. It was not until the McFadden Act was passed in 1927 that commercial banks were permitted to go beyond one year in the maturities of their nonfarm mortgage loans, and even then the outer limit was set at five years. Within that framework it was obviously impossible to require any substantial repayment. It was because of statutory restrictions that the practice grew of taking what reduction could be obtained in a mortgage loan at its maturity and then remaking it for another short span of years. There were good reasons, of course, why such severe limitations were written into the banking statutes, but the debacle of the thirties proved beyond question that they were inadequate for the task for which they were designed; what was required was a set of terms more closely adapted to the realities of the family budget.

The change that came with the initiation of federal mortgage loan insurance was nowhere more striking than in the adoption of full-amortization repayment plans. Insured and guaranteed loans are necessarily made on a full-amortization basis, but the interesting fact is that conventional loans are now, in the majority of cases, similarly written. Of the conventional loans secured by one- to four-family properties that were outstanding in the portfolios of insurance companies and commercial banks in 1946-47, only about a tenth were nonamortized, only about 25 percent were partially amortized, and the remainder provided for full repayment by maturity. Straight loans providing for no amortization are also infrequent in lending on income properties by insurance companies and commercial banks, but in this case contracts calling for only partial amortization by maturity are fairly common, especially on the larger loans. Even so, about one-half of the number of loans on commercial and multi-family structures called for full repayment by maturity.

The wide adoption of the amortization principle is regarded by many observers as having placed the urban mortgage loan on a greatly improved level of investment quality, as contrasted with the nonamortized loans so characteristic of the twenties. A judgment on the merits of this view must, however, take into account the fact that the trend to full amortization is but one side of the revolution in home mortgage lending practices that has occurred in the last twenty years. As has been pointed out above, it was the legal requirement of short maturities that required nonamortization clauses, and with the release of this restriction the lending institutions were in a position to require full or partial repayment by maturity. In fact, the much lauded feature of full repayment by maturity has been won at the price of extended maturities and has been accompanied also by a substantial rise in ratios of amount of debt contracted under the mortgage to the value of the underlying security.

Dr. Morton's data are fortunately very illuminating of both of these trends. He shows not only that large segments of the conventional loans outstanding around 1946-47 carried long repayment terms, but that they had been made on the basis of quite high loan-to-value ratios. Thus, of the amount of conventional credit on one- to four-family dwellings outstanding when the recent surveys were taken, 68 percent of that held by insurance companies and 47 percent of the savings and loan association total had an original contract maturity of fifteen years or more. Only 8 percent of the amount of commercial bank credit was of comparable length, but 44 percent of the banks' home loan volume had an original contract maturity of from ten to fourteen years. As for loan-to-value ratios, nearly 80 percent of the amount of combined conventional and insured home mortgage credit outstanding in 1946-47 on the books of three institutional lenders—insurance companies, commercial banks, and savings and loan associations—involved borrower equities at the time the loans were made of less than 40 percent.

Although there have been times—notably in the housing boom of the late forties—when the liberalization of home financing terms produced some increase in housing prices, the liberal terms on which mortgage loans are currently made have doubtless broadened the market for sales of homes and made it possible for families with a given income and savings to acquire, and eventually to own outright, a better residence than they could otherwise afford. Yet there is another side to the story: namely, the impact of more liberal terms on the investment quality of mortgage loans. To Dr. Morton's chapter on this matter many students of mortgage finance may turn for guidance, for he summarizes a mass of new facts on the effect of various characteristics of loan contracts, borrowers, and underlying properties on the investor's experience with mortgages.

Considering the whole body of evidence which the author reviews, the factor of predominant importance in mortgage loan experience appears to be the phase of the business cycle in which the loan is made. The facts suggest that the closer a loan is made to a major downturn in consumer income and in real estate values, the greater the chance that it will end in default. It is far from clear, however, why this is the case. It may be said that the record of the twenties merely confirms a credit principle of long standing, namely that a seasoned loan—certainly one on which an appreciable reduction of debt had been made—is of much higher quality than an otherwise similar loan that is unseasoned. Reassuring as this is when one contemplates the fact that most loans are nowadays made on an installment basis, it raises doubts concerning the inherent quality of loan portfolios in times when the turnover of loans is high and only a small proportion of those outstanding have been on the books of lending institutions long enough to have had any appreciable degree of seasoning. The fact is that even fully amortized loans made shortly before the 1929 crash fared poorly in the thirties; indeed, only very little better than those made on a nonamortized basis. Perhaps the chief lesson to be drawn from the studies is that a sustained level of aggregate income, and the limitation of individual loans to amounts that are moderate in relation to borrower income, are the foundations of favorable loan experience, and that full amortization, for all its advantages, is an uncertain protection against default in an economy which experiences sudden and severe deflation.

There is also the possibility—and this is in no sense inconsistent with the seasoning hypothesis—that the high rate of foreclosure on loans made just before the 1929 reversal may have been due to a deterioration in the quality of new loans which occurred at that time—and which may be characteristic of cycles generally. It is known, at any rate, that there was some tendency in the second half of the twenties for loan-to-value ratios to rise, and for maturities to lengthen; other things may have occurred to lower credit quality, such as more liberal appraisals of property and less rigorous standards in screening loan applications, though we have no systematic evidence for these points. There can be no certainty that a deterioration of credit terms is a recurring cyclical phenomenon, since the liberalization of terms which occurred in the twenties was in part a secular movement and in part a fortuitous legal development—the McFadden Act opened the road for more liberal bank lending in 1927. At the same time, *a priori* considerations, and the experience with domestic corporate bonds and foreign bonds in the twenties, suggest this as a strong likelihood.

Supporting the belief that a pre-1929 lowering of loan quality was significantly implicated in the mortgage difficulties of the early thirties is the fact that among the loans made in the years 1920-29 the frequency of default increased with increases in contract maturity and in loan-to-value ratios. It may be argued that a loan on which the original maturity is realistically geared to feasible repayment possibilities is a better loan than one that requires successive extensions, and that a liberal loan-to-value ratio on a first mortgage loan is to be desired—even on grounds of investment quality—over a more conservative first mortgage supplemented by high cost borrowing on a secondary lien. Yet the fact is that the experience on the more liberally designed loans was less favorable than on those of a more conservative cast. Again, experience suggests that the advantages of liberal lending can be safely indulged in only when consumer income is maintained or increased.

There are other characteristics of loan contracts that *a priori* considerations suggest have a significant bearing on the quality of loans, but the importance of most of these could not be evaluated in the Project's experience studies for lack of relevant information. The quality and trend of the neighborhood in which the property is located, and the condition of the property itself, are doubtless critical factors, but there is no systematic information on these points. Nor is a great deal known as to the relation between the personal characteristics of borrowers and loan experience. A special analysis of loans made by the Home Owners' Loan Corporation showed that age exerts an appreciable influence on loan experience —young and old persons proved to have much less favorable records as mortgagors than those of middle age—but such matters as the occupation, employment stability, etc., of the borrower could not be evaluated.

For all of the gaps that inadequate data make inevitable, there is much in the account that Dr. Morton gives here of factors affecting loan experience that will interest the practical man engaged in lending money on the security of real estate; there is a good deal, also, that should interest the economic theoretician, especially in connection with interest theory. The study makes it possible to test, at least tentatively, whether mortgage lenders have been able to make adjustments in the interest rates that they charge mortgagors that properly compensate for the differences in the losses actually realized on various categories of loans. Presumably, most lenders attempt to make such adjustments, at least as between broad classes of loans. It would be a mistake, however, to picture them as unerring calculators of the probabilities involved, or even as being in a position exactly to make the adjustments that would be dictated by perfect knowledge and foresight when they must somehow survive in competition with less knowledgeable and prescient competitors. Yet it is reasonable to expect that there would be some effort to make appropriate adjustments, and it may be asked whether the record reveals any appreciable success.

Our basis for testing the success or failure of mortgage lenders in making such adjustments is far from perfect, but the record does show that differences in contract interest rates as between groups of loans were as often as not the opposite of what would have been necessary to adjust for differences in eventual loss rates. Referring to the author's Table 46, twenty-seven comparisons can be made of differences in interest rates and in loss rates as between pairs of loan categories—fifteen for life insurance companies and twelve for commercial banks. Among the 27, there were 12 cases in which the differences in contract rates were the opposite of what subsequent experience shows would have been necessary to correct for differences in losses. In 15 cases the differences in contract rates were in the right direction, but for the most part they did not go far enough: 13 were less than what experience eventually showed was necessary, 1 was more than necessary, and only 1 sufficed to equate the realized yields on the two groups of loans being compared. In short, the lenders made the wrong adjustments about as frequently as they made the right ones, and where they made the right ones they almost always failed to go as far as they should. Life insurance company experience in this respect was almost exactly the same as that of commercial banks; both groups of lenders seemed to have greater success in making the needed adjustments on loans secured by income properties than on loans secured by one- to four-family residences.

Before formulating any conclusions on the basis of this record, it should be recalled that the loan officer must make interest rate adjustments for differences in lending costs as well as for differences in probable losses. Our lack of information concerning cost differentials seriously impairs our ability, therefore, to make judgments as to the success or failure of the adjustment effort. Cost differentials would certainly have to be taken into account in some of the comparisons that can be made in Table 46—for example, as between loans secured by one- to four-family properties and those otherwise secured—though there is presumably much less need for taking them into account in comparing loans that differ, for example, with respect to loan-to-value ratios.

There is much else in the materials of this study which the economic theorist should find useful. There is the evidence on the extent to which contract rates of interest are modified before loans are actually extinguished, the tendency for lender competition to be increased in recent years, doubtless as a result of loan insurance and guarantee programs, and the tendency for regional differences in interest rates to become less marked. The evidence on the relation of lending costs to portfolio size is interesting, though hardly as elaborate (if that could ever be) as would be necessary to test conventional beliefs concerning the relation of cost to scale of operations. Like many empirical studies, however, the one in hand will serve best to clarify specific problems of practice and policy as these arise.

≺ 1 ≻

THE NONFARM MORTGAGE DEBT

THE importance of urban mortgages for the debt structure of the United States can hardly be overrated. Considering size only, we find that more than one-half of the entire privately issued and privately held long-term debt of this country, corporate and noncorporate, is in the form of mortgages. In turn, about nine-tenths of the mortgage debt is secured by urban (nonfarm) real estate. It is not at all surprising, therefore, that the problems connected with urban mortgage financing should have commanded much attention, not only in connection with the real estate market, which depends heavily on mortgage financing, but also within the wider framework of the economy as a whole. The present chapter sketches the main lines of growth and change in nonfarm mortgage debt and its components since 1920.

Trends in Nonfarm Mortgage Debt

The flow of mortgage funds into the urban real estate market has undergone substantial changes since 1920, affecting both the absolute and the relative size of the urban mortgage debt. Not only the dollar amount of nonfarm mortgage debt, but also its ratio to the total private long-term debt, is considerably larger today than it was thirty some years ago.

After a spectacular rise during the early twenties the volume of outstanding urban mortgage debt reached a peak in 1930, declined somewhat during the depression, and found a level in 1936 well above its level after World War I (Table 1). A second wave of growth, which started in 1939 and was proceeding by 1941 at a fairly modest rate, was interrupted by World War II, only to be resumed after the war at a considerably more rapid rate of increase.

Thus the urban mortgage debt increased from 1920 through 1953 by nearly $80 billion, to an amount six times its earlier size, while total private long-term debt about tripled. Nonfarm mortgages, which represented less than three-tenths of the private long-term debt in 1920, constituted over one-half of the entire private long-term debt by 1953. Urban mortgages had become one of the most important components of the nation's credit structure, exceeding in size the net long-term debt of the entire corporate sector of the economy.

TABLE 1
Relation of Nonfarm Mortgage Debt to Total Long-Term Debt, 1920-53
(*dollar figures in billions*)

		NONFARM MORTGAGE DEBT			
END OF YEAR	PRIVATE LONG-TERM DEBT[a]	*Corporate and Non-corporate*[b]	*As Per-cent of Private Debt*	*Ratio to Farm Mortgage Debt*	FARM MORTGAGE DEBT[c]
1920	$54.5	$15.3	28.1%	1.5	$10.2
1921	57.3	16.5	28.8	1.5	10.7
1922	59.3	17.9	30.2	1.7	10.8
1923	63.2	20.3	32.1	1.9	10.7
1924	67.0	22.8	34.0	2.3	9.9
1925	70.7	25.7	36.4	2.6	9.7
1926	75.4	28.6	37.9	2.9	9.7
1927	81.1	31.8	39.2	3.2	9.8
1928	85.5	34.7	40.6	3.5	9.8
1929	88.1	36.9	41.9	3.8	9.6
1930	92.5	37.7	40.8	4.0	9.4
1931	90.3	36.5	40.4	4.0	9.1
1932	86.7	34.4	39.7	4.0	8.5
1933	81.9	30.5	37.2	4.0	7.7
1934	77.7	29.5	38.0	3.9	7.6
1935	75.7	28.4	37.5	3.8	7.4
1936	74.1	28.0	37.8	3.9	7.2
1937	74.8	28.0	37.4	4.0	7.0
1938	76.1	28.2	37.1	4.1	6.8
1939	76.0	28.9	38.0	4.4	6.6
1940	76.2	30.0	39.4	4.6	6.5
1941	77.2	31.3	40.5	4.9	6.4
1942	75.5	30.8	40.8	5.1	6.0
1943	72.6	29.9	41.2	5.5	5.4
1944	70.8	29.7	41.9	6.1	4.9
1945	70.1	30.8	43.9	6.4	4.8
1946	78.6	36.9	46.9	7.5	4.9
1947	89.9	43.9	48.8	8.6	5.1
1948	102.9	50.9	49.5	9.6	5.3
1949	112.7	57.1	50.7	10.2	5.6
1950	125.5	66.7	53.1	10.9	6.1
1951	140.3	75.6	53.9	11.5	6.6
1952	155.5	84.0	54.0	11.7	7.2
1953	170.7	93.4	54.7	12.1	7.7

From *Survey of Current Business* (Department of Commerce), September 1953, Tables 1 and 6, pp. 14 and 18, and October 1954, Tables 1 and 6, pp. 14 and 19. Ratios computed after rounding to nearest tenth of a billion.

[a] Includes net corporate long-term debt plus individual and noncorporate mortgage debt.

[b] The corporate nonfarm mortgage component for 1920-28, not available in the Department of Commerce series, was estimated by applying to the data on net corporate long-term debt the 1945-49 ratio of corporate nonfarm mortgage debt to corporate long-term debt. Excludes real estate mortgage bonds and mortgages held by nonfinancial corporations on corporate-owned multifamily and commercial properties.

[c] Includes individual and noncorporate mortgage debt.

During the same period farm mortgage debt declined by 25 percent. Whereas urban mortgage debt at the end of World War I was only about half again as large as the total of farm mortgages outstanding, by 1953 it had grown to about twelve times the size of the farm mortgage debt.

The decline in farm mortgage debt, though gradual, was persistent, reflecting, in the main, slow, long-range downward trends in the agricultural sector of the economy. Nonfarm mortgage debt, on the other hand, differed from the farm debt not only in the direction of its long-range trend; it also displayed less regular changes, suggesting that the more erratic pattern of urban economic growth exerted its effect on the corresponding debt component.

Composition of Urban Mortgage Debt

So far we have been looking at the order of magnitude of the urban real estate debt without considering the particular kind of real estate involved. In evaluating structural and short-term changes it is helpful to know the composition of the debt according to major categories of properties that serve as security. Available material does not permit a detailed description, but it is possible to outline major traits if we are satisfied with a rough breakdown.

Urban real estate has some characteristics of a durable consumer good and corresponds in other respects more nearly to a producer good. From the financing point of view an owner-occupied one-family residence differs markedly, of course, from, say, a loft building; this difference is likely to affect not only the demand for credit and the financial characteristics of the mortgage transaction but also its outcome. It stands to reason, for example, that borrower characteristics are much more important for the outcome of a credit transaction where a consumer good is involved than where the property being financed is of the income-producing type, and that other factors of a more general economic nature might influence the result of a loan contract pertaining to an industrial or commercial property.

A classification of properties into those that are income-producing in character and those of the consumer good type—useful also in studying the social implications of lending activities in the real estate market—is not available. In most cases it is possible to study only one- to four-family properties as against all others, combining residential structures having five or more dwelling units with commercial and industrial properties. In some instances a three-way classification is possible in which "all other" properties are divided into residential structures with five or more dwelling units and those income-producing structures that are nonresidential in character. As an approximation, therefore, properties falling in the category of one- to four-family homes will be considered as roughly corresponding to consumer goods, and the remainder to the income-producing or producer category of goods; but it will be understood that there are some small amounts of income-producing properties included in the one- to four-family group.

By far the greater part of all urban mortgage funds in 1953 were invested in one- to four-family homes (71 percent, as shown in Table 2). Of the remaining funds, two-fifths were invested in multifamily residences (structures with five or more dwelling units) and three-fifths in nonresidential properties. Over the preceding twenty years the one- to four-family group had increased in importance; the remainder, to which we shall refer somewhat loosely as income-producing property, underwent a relative decline, especially in its nonresidential part (Table 2). Between 1925 and 1953 both the outstanding debt secured by income-producing properties and that secured by one- to four-family homes have grown, but the latter much more markedly. Thus, as percentages of total mortgage debt the share secured by structures of the consumer goods type increased while the share secured by income-producing properties diminished.

Summarizing, it may be said that at virtually all times since 1925 the volume of outstanding mortgage debt on one- to four-family homes has exceeded that on income-producing property, and also that the excess increased throughout the period. This increase was particularly pronounced during the depression years and after World War II. By the end of 1953, loan funds secured by one- to four-family residences represented over two-thirds of the total nonfarm real estate debt, and as yet there is no observable tendency for the ratio to decrease.

Debt-to-Value Ratios in Real Estate Finance

There are many connections in which it would be useful to know the equity of owners in urban properties and to be able to trace trends in the ratio of debt outstanding against these properties to their values. A number of difficulties stand in the way of constructing such an index, chief of which is the problem of estimating, year by year, the values that should be attached to the properties. Two sets

TABLE 2
Distribution of Nonfarm Mortgage Debt by Type of Property, 1925-53

END OF YEAR	AMOUNT OUTSTANDING (*billions*)				PERCENTAGE DISTRIBUTION			
	1- to 4-Family	*Multi-family*	*Commer-cial*	*Multifamily and Commercial*	*1- to 4-Family*	*Multi-family*	*Commer-cial*	*Multifamily and Commercial*
1925	$13.0	a	a	$12.7	50.6%	a	a	49.4%
1926	14.8	a	a	13.8	51.7	a	a	48.3
1927	16.4	a	a	15.4	51.6	a	a	48.4
1928	17.9	a	a	16.8	51.6	a	a	48.4
1929	18.9	$6.0	$11.9	17.9	51.4	16.3%	32.3%	48.6
1930	18.9	6.5	12.3	18.8	50.1	17.3	32.6	49.9
1931	18.1	6.2	12.2	18.4	49.6	17.0	33.4	50.4
1932	16.7	6.0	11.7	17.7	48.5	17.5	34.0	51.5
1933	15.4	5.7	9.4	15.1	50.5	18.7	30.8	49.5
1934	15.6	5.1	8.8	13.9	52.9	17.3	29.8	47.1
1935	15.4	4.8	8.2	13.0	54.2	16.9	28.9	45.8
1936	15.4	4.6	8.1	12.7	54.8	16.4	28.8	45.2
1937	15.5	4.5	8.0	12.5	55.4	16.1	28.6	44.6
1938	15.8	4.4	8.1	12.5	55.8	15.6	28.6	44.2
1939	16.3	4.5	8.1	12.6	56.4	15.6	28.0	43.6
1940	17.3	4.6	8.0	12.6	58.0	15.3	26.7	42.0
1941	18.4	4.8	8.1	12.9	58.8	15.3	25.9	41.2
1942	18.2	4.7	7.8	12.5	59.1	15.3	25.6	40.9
1943	17.8	4.6	7.5	12.1	59.5	15.4	25.1	40.5
1944	17.9	4.5	7.3	11.8	60.3	15.1	24.6	39.7
1945	18.5	4.5	7.7	12.2	60.4	14.6	25.0	39.6
1946	23.1	4.9	8.9	13.8	62.6	13.3	24.1	37.4
1947	28.2	5.4	10.3	15.7	64.2	12.3	23.5	35.8
1948	33.3	6.2	11.4	17.6	65.4	12.2	22.4	34.6
1949	37.5	7.1	12.5	19.6	65.7	12.4	21.9	34.3
1950	45.1	8.7	12.9	21.6	67.6	13.1	19.3	32.4
1951	51.9	9.8	13.9	23.7	68.6	13.0	18.4	31.4
1952	58.7	10.6	14.7	25.3	69.9	12.6	17.5	30.1
1953	65.9	11.5	16.0	27.5	70.6	12.3	17.1	29.4

Data for one- to four-family homes are from *Housing Statistics* (Housing and Home Finance Agency), January 1954, p. 20, and *Survey of Current Business* (Department of Commerce), October 1954, Table 6, p. 19. Data for multifamily and commercial properties combined are from the *Survey of Current Business*, September 1953, Table 6, p. 18, and October 1954, Table 6, p. 18, with additional figures, for 1925-28, computed by subtraction of the debt secured by one- to four-family homes from total nonfarm mortgage debt (the latter as shown in Table 1).

Breakdown for multifamily and for commercial properties for the period 1938-53 is from the Board of Governors of the Federal Reserve System, with minor adjustments to the data for 1943, 1944, 1951, and 1952; figures for 1929-37 were developed from earlier estimates published in the *Survey of Current Business*, September 1946, Table 9, p. 17, as follows. The 1938 relationship between the Federal Reserve and the Commerce series of the ratio of debt on multifamily properties to that on multifamily and commercial properties combined was used to adjust yearly percentage ratios—based on the Commerce series—of debt on multifamily residences to the estimated debt on both property types. The adjusted percentages were then applied to the revised estimates of the combined total from the sources noted above.

[a] Not available.

of data on this matter are at hand, different in coverage and involving critical differences in the manner in which valuations are placed on property. The first is a series showing the ratio of mortgage debt on nonfarm residences (inclusive of multifamily structures) to an estimate of the value of nonfarm residential wealth for the years 1896-1952.[1] These data are shown in Chart 1, where it will be seen

CHART 1

Average Ratios of Nonfarm Residential Mortgage Debt to Nonfarm Residential Wealth, 1896-1952

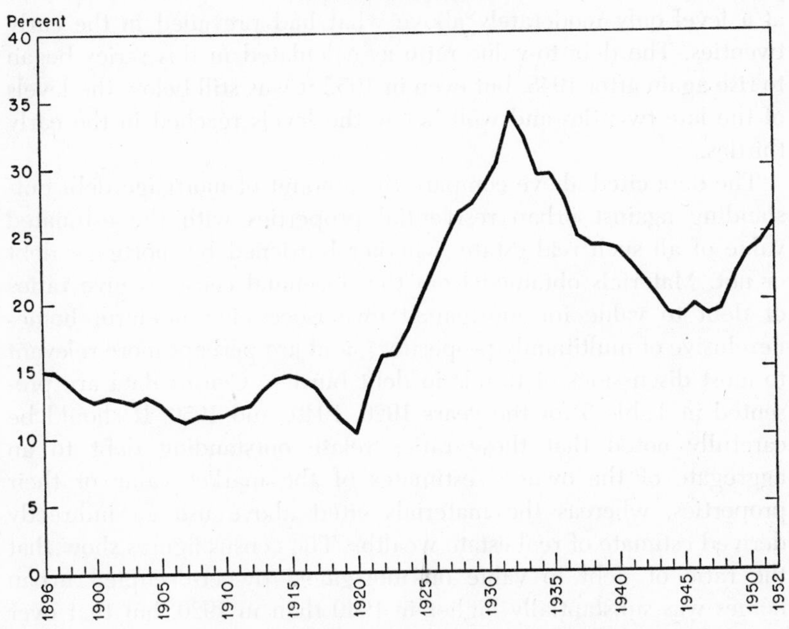

From *Capital Formation in Residential Real Estate: Trends and Prospects*, by Leo Grebler, David M. Blank, and Louis Winnick (Princeton University Press for the National Bureau of Economic Research, in press), Table L-6. The wealth estimates were derived by cumulating residential construction expenditures and include estimated land value.

that the ratio of debt to value is distinctly higher now than it was in the 1890's and in the first two decades of this century. It is important to observe, however, that the ratios of debt to value were substantially lower after World War II than they were in the early thirties.

[1] Leo Grebler, David M. Blank, and Louis Winnick, *Capital Formation in Residential Real Estate: Trends and Prospects* (Princeton University Press for the National Bureau of Economic Research, in press), Appendixes D and L.

The sharp increase of the ratios in the late twenties and early thirties was due at first to an increase in urban residential mortgage debt in the last half of the twenties much more rapid than the increase in the value of urban residential wealth, and then, in the early thirties, to a much sharper decline in the value of the properties than in the amount of the debt. The decline in the ratio thereafter, which continued through much of the forties, was due in the main to a much more rapid increase in the value of properties than in the amount of debt outstanding. The result of these changes was to place the ratio of debt to value at the end of World War II (1945-48) at a level only moderately above what had prevailed in the early twenties. The debt-to-value ratio as calculated in this series began to rise again after 1948, but even in 1952 it was still below the levels of the late twenties and well below the levels reached in the early thirties.

The data cited above compare the amount of mortgage debt outstanding against urban residential properties with the estimated value of all such real estate, whether burdened by mortgage debt or not. Materials obtained from the decennial censuses give ratios of debt to value for mortgaged owner-occupied nonfarm homes (exclusive of multifamily properties), and are perhaps more relevant to most discussions of trends in debt burden. Census data are presented in Table 3 for the years 1920, 1940, and 1950. It should be carefully noted that these ratios relate outstanding debt to an aggregate of the owners' estimates of the market value of their properties, whereas the materials cited above use an indirectly derived estimate of real estate wealth.[2] The census figures show that the ratio of debt to value on mortgaged owner-occupied urban homes was substantially higher in 1940 than in 1920, but that over the decade 1940-50 the ratio fell from over 52 percent to about 45 percent (the comparison is somewhat imprecise because data from the 1950 census are not homogeneous with the earlier figures). It is almost certain that similar information for the years following 1950 would show a rise in this ratio, but unlikely that it would stand at the present time above the 1940 level. The primary reason for the improvement in the debt-to-value position of mortgaged owner-occupied homes over the decade 1940-50 lies, of course, in the twin facts of rising incomes, which made it possible to retire debt at increasing rates, and of inflation in the values of the properties.

[2] For the method used, see Grebler, Blank, and Winnick, *op. cit.*, Appendix D, especially the opening section.

TABLE 3

Regional Differences in the Percentage of Owner-Occupied Nonfarm Homes Mortgaged, and in Debt-to-Value Ratios, 1920, 1940, and 1950

CENSUS DIVISION[a]	PERCENTAGE OF NONFARM HOMES MORTGAGED[b] 1920	1940	1950	DEBT-TO-VALUE RATIO[c] 1920	1940	1950
New England	51.7%	57.6%	56.6%	43.9%	51.4%	41.2% (New England and Middle Atlantic)
Middle Atlantic	51.3	52.0	48.9	44.8	54.5	
East North Central	41.6	47.3	42.9	41.0	51.3	43.1 (East and West North Central)
West North Central	32.4	38.0	36.2	40.4	51.0	
South Atlantic	29.3	39.1	42.0	41.1	51.3	49.0 (South Atlantic, East and West South Central)
East South Central	22.7	33.5	34.9	42.0	51.8	
West South Central	26.0	33.5	37.3	39.2	54.2	
Mountain	29.5	35.0	38.8	41.8	50.2	49.5 (Mountain and Pacific)
Pacific	38.9	48.8	49.9	41.4	51.8	
United States	39.7%	45.3%	44.0%	42.6%	52.4%	45.0%

From various compilations by the Bureau of the Census: *Mortgages on Homes in the United States, 1920,* Monograph No. 2 (Tables 6 and 7, pp. 41 and 45); 16th Census: 1940, *Housing,* Vol. 4, Part 1 (Tables 14 and 15, pp. 63 and 65); and *1950 Census of Housing,* Vol. 1, General Characteristics, Part 1 (Table 1, p. 1-1), and Vol. 4, Residential Financing, Part 1, Chapter 2 (Table 3, pp. 61, 64, 67, 70, and 73).

[a] States included in the census divisions are as follows: *New England*—Maine, New Hampshire, Vermont, Massachusetts, Rhode Island, Connecticut; *Middle Atlantic*—New York, New Jersey, Pennsylvania; *East North Central*—Ohio, Indiana, Illinois, Michigan, Wisconsin; *West North Central*—Minnesota, Iowa, Missouri, North Dakota, South Dakota, Nebraska, Kansas; *South Atlantic*—Delaware, Maryland, District of Columbia, Virginia, West Virginia, North Carolina, South Carolina, Georgia, Florida; *East South Central*—Kentucky, Tennessee, Alabama, Mississippi; *West South Central*—Arkansas, Louisiana, Oklahoma, Texas; *Mountain*—Montana, Idaho, Wyoming, Colorado, New Mexico, Arizona, Utah, Nevada; *Pacific*—Washington, Oregon, California.

[b] Covers owner-occupied homes whose mortgage status was reported (cf. Table 4). Data for 1940 and 1950 cover one- to four-family homes without business use; data for 1920 include some other types of structure.

[c] Represents outstanding mortgage debt as a percentage of the reported value of mortgaged owner-occupied homes. Data for 1940 cover only one-family homes whose owners reported both value of property and indebtedness (including first and junior mortgages). Data for 1920 differ as noted above. Figures for 1950 are mean averages computed from frequency distributions of the number of mortgaged owner-occupied one- to four-family properties by size class of debt-to-value ratio.

Data confirming these trends in mortgage indebtedness are given in Table 4, where it will be seen that the percentage of owner-occupied urban dwellings that were mortgaged was somewhat higher in 1940 than in 1920, though not appreciably so, and that there was a slight decrease in the percentage between 1940 and 1950. The recent Survey of Consumer Finances indicates a moderate increase between 1950 and early 1955.

Materials with which to trace the trend of debt-to-value ratios for tenant-occupied residences are not available; but it appeared from

TABLE 4
Number and Percent of Nonfarm Homes Owner-Occupied and Mortgaged, 1890-1950

	MILLIONS OF OCCUPIED DWELLING UNITS					PERCENTAGE OF:	
			Owner-Occupied				
YEAR	*Total*	*Reporting Tenure*	*Total*	*Reporting Mortgage Status*	*Mortgaged*	*Units of Known Tenure Owner-Occupied*	*Owner-Occupied Dwellings of Known Mortgage Status Mortgaged*
1890	7.9	7.9	2.9	2.9	0.8	37%	28%
1900	10.3	9.8	3.6	3.4	1.1	37	32
1910	14.1	13.7	5.2	5.1	1.7	38	33
1920	17.6	17.2	7.0	6.9	2.7	41	40
1930	23.3	22.9	10.5	[a]	[a]	46	[a]
1940	27.7	27.7	11.4	10.6[b]	4.8[b]	41	45
1950	37.1	37.1	19.8	17.8[b]	7.8[b]	53	44

From the *1950 Census of Housing*, Vol. 1, General Characteristics, Part 1, Tables J, L, and T, pp. XXVIII, XXX, and XXXVI.

[a] Not available.

[b] Figures represent number of owner-occupied dwelling units in one- to four-family structures without business use and are imperfectly comparable with the data for prior years, which represent owners' residences in some other types of structure as well; but the differences are not large enough to invalidate comparisons.

spot checks for urban areas in 1929 and 1933 that the ratios for these properties were at least as high as those for owner-occupied residences,[3] and results from the 1950 census Survey of Residential Financing show similar ratios for the owner-occupied and the rental properties.[4]

[3] Sample data based on a survey of owner-occupied homes in 52 cities and on a survey of tenant-occupied nonfarm homes in 44 cities reveal that the debt-to-value ratios for owner-occupied and for tenant-occupied homes were approximately the same at the end of 1929 (50.8 percent and 51.9 percent, respectively). By the end of 1933 the ratio for tenant-occupied homes was 60.4 percent; for owner-occupied homes, 55.6 percent. (David L. Wickens, *Residential Real Estate*, National Bureau of Economic Research, 1941, Table D3, p. 204.)

[4] The median debt-to-value ratio for two- to four-family owner-occupied nonfarm homes in 1950 was 38 percent, which compares closely with a median

Some interesting differences in mortgage financing trends in different regions of the country appear in Table 3. It will be observed that between 1940 and 1950 there was a tendency for the percentage of nonfarm homes mortgaged to decline in the older and more industrialized regions of the country, and for the frequency of use of mortgage debt to rise in those areas—notably the Southwest and the Far West—where in recent years the increase of urban population has been most rapid; only in the Pacific coast region was a striking growth in urban population accompanied by but a small increase in the already high percentage of mortgaged homes. Thus, the fact that there was a small decline in the national index of mortgage debt frequency between 1940 and 1950 veils important regional differences. It is also true that ratios of debt to value declined much more sharply between 1940 and 1950 in the New England, Middle Atlantic, and North Central sections of the country than in other areas. All of this suggests a close connection of both the frequency of mortgage indebtedness and the ratio of debt to value with rates of industrial and population growth.

Data are not available for 1950 on the debt-to-value ratio for mortgaged properties classified according to the size of the city in which the property is located, but information of this type is presented in Table 5 for 1920 and 1940. These data show that, in

TABLE 5

Debt-to-Value Ratios for Mortgaged Owner-Occupied Homes, 1920 and 1940, by Size of City

<table>
<tr><th>Size of City</th><th>All Owner-Occupied Nonfarm Homes, 1920</th><th>One-Family Owner-Occupied Nonfarm Homes, 1940</th></tr>
<tr><td>100,000 and over</td><td>44.6%</td><td>54.5%</td></tr>
<tr><td>50,000 - 99,999</td><td rowspan="2">42.8</td><td>52.6</td></tr>
<tr><td>25,000 - 49,999</td><td rowspan="2">48.4</td></tr>
<tr><td>Under 25,000</td><td>39.9</td></tr>
<tr><td>United States</td><td>42.6%</td><td>52.4%</td></tr>
</table>

From *Mortgages on Homes in the United States, 1920*, Monograph No. 2 (Bureau of the Census, 1923), p. 102; and 16th Census: 1940, *Housing*, Vol. 4, Part 1, pp. 7, 18, 23, 33, and 88. For coverage and for a definition of the debt-to-value ratio, see Table 3, notes b and c.

ratio of 40 percent reported for urban rental properties with two to four dwelling units which were either vacant or tenant-occupied. (*1950 Census of Housing*, Vol. 4, Residential Financing, Part 1, pp. 323 and 554.)

general, the equity ratios have been somewhat lower in larger cities than in places of relatively small size.

Insured versus Conventional Mortgage Markets

Of the many factors that have affected the structure of the mortgage market since 1920 the most important was the introduction in 1934 of home mortgage insurance. The Federal Housing Administration's insurance program, and, ten years later, the Veterans' Administration loan guaranty program, created and developed a new mortgage market characterized by more liberal credit terms than were usual for conventionally financed (that is, noninsured) loans, and by a new risk-spreading device intended to appeal to both lender and borrower. Since this new market was open to lenders who in the past had been confined through statute and administrative regulation to more stringent lending policies, a description of it is essential for an understanding of the growth and changing composition of institutionally held urban real estate debt.

Though the importance of the new market can hardly be overrated—for instance, by 1953 government-insured loans constituted over one-third of the total outstanding nonfarm real estate debt and about 40 percent of the debt on one- to four-family homes—it is worth noticing that here, as for the home mortgage debt as a whole, a slowing down of the rate of increase is clearly recognizable (Table 6). Like the increase in the ratio of mortgaged to all homes, the increase in the ratio of government-insured to total outstanding home mortgage debt has been leveling off after a period of spectacular rise.

A comparison of the two markets, the government-insured and the conventionally financed, is now possible for mortgages outstanding in 1950 on single family owner-occupied homes. Within that group, conventional loans appear to have been more important than government-insured loans for borrowers with properties at the bottom and at the top of the distributions by market value, purchase price, and number of rooms (Table 7). Conventional mortgage loans also predominated both among borrowers of low socio-economic status—those with incomes of $2,500 or less, and those listed occupationally as operatives, service workers, and laborers—and among the small group at the upper end of the scale, the self-employed managers of business firms.

Socio-economic differences between conventional and insured bor-

TABLE 6

Amount of Government-Insured Nonfarm Mortgage Debt and Its Ratio to Total Nonfarm Mortgage Debt, 1935-53

(*dollar figures in millions*)

Year	*FHA and VA Home Mortgage Debt*[a]	*As Percent of Total Home Mortgage Debt*[b]	*Total FHA and VA Mortgage Debt*[a]	*As Percent of Total Nonfarm Mortgage Debt*[b]
1935	$ 12	0.1%	$ 13	[c]
1936	203	1.3	205	0.7%
1937	594	3.8	600	2.1
1938	967	6.2	1,003	3.6
1939	1,755	10.7	1,860	6.4
1940	2,349	13.5	2,453	8.2
1941	3,030	16.5	3,137	10.0
1942	3,742	20.5	3,868	12.6
1943	4,060	22.8	4,262	14.3
1944	4,190	23.3	4,431	14.9
1945	4,578	24.7	4,815	15.6
1946	6,292	27.3	6,505	17.6
1947	9,581	34.0	10,130	23.1
1948	12,469	37.5	13,611	26.7
1949	15,006	40.0	17,140	30.0
1950	18,863	41.9	22,082	33.1
1951	22,877	44.1	26,583	35.2
1952	25,370	43.2	29,290	34.9
1953	28,090	42.6	32,118	34.4

[a] For 1935-38, estimates from the Annual Reports of the Federal Housing Administration as of June 30. For 1939-53, end-of-year data from *Housing Statistics* (Housing and Home Finance Agency), January 1954, pp. 37 and 41.

[b] Refers to mortgage debt outstanding on one- to four-family residential properties, and on nonfarm residential and commercial properties combined, as given in *Survey of Current Business* (Department of Commerce), September 1953, Table 6, p. 18, and October 1954, Table 6, p. 19.

[c] Less than 0.05 per cent.

rowers may be detected also within different regions. Regional differences in the economic status of mortgagors reflect, of course, regional differences in the general distribution of income, namely the relative predominance of lower incomes in the South and of middle and upper middle incomes in the West. Within that setting there are also differences between the government-insured and the conventional sectors of the regional mortgage markets. In 1950 for the United States as a whole about one-sixth of the mortgages on single family owner-occupied homes were FHA-insured; a somewhat smaller proportion were VA-guaranteed, and two-thirds were

TABLE 7

Distribution of Owner-Occupied One-Family Homes with Conventional and with Insured Mortgages, 1950, by Value of Property, Borrower's Income, etc.

CHARACTERISTICS OF PROPERTY AND OWNER	CONVENTIONAL	INSURED *FHA*	INSURED *VA*	ALL
Market Value of Home				
Less than $5,000	24%	2%	11%	18%
$5,000 - 9,999	41	49	56	44
10,000 - 14,999	21	38	27	25
15,000 - 19,999	8	8	5	8
20,000 and over	6	3	1	5
Purchase Price of Home				
Less than $5,000	45	14	17	36
$5,000 - 9,999	35	61	61	43
10,000 - 14,999	12	21	18	14
15,000 - 19,999	4	3	2	4
20,000 and over	3	1	1	2
Not acquired by purchase	1	a	a	1
Number of Rooms				
Less than 4	7	2	3	6
4	18	27	28	21
5	25	38	33	29
6	27	24	25	26
7 and over	23	9	11	18
Income of Owner[b]				
Less than $2,500	31	13	18	26
$2,500 - 3,999	38	39	49	40
4,000 - 5,999	20	34	26	24
6,000 - 7,999	5	8	4	5
8,000 - 9,999	2	2	1	2
10,000 and over	4	3	1	3
Occupation of Owner[b]				
Professional and technical workers, salaried	8	13	10	9
Professional and technical workers, self-employed	2	2	2	2
Managers and officials, salaried	9	13	10	10
Managers, officials, and proprietors, self-employed	8	6	4	7
Clerical and kindred workers	7	9	9	8
Sales workers	8	12	9	9
Craftsmen, foremen	24	25	27	25
Operatives	21	15	21	20
Service workers	6	4	5	5
Laborers (except miners)	6	2	3	5
Total	100%	100%	100%	100%

Refers to nonfarm properties, first mortgages only. Based on data from *1950 Census of Housing*, Vol. 4, Residential Financing, Part 1, Chapter 3, Table 3, pp. 162 and 165. Mortgaged properties for which the required information was not reported are excluded.

[a] Less than 0.5 percent. [b] Refers to owner who is head of the household.

conventionally financed (Table 8).[5] The proportion of outstanding mortgages that were FHA-insured was higher in the South and the West than elsewhere; yet in both regions it comprised less than one-fourth of all single family home mortgages. In the South about one-third of the FHA-insured, but over one-half of the conven-

TABLE 8

Regional Differences in the Percentages of Owner-Occupied One-Family Homes with Conventional and with Insured Mortgages, 1950

Type of Loan	*North-east*	*North Central*	*South*	*West*	*United States*
Conventional	*73%*	*72%*	*64%*	*63%*	*68%*
Insured	27	28	36	37	32
FHA	10	14	22	23	17
VA	17	14	14	14	15
Total	100%	100%	100%	100%	100%

Refers to nonfarm properties, first mortgages only. Based on data from *1950 Census of Housing*, Vol. 4, Residential Financing, Part 1, Chapter 3, Table 3, pp. 162-68. For states included in the regions, see note to Table 9.

tionally financed, mortgages represented loans made to borrowers in the lower income brackets (reporting family incomes of less than $3,500 at the time of the 1950 census; see Table 9).

It may, of course, be argued that the primary purpose of the government loan insurance program was to encourage higher housing standards without incurring high risks; the fact remains that so far as can be told from the outstanding debt, the low income borrower and the low-price housing market have remained the domain of conventionally supplied credit. This impression is reinforced by glancing at the housing cost to mortgagors in various economic groups as they are reflected in the ratio of mortgage payments (interest and principal) to borrower's income. Since conventionally supplied credit was as a rule extended on shorter terms than insured credit, and to a higher proportion of borrowers with small incomes, mortgage payments on the conventional loans were relatively large as compared with mortgagors' incomes, especially for borrowers in the lower income brackets. This was true for the nation as well as

[5] Comparisons in the present chapter between insured and conventional lending refer to first mortgages only, a restriction imposed by the data of Tables 7 through 11 and Table 13. About one-fourth of the FHA-insured mortgages were on properties also encumbered by VA-guaranteed second mortgages; hence from the standpoint of all mortgages, secondary liens included, the percentages given above tend to understate the importance of the VA-guaranteed loans.

TABLE 9
Regional Differences in Distribution of Owner-Occupied One-Family Homes with Conventional and with Insured Mortgages, 1950, by Borrower's Income

BORROWER'S INCOME[a]	CONVEN-TIONAL	INSURED *FHA*	INSURED *VA*	ALL
		Northeast		
Less than $2,000	11%	4%	5%	9%
$2,000 - 3,499	29	20	37	29
3,500 - 4,999	25	34	32	27
5,000 - 7,999	23	30	21	23
8,000 - 9,999	5	5	3	5
10,000 and over	7	7	2	6
		North Central		
Less than $2,000	12	4	5	10
$2,000 - 3,499	31	17	37	30
3,500 - 4,999	28	35	36	30
5,000 - 7,999	21	33	18	22
8,000 - 9,999	3	5	2	3
10,000 and over	4	6	2	4
		South		
Less than $2,000	20	6	8	15
$2,000 - 3,499	34	27	36	33
3,500 - 4,999	21	34	33	26
5,000 - 7,999	17	28	19	20
8,000 - 9,999	3	3	2	3
10,000 and over	4	3	2	3
		West		
Less than $2,000	14	5	4	10
$2,000 - 3,499	28	18	30	26
3,500 - 4,999	29	35	41	32
5,000 - 7,999	22	33	22	25
8,000 - 9,999	3	5	1	3
10,000 and over	4	4	2	4
		United States		
Less than $2,000	14	4	5	11
$2,000 - 3,499	31	21	36	30
3,500 - 4,999	26	34	35	29
5,000 - 7,999	21	31	20	22
8,000 - 9,999	4	4	2	3
10,000 and over	5	5	2	5
Total	100%	100%	100%	100%

Refers to nonfarm properties, first mortgages only. Based on data from *1950 Census of Housing*, Vol. 4, Residential Financing, Part 1, Chapter 3, Table 3, pp. 165-168. Mortgaged properties for which owner's income was not reported are excluded.

The Northeast includes New England, New York, New Jersey, and Pennsylvania. The South includes states south of the northeastern group and the Ohio River, and westward to Texas and Oklahoma. The North Central group region extends from Ohio and Michigan west to Kansas, Nebraska, and the Dakotas. The West is the Mountain and Pacific states.

[a] Refers to income of owner and his immediate family in 1949.

for individual regions. For example, in 1950 for the United States as a whole, one-eighth of all mortgagors under conventional arrangements, but only one-twentieth and one-sixteenth, respectively, of mortgagors under FHA and VA arrangements, made current payments on interest and principal which exceeded 25 percent of their income (Table 10).

Also, in the two major regions in which the proportion of government-insured loans was higher than the national average—the South and the West—the proportion of conventional mortgages on which regular payments exceeded 25 percent of borrower's income was substantially higher than for the nation as a whole. Thus, although properties with government-insured mortgages in 1950 were most numerous in the regions of comparatively low incomes, it appears improbable, from the ratios of mortgage payments to income, that government-insured lending tended especially toward properties in the lower price brackets or toward borrowers presenting higher risks than those involved in conventional lending in comparable price brackets.

Other suggestive differences between FHA and conventional mortgages outstanding in 1950 are the following: (1) The government-insured loans had been made predominantly on new homes, but the conventional loans most frequently on existing properties. For example, about three-quarters of all conventional mortgages on single family owner-occupied homes, but only four-tenths of FHA-insured mortgages, represented loans on previously occcupied homes (Table 11). (2) The proportion of loans originated by one lender and later sold to another was noticeably higher for FHA-insured than for conventional loans. Nearly nine-tenths of the conventional mortgages secured by one-family homes and held by various lenders in 1950 were loans which they originated rather than purchased, whereas slightly less than three-fifths of the FHA-insured mortgages fell into that category.

All of these differences taken together, though small individually, point toward the possibility of a real functional difference between the government-insured and conventional loan markets, a difference that to a considerable extent is due to the legal framework within which the FHA must operate. This difference is seen in a tendency for the government-insured loan market to be oriented somewhat more than the conventional loan market toward the financing of new construction; toward medium-priced properties, and toward borrowers in the middle brackets of income and socio-economic

TABLE 10

Regional Differences in Distribution of Owner-Occupied One-Family Homes with Conventional and with Insured Mortgages, 1950, by Ratio of Repayments to Borrower's Income

RATIO OF PAYMENTS OF INTEREST AND PRINCIPAL TO INCOME[a]	CONVENTIONAL	INSURED		
		FHA	*VA*	ALL
		Northeast		
Less than 5%	14%	9%	2%	11%
5 - 9	37	46	24	35
10 - 14	25	27	37	28
15 - 19	10	12	23	13
20 - 24	5	3	7	5
25 and over	9	4	6	8
		North Central		
Less than 5%	9	7	1	7
5 - 9	33	43	25	34
10 - 14	28	31	39	30
15 - 19	13	12	25	15
20 - 24	6	4	6	6
25 and over	11	3	4	9
		South		
Less than 5%	8	7	1	7
5 - 9	27	35	25	29
10 - 14	23	35	37	28
15 - 19	16	15	22	17
20 - 24	8	3	7	7
25 and over	17	5	8	13
		West		
Less than 5%	4	6	b	4
5 - 9	24	40	19	27
10 - 14	26	30	42	30
15 - 19	18	15	25	18
20 - 24	9	3	8	8
25 and over	18	6	6	13
		United States		
Less than 5%	9	7	1	7
5 - 9	31	41	24	32
10 - 14	26	31	38	29
15 - 19	14	14	24	15
20 - 24	7	3	7	6
25 and over	13	5	6	10
Total	100%	100%	100%	100%

Refers to nonfarm properties, first mortgages only. Based on data from *1950 Census of Housing*, Vol. 4, Residential Financing, Part 1, Chapter 3, Table 3, pp. 165-68. Mortgaged properties for which the required information was not reported are excluded. For states included in the regions, see note to Table 9.

[a] Income refers to earnings of less than $10,000 by the owner and his immediate family in 1949.

[b] Less than 0.5 percent.

status; and toward average and perhaps better than average risks. The loans, of course, have a higher degree of market negotiability because of their insurance or guaranty features.

TABLE 11

Percentage of New versus Existing Structures and Purchased versus Originated Mortgages for Owner-Occupied One-Family Homes with Conventional and with Insured Mortgages, 1950

CHARACTERISTICS OF STRUCTURE AND MORTGAGE	CONVENTIONAL	INSURED		ALL
		FHA	*VA*	
Structure as Acquired by Owner				
New	27%	60%	39%	34%
Previously occupied	73	40	61	66
Mortgage as Acquired by Holder				
Purchased	11	41	27	18
Originated	89	59	73	82
Total	100%	100%	100%	100%

Refers to nonfarm properties, first mortgages only. Based on data from *1950 Census of Housing*, Vol. 4, Residential Financing, Part 1, Chapter 3, Tables 2 and 3, pp. 159 and 162.

Since appraising the growth and changing composition of urban mortgage debt was the primary function of the present chapter, a word of caution is now in order should the data be used for other purposes. In interpreting the material on the preceding pages it is necessary to keep in mind that at no time has home mortgage credit been used exclusively for the financing of home purchases and home maintenance. During the twenties, for example, the practice of funding previously contracted debts through loans with real estate as collateral was quite common. For later years some quantitative information on the purposes for which mortgage loans are made is available from a continuous sample of savings and loan associations, compiled by the Home Loan Bank Board. These data show that even in the years of high home-purchase activity immediately following World War II, some 20 percent of the loans were made for other purposes than construction of new or acquisition of existing homes, and that at least one out of every fourteen loans was made for purposes not connected with housing expenditures even in a broad sense of the term (Table 12).

TABLE 12

Distribution of Annual Dollar Volume of Mortgage Loans by Savings and Loan Associations, 1936-50, by Purpose of Loan

Year	*Construction*	*Home Purchase*	*Refinancing*	*Reconditioning*	*Other Purposes*
1936	23%	30%	24%	9%	14%
1937	26	37	20	7	10
1938	28	33	20	7	12
1939	31	34	18	6	11
1940	33	36	17	5	9
1941	32	42	14	4	8
1942	18	55	16	4	7
1943	9	68	14	3	6
1944	7	73	11	2	7
1945	10	71	10	2	7
1946	17	66	8	2	7
1947	24	56	8	3	9
1948	29	47	9	4	11
1949	30	43	10	5	12
1950	34	43	8	4	11
1951	31	45	9	4	11
1952	32	45	9	4	11
1953	32	45	8	4	11

Based on the Home Loan Bank Board's *Statistical Summary, 1949*, Table 11, p. 12, and the Housing and Home Finance Agency's *Housing Statistics*, January 1954, p. 45. The data were compiled by the Operating Analysis Division from reports of approximately 3,000 savings and loan associations whose combined assets represented about four-fifths of the total assets of all such associations.

Mortgage lending by the associations is predominantly on nonfarm residential properties; cf. Table 27.

Similarly, census data for 1950 (Table 13) indicate that for all lenders, nearly one out of every six of the then outstanding mortgages on single family owner-occupied homes was made for other purposes than for acquisition or improvement and repairs of the home; that the mortgages made after the property had been acquired by the owner—including refinancings—accounted for over one-fourth of all loans (and for over one-third of all conventional loans); and that 70 percent of the refinancings and renewals, and over 50 percent of the new mortgages placed after acquisition of the property, had been taken out by the borrower for financial reasons (securing better terms, investing in other property, in business, etc.) and for other reasons not directly related to the purchase or improvement of his home.

TABLE 13

Distribution of Owner-Occupied One-Family Homes with Conventional and with Insured Mortgages, 1950, by Origin and Purpose of Loan

ORIGIN AND PURPOSE OF LOAN	CONVEN-TIONAL	INSURED *FHA*	INSURED *VA*	ALL LOANS
ORIGIN OF LOAN				
Made or Assumed at Time of Property Acquisition	*64%*	*93%*	*97%*	*73%*
Refinanced or Renewed	*21*	*5*	*2*	*16*
Improve or repair property	6	1	1	5
Secure better terms	5	3	1	4
Renew or extend term	4	a	a	3
Other	6	1	a	4
Placed after Property Acquisition	*15*	*2*	*1*	*11*
Improve or repair property	7	1	1	5
Invest in other properties	1	a	..	1
Invest in business other than real estate	2	a	a	1
Other	5	1	a	4
Total	100%	100%	100%	100%
PURPOSE OF REFINANCED LOANS				
Improve or repair property	30	24	44	30
Secure better terms	25	48	29	27
Renew or extend term	18	4	4	17
Other	27	24	22	26
Total	100%	100%	100%	100%
PURPOSE OF MORTGAGES PLACED AFTER PROPERTY ACQUISITION				
Improve or repair property	47	43	66	47
Invest in other properties	7	4	..	7
Invest in business other than real estate	11	8	5	11
Other	35	45	29	35
Total	100%	100%	100%	100%

Refers to nonfarm properties, first mortgages only. Based on data from *1950 Census of Housing*, Vol. 4, Residential Financing, Part 1, Chapter 3, Table 3, p. 163.

[a] Less than 0.5 percent.

Notwithstanding the above qualifications, the data we have reviewed suggest a general, long-range pattern which, over the past thirty years or more, has been characterized by: (1) growth of mortgage debt, not only in absolute terms but—more importantly—in relation to the other components of private long-term debt; (2) within the growing mortgage debt, a rapid increase of the nonfarm or urban as compared with the farm sector; and (3) within the nonfarm sector, a steady rise of the residential as against the nonresidential debt, and a sustained decline in the importance of income-producing real estate as compared with the consumer type of shelter, i.e. the owner-occupied single family home.

This long-range development has been encouraged by the government through what was originally an emergency measure but has since become an integral part of the real estate finance structure of the economy. To what extent the pattern is also the outcome of growing urbanization, and with it an increasing willingness to make use of long-term debt financing, or of the maturing of an intensified demand for shelter as a reflection of the continuing struggle for rising standards of living, and to what extent it is due to the many accidental circumstances of the past which, in joint interaction, have helped shape the present, cannot be accurately judged. In any case, some implications of the development clearly point to a more pronounced impact of the vagaries of changing consumer demand and changing consumer incomes upon the financial structure of the economy than has been observable in the past. Whether and to what degree it will be possible to cushion such impacts—should this become necessary—through government or other action is a matter of conjecture. In any event, it would seem that the observed changes in urban mortgage financing have tended toward shifting major risks from the spender to the saver, from the younger to the older age groups, and—in general—from the present to the future.

⤙ 2 ⤚

STRUCTURE OF URBAN MORTGAGE MARKETS

NONFARM real estate credit is supplied by a variety of lenders who may conveniently be grouped into two major categories: institutions and individuals; the former, in turn, may be divided into private and public lending institutions. In terms of volume, the principal institutional lenders have been the life insurance companies, the commercial banks, the mutual savings banks, and the savings and loan associations. A number of other lenders are known to have supplied the mortgage market with funds (for example, real estate and bond companies, fiduciaries, title and mortgage companies, construction companies, the Reconstruction Finance Corporation Mortgage Company, the Federal National Mortgage Association, and some philanthropic, educational, and fraternal organizations); but relatively their combined volume is very small.[1] In the present and following chapters, therefore, the term institutional lender will be limited to the following: legal reserve life insurance companies, commercial banks, mutual savings banks, and savings and loan associations. Institutionally held debt will refer to the nonfarm mortgage debt held by such lenders.

Trends in the Institutional Distribution of Urban Mortgage Debt

Institutional lenders hold a substantial part of the nation's aggregate nonfarm mortgage portfolio. By the end of 1953 over three-fourths of the entire urban mortgage debt was held by the four principal lenders, and the general tendency, observable over the thirty-odd years preceding 1953, was one of continuously increasing participation by these institutions in the country's urban mortgage holdings (Table 14). Within that slowly changing framework, however, the portfolios of the principal types of lender differed markedly in their behavior, with respect to both long-run and cyclical changes.

In long-run change, the spectacular feature of the period was the growth of life insurance company holdings (Chart 2, Panel A).

[1] For data on the importance of other private lenders in 1951 as compared with the four major lenders, see "Real Estate Loans of Registrants under Regulation X," by Doris P. Warner, *Federal Reserve Bulletin*, June 1952, Table 5, p. 626.

TABLE 14
Share of Nonfarm Mortgage Debt
Institutionally Held, 1920-53
(*dollar figures in billions*)

END OF YEAR	TOTAL NONFARM MORTGAGE DEBT[a]	INSTITUTIONALLY HELD[b]	
		Amount	*As Percent of Total*
1920	$15.3	$ 7.9	52%
1921	16.5	8.4	51
1922	17.9	9.4	53
1923	20.3	11.0	54
1924	22.8	13.0	57
1925	25.7	15.2	59
1926	28.6	17.2	60
1927	31.8	19.1	60
1928	34.7	21.1	61
1929	36.9	22.6	61
1930	37.7	22.7	60
1931	36.5	22.2	61
1932	34.4	20.6	60
1933	30.5	18.1	59
1934	29.5	16.4	55
1935	28.4	15.5	55
1936	28.0	15.4	55
1937	28.0	15.8	56
1938	28.2	16.4	58
1939	28.9	17.1	59
1940	30.0	18.0	60
1941	31.3	19.2	61
1942	30.8	19.3	63
1943	29.9	18.9	63
1944	29.7	18.9	64
1945	30.8	19.7	64
1946	36.9	24.4	66
1947	43.9	30.1	69
1948	50.9	35.9	71
1949	57.1	40.8	71
1950	66.7	49.3	74
1951	75.6	56.9	75
1952	84.0	64.0	76
1953	93.4	72.0	77

[a] From *Survey of Current Business* (Department of Commerce), September 1953, Tables 1 and 6, pp. 14 and 18, and October 1954, Tables 1 and 6, pp. 14 and 19. For 1920-28 the corporate nonfarm mortgage component was estimated; details are given in Table 1, note b.

[b] Includes holdings of life insurance companies, commercial banks, mutual savings banks, and savings and loan associations, from Table C-1.

CHART 2

Shares of Institutional Lenders in Nonfarm Mortgage Debt, 1920-53

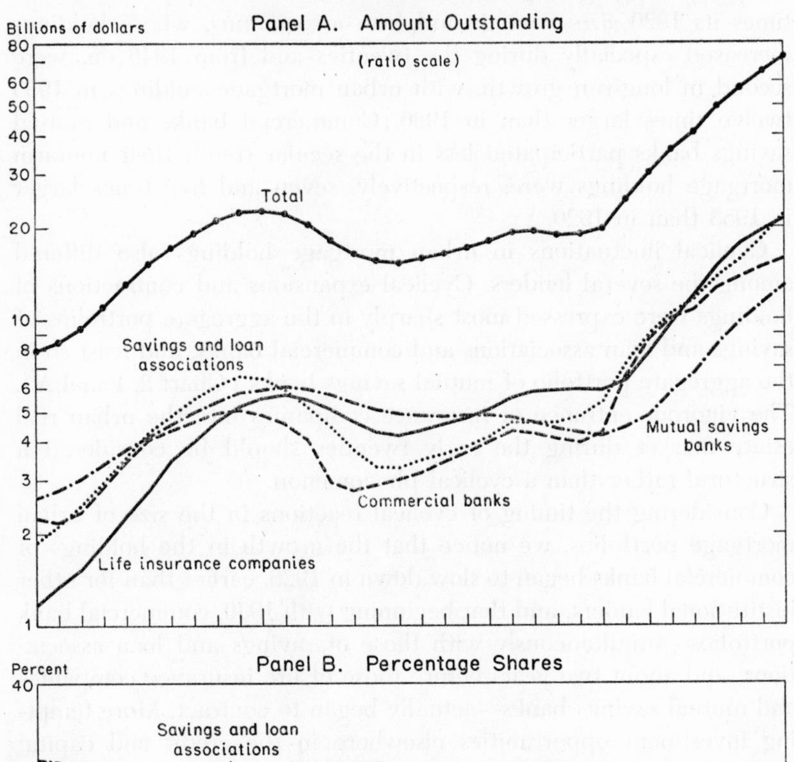

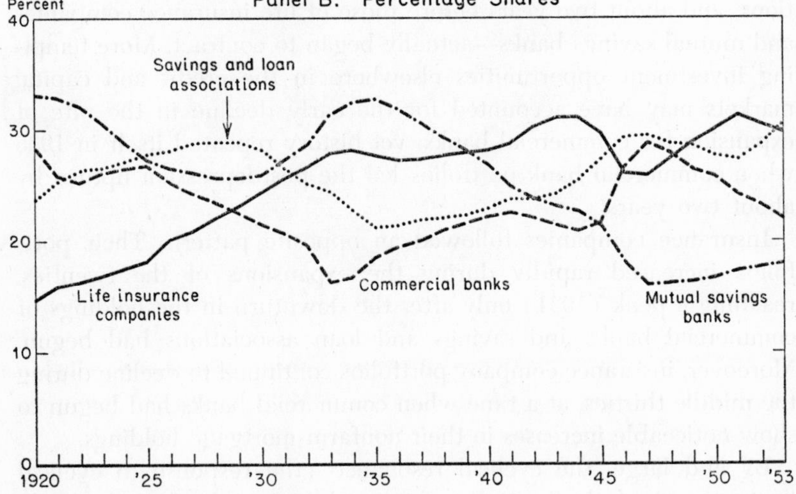

From end-of-year data given in Table C-1.

While the total of institutionally held nonfarm mortgage debt increased by the end of 1953 to nine times its 1920 amount, the life companies' aggregate portfolio rose even more steeply, to eighteen times its 1920 size. Savings and loan associations, whose holdings increased especially during the twenties and from 1946 on, were second in long-run growth, with urban mortgage holdings in 1953 twelve times larger than in 1920. Commercial banks and mutual savings banks participated less in the secular trend; their nonfarm mortgage holdings were, respectively, seven and five times larger in 1953 than in 1920.

Cyclical fluctuations in urban mortgage holdings also differed among the several lenders. Cyclical expansions and contractions of holdings were expressed most sharply in the aggregate portfolios of savings and loan associations and commercial banks, and least so in the aggregate portfolio of mutual savings banks (Chart 2, Panel A). The vigorous entrance of insurance companies into the urban real estate market during the early twenties should be considered a structural rather than a cyclical phenomenon.

Considering the timing of cyclical reactions in the size of urban mortgage portfolios, we notice that the growth in the holdings of commercial banks began to slow down in 1926, earlier than for other institutional lenders; and that beginning with 1930, commercial bank portfolios—simultaneously with those of savings and loan associations, and about two years before those of life insurance companies and mutual savings banks—actually began to contract. More tempting investment opportunities elsewhere in the credit and capital markets may have accounted for the early decline in the rate of expansion for commercial banks; yet history repeated itself in 1935 when commercial bank portfolios led the postdepression upturn by about two years.

Insurance companies followed an opposite pattern. Their portfolios increased rapidly during the expansions of the twenties, reaching a peak (1931) only after the downturn in the holdings of commercial banks and savings and loan associations had begun. Moreover, insurance company portfolios continued to decline during the middle thirties, at a time when commercial banks had begun to show noticeable increases in their nonfarm mortgage holdings.

By and large, the cyclical resonance (the response to cyclical fluctuations) of the portfolio of mutual savings banks was weak, and that of commercial banks and savings and loan associations rather pronounced, with insurance companies taking an intermediate position. Differences among lenders in policy and in availability of investable funds, as well as in the composition of their portfolios and the characteristics of their outstanding mortgage loans, are likely to have contributed to the differences in cyclical patterns.

Such differences in the behavior of urban mortgage portfolios held by different institutional lenders become even more apparent if we observe, instead of changes in the absolute amounts, changes in their respective percentage shares of the combined holdings (Chart 2, Panel B). Again we find that savings and loan associations were usually the most important lending group during years of peak peacetime activity, holding nearly three-tenths of the combined institutional nonfarm mortgage portfolio, and that commercial banks anticipated the other lenders at the turning points. In addition, the data clearly reveal the rapidly growing importance of insurance companies, and the cyclically complementary behavior of commercial banks and savings and loan associations on the one hand and mutual savings banks on the other. That is, while the shares of commercial banks and savings and loan associations in the combined institutional mortgage portfolio moved in conformity with the ups and downs of the cycle, the pattern for mutual savings banks was opposite; the latter held their biggest shares during periods of greatest mortgage and real estate distress and their smallest shares in times of highest activity in the mortgage market.

Regional Distribution of Institutional Mortgage Holdings

A detailed study of the regional distribution of urban mortgage debt would require complete knowledge of the location of mortgaged properties throughout the country. While such information is not presently available except in the case of life insurance companies, reasonably satisfactory estimates of the geographic structure of the nonfarm mortgage debt can be made by using in other cases the location of the lender rather than of the real estate. Since commercial banks, mutual savings banks, and savings and loan associations are primarily short-distance lenders, the location of the institution should approximate the location of mortgaged properties rather closely when the unit areas observed are extensive.

Almost half of the institutionally held nonfarm mortgage debt in 1950 was concentrated in the Middle Atlantic and East North Central states, the first group accounting for three-tenths of the total and the second for nearly one-fifth (Table 15). The Pacific

TABLE 15
Regional Distribution of Institutionally Held Nonfarm Mortgage Debt, 1928-50

Region and Census Division[a]	*1928*	*1933*	*1934*	*1939*	*1946*	*1950*
North	*79%*	*82%*	*81%*	*77%*	*70%*	*64%*
New England	27	15	15	14	11	9
Middle Atlantic	27	47	46	42	34	30
East North Central	21	16	16	16	19	19
West North Central	4	4	4	5	6	6
South	*10*	*10*	*10*	*13*	*17*	*20*
South Atlantic	5	5	6	8	10	11
East South Central	2	2	2	2	3	3
West South Central	3	3	2	3	4	6
West	*11*	*8*	*9*	*10*	*13*	*16*
Mountain	1	1	1	1	2	2
Pacific	10	7	8	9	11	14
Total debt	100%	100%	100%	100%	100%	100%

Refers to combined mortgage holdings of mutual savings banks, commercial banks, life insurance companies, and savings and loan associations. Regional distributions as compiled from sources cited in Table 24 were applied to estimates of each lender's holdings. Data of holdings for 1933-50 are from *Survey of Current Business* (Department of Commerce), September 1953, Table 6, p. 18, and October 1954, Table 6, p. 19. Data on holdings of commercial banks and mutual savings banks in 1928 are the author's estimates: in the first case, from total mortgage holdings as given in *Long-Term Debt in the United States,* by Donald C. Horton (pp. 111, 130), adjusted to exclude farm mortgage holdings as estimated by the Bureau of Agricultural Economics; in the second case, made by relating data on urban mortgage loans outstanding in 1931 (supplied by the National Association of Mutual Savings Banks) to total loans outstanding then (*Banking and Monetary Statistics,* p. 23) and applying that ratio to total outstandings in 1928, from the source last named. Other 1928 data are from the *Life Insurance Fact Book, 1954* (Institute of Life Insurance), p. 74, and from *Trends in the Savings and Loan Field, 1953* (Home Loan Bank Board), Table 1, p. 4.

[a] Refers to location of institution except in the case of life insurance companies, where reference is to the location of the mortgaged properties. For a listing of states included in the census divisions, see Table 3, note a.

states had about one-seventh, and the other census divisions still smaller shares. In terms of broader groupings, over 60 percent of the debt was located in the North; the South had somewhat more of the remainder than the West.

If attention is centered on time changes in the regional pattern, it is seen that the South and the West have been increasing in importance, whereas the North has been decreasing (Table 15). These long-range shifts are particularly noticeable if viewed in the light of the changes produced by the depression of the thirties, which had a sharp effect on the relative position of the New England states and an equally pronounced, though less lasting, effect on the Middle Atlantic region.

The relative importance of various types of lenders also varies in the different regional markets. Thus it appears that in the older market of the New England and Middle Atlantic states, mutual savings banks have remained the principal lender. As late as 1950, and after having given way gradually to the other three lenders, they held nearly one-half of the entire institutional urban mortgage debt in the New England states (Table 16).

In the comparatively new markets of the west coast, commercial banks, which from the late twenties on accounted for about one-half of the institutional debt, still ranked first among institutional lenders in 1950, although their share was declining under pressure from life insurance companies and savings and loan associations.

In the South, life insurance companies were the foremost lenders east of the Mississippi in the twenties, and throughout in the middle thirties. By 1950 they had acquired over one-half of the institutional debt of the two South Central divisions and had regained first rank in the South Atlantic states in successful competition with commercial banks and, especially, savings and loan associations.

In predepression days the two North Central divisions were markets served primarily by savings and loan associations. They are today. Although at one time exceeded by insurance companies, savings and loan associations have been able to maintain their regional supremacy in the North Central states.

All regional markets were deeply affected by the depression of the thirties. Comparison of the pre- with the postdepression period suggests that in spite of the pronounced features of the different regional markets, there has been a long-range tendency for differences both within and among the three major regions to become less pronounced. Differences as between lenders' shares have tended in general (though not without exception) to become smaller and more uniform, in the historically older markets of the North more so than in the South, and in the East more so than in the West.

Patterns which themselves are the result of a complex matrix of economic conditions, social development, and historical accident do not lend themselves to simple interpretations. It is noteworthy, however, that in most of the regions a tendency toward equalization among the various institutional lenders is clearly recognizable for

TABLE 16

Distribution of Institutionally Held Nonfarm Mortgage Debt within Region by Type of Lender, 1928-50

Type of Lender	*New England*	*Middle Atlantic*	*East North Central*	*West North Central*	*South Atlantic*	*East South Central*	*West South Central*	*Mountain*	*Pacific*	*United States*
1928										
Mutual savings banks	78%	12%	3%	..	3%	..	..	..	6%	26%
Commercial banks	12	19	34	11%	16	7%	15%	38%	59	23
Life insurance companies	2	32	23	42	43	58	28	21	19	22
Savings & loan associations	8	37	40	47	38	35	57	41	16	29
1933										
Mutual savings banks	67	44	1	..	8	..	..	..	4	31
Commercial banks	13	15	16	8	11	7	14	29	47	17
Life insurance companies	6	24	40	48	48	58	40	35	32	28
Savings & loan associations	15	18	42	44	34	35	46	36	17	24
1934										
Mutual savings banks	67	45	2	1	7	..	..	..	5	32
Commercial banks	14	13	18	17	18	21	15	20	52	18
Life insurance companies	5	25	41	46	43	48	46	38	30	28
Savings & loan associations	15	17	39	36	31	31	39	43	13	22
1939										
Mutual savings banks	60	45	1	2	3	..	..	..	2	28
Commercial banks	14	14	25	26	23	26	17	38	57	22
Life insurance companies	8	29	37	34	36	42	42	25	24	28
Savings & loan associations	18	12	37	38	38	32	41	37	17	22
1946										
Mutual savings banks	46	36	1	3	1	..	..	..	2	18
Commercial banks	16	17	31	37	25	32	21	45	53	27
Life insurance companies	11	30	25	22	32	34	42	17	20	26
Savings & loan associations	27	17	43	38	42	34	37	38	25	29
1950										
Mutual savings banks	47	39	1	2	2	..	..	..	1	17
Commercial banks	17	20	29	35	21	24	14	32	43	26
Life insurance companies	11	23	28	29	42	47	60	40	32	30
Savings & loan associations	25	18	42	34	35	29	26	28	23	28

(notes on next page)

Notes to Table 16

For sources of data see note under Table 15. Regional breakdown refers to location of institution except in the case of life insurance companies, where reference is to the location of the mortgaged properties. For a listing of states included in the census divisions, see Table 3, note a.

the period under review, pointing toward a debt more uniformly distributed among all the major lenders. Federal programs of loan insurance and guarantee doubtless have contributed to this result, having enforced a substantial uniformity in credit practices and promoted increased competition among lending institutions. Thus, taking each of the regional markets, we find that by 1946 all of them but one were supported by components of a more evenly articulated mortgage credit system than in earlier years. The exception is the West South Central region, where the vigorous entrance of life insurance companies at the expense of savings and loan associations resulted in a switch of relative positions but not in a more even distribution.

Distribution of Institutional Mortgage Holdings by Type of Property

As has already been seen, over two-thirds of the country's nonfarm mortgage debt represents debt secured by family-sized homes and small residential properties. Institutional lenders play an important role in the financing of this debt. Their holdings of mortgages on one- to four-family homes increased from about $8 billion in 1925 to $53 billion at the end of 1953 (Chart 3, Panel A). The growth of institutional holdings was due in the main to the growth of the debt itself. Partly, however, it marks a relative change as well, since lending institutions have been absorbing an increasing portion of the growing home mortgage debt. By 1953 the major institutional lenders held four-fifths of the mortgage debt on one- to four-family nonfarm homes.[2]

Within the group of institutional lenders the behavior of the several types of institution has varied markedly. As holders of debt on one- to four-family homes, savings and loan associations held first place throughout the period from 1925 to 1953 (Chart 3, Panel B). Mutual savings banks, which ranked second at the beginning of the period, became the least important holder after 1941. Commercial banks and insurance companies expanded their shares over the years

[2] *Survey of Current Business* (Department of Commerce), October 1954, Table 6, p. 19.

CHART 3

Shares of Institutional Lenders in Mortgage Debt on Nonfarm Homes, 1925-53

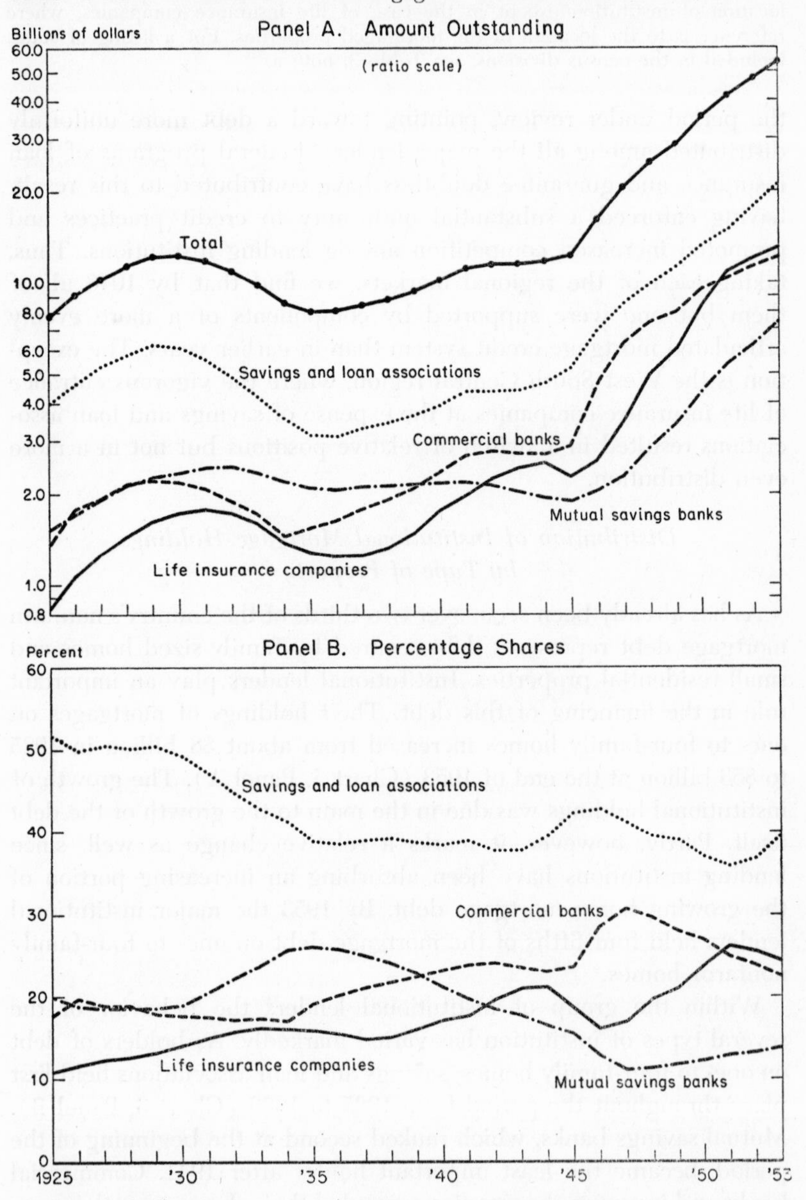

From end-of-year data given in Table C-2. Refers to loans secured by one- to four-family homes.

preceding World War II. By 1940, commercial bank holdings were second in importance, and they remained so until 1951, when the share of life insurance companies, having increased sharply in the late forties, rose somewhat above that of commercial banks.

The impact of cyclical expansions and contractions on the volume of mortgages outstanding on one- to four-family homes was most pronounced for commercial banks and savings and loan associations, somewhat less for life insurance companies, and least for mutual savings banks. The volume of outstanding home loans both of commercial banks and of savings and loan associations reached a peak in 1929, and contracted sharply during the depression years; mutual savings banks and insurance companies reached the peak of their outstandings two to three years later and reduced their volume of outstanding home mortgages more gradually than did the other two lenders during the same period.

The data on mortgages on multifamily and commercial properties are less reliable, since they are residuals obtained by subtracting one estimate (one- to four-family home mortgage debt) from another (total urban real estate debt); but with that reservation in mind the major aspects of changes in institutionally held mortgage debt on income-producing properties can be traced.

Since 1929, life insurance companies have been the leading mortgage lender on nonfarm income-producing properties, with mutual savings banks and commercial banks following, and savings and loan associations the least important of all (Chart 4, Panel A). It is also apparent that both commercial banks and mutual savings banks steadily lost ground, the former contracting sharply during the depression and re-entering the market for commercial and large residential mortgages only gradually during the thirties and on a level substantially below that of the predepression years. Despite the forceful re-entry into this market—beginning with 1946—by both types of bank, neither was able to recapture its relative position as of the mid-twenties (Chart 4, Panel B).

In 1925, commercial banks and mutual savings banks each held over one-third, insurance companies one-fourth, and savings and loan associations less than one-twentieth of all institutionally held mortgage debt secured by nonfarm income-producing property (Chart 4, Panel B). By the end of 1940, life insurance companies had become by far the most important holder (42 percent); mutual savings banks and commercial banks came next (with about one-third and one-fifth, respectively); savings and loan associations still con-

CHART 4

Shares of Institutional Lenders in Mortgage Debt on Nonfarm Income-Producing Properties, 1925-53

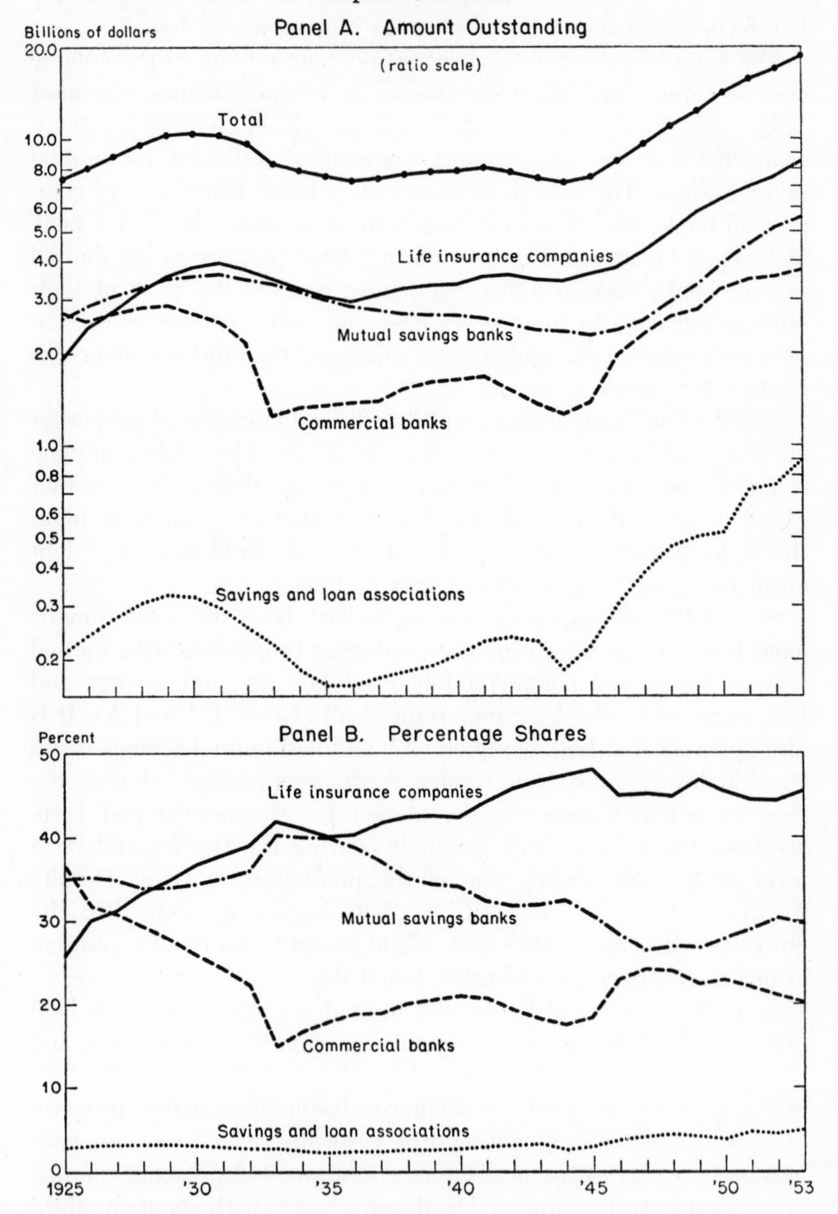

From end-of-year data given in Table C-3. Refers to loans secured by properties other than one- to four-family homes.

centrated, as they had throughout the entire period, on one- to four-family home mortgages, having little or no impact on the market for nonresidential mortgages.

Summarizing, we find that during the period 1925-53 the relative importance of the major institutional lenders has undergone changes both in the market for small residential mortgages and in that concerned with income-producing properties. In the home mortgage market the tendency has been for the various lenders to become more nearly equal in importance. Insurance companies and commercial banks have tended to increase their shares; mutual savings banks and savings and loan associations have reduced theirs. Savings and loan associations have remained, throughout the period, however, clearly the most important holder of one- to four-family home mortgages.

In the market for mortgages on income-producing properties, life insurance companies have increased their shares; commercial banks and mutual savings banks have again contracted theirs. The result has been a tendency toward greater diversity: toward a wider spread in the relative positions of different types of lender at the end of the period than existed just before the depression.

In general, participation in the outstanding nonfarm mortgage debt by the principal institutional lenders has been increasing over time. Concurrently with the expansion of the institutional sector of the market, the relative dominance of the market by any one lender —especially of the market for home mortgages—has lessened. Some of the implications of this development, which may be expressed also as a decline in the importance of individuals as mortgage investors, may be a retreat from a more nearly speculative mortgage lending policy to one in which major emphasis is on safety, even at the cost of a somewhat lower investment return, and, correspondingly, a move toward greater uniformity in credit standards.

3

STRUCTURE OF THE LENDING INDUSTRY

As we have seen, four private institutional lenders—insurance companies, commercial banks, mutual savings banks, and savings and loan associations—represent a substantial part of the urban mortgage lending industry. In 1946, the year the National Bureau's sample was drawn,[1] they held nearly two-thirds of the entire nonfarm real estate debt (66 percent) and a similar fraction of the debt on one- to four-family homes (69 percent); they also accounted in that year for about three-fourths (73 percent) of all lending activity on one- to four-family homes.[2] The total number of such institutions in 1946 was around 21,000, of which approximately two-thirds were commercial banks and somewhat less than three-tenths were savings and loan associations (Table 17). The small remainder was divided between mutual savings banks and life insurance companies in the approximate ratio of three to two.

The two most numerous groups of private institutional lenders—commercial banks and savings and loan associations—have contracted sharply in number since 1930, through failures and consolidations. For commercial banks the contraction was sharper and took place earlier than for savings and loan associations, largely because of differences in statutes governing the two types of institutions.[3] Life insurance companies, on the other hand, have increased in number and have simultaneously increased their outlets by setting up field office and correspondent systems, while mutual savings banks displayed a relatively stable pattern, though their number decreased slowly from 620 in 1920 to about 528 in 1953.

Size Comparisons of Lending Institutions

Dividing lending institutions into three broad size groups—those with urban mortgage portfolios of less than a quarter million dollars, one-quarter of a million to $50 million, and $50 million or more—

[1] See the opening section of Chapter 4.

[2] By 1950 these ratios had increased to 74, 78, and 74 percent, respectively. (Department of Commerce, *Survey of Current Business*, October 1954, Table 6, p. 19; Home Loan Bank Board, *Estimated Home Mortgage Debt and Lending Activity*, 1950, p. 3.)

[3] In cases of insolvency the applicable statutes compelled banks to close more promptly than associations.

TABLE 17

Number of Mutual Savings Banks, Commercial Banks, Life Insurance Companies, and Savings and Loan Associations, 1920-53

Year[a]	*Mutual Savings Banks*	*Commercial Banks*	*Life Insurance Companies*[b]	*Savings and Loan Associations*
1920	620	29,519	272	8,633
1921	623	30,189	288	9,255
1922	619	29,770	286	10,009
1923	618	29,560	291	10,744
1924	613	28,735	297	11,844
1925	611	28,230	308	12,403
1926	620	27,526	322	12,626
1927	618	26,443	319	12,804
1928	616	25,597	331	12,666
1929	611	24,719	353	12,342
1930	606	23,473	352	11,777
1931	600	21,471	342	11,442
1932	594	18,569	328	10,915
1933	576	14,048	318	10,596
1934	578	15,316	313	10,744
1935	571	15,482	340	10,266
1936	566	15,237	315	10,042
1937	564	15,016	308	9,225
1938	562	14,779	306	8,762
1939	552	14,594	306	8,006
1940	551	14,466	305	7,521
1941	550	14,369	304	7,211
1942	538	14,277	303	6,941
1943	537	14,129	305	6,498
1944	536	14,072	305	6,279
1945	534	14,067	348	6,149
1946	533	14,100	370	6,093
1947	533	14,222	398	6,045
1948	532	14,240	380	6,011
1949	530	14,199	435	5,983
1950	530	14,187	440	5,992
1951	529	14,151	418	5,995
1952	529	14,112	573	6,004
1953	528	14,051	580	6,010

Includes institutions in the United States and its possessions. Data for commercial and mutual savings banks are from *Annual Reports* of the Comptroller of the Currency and of the Federal Deposit Insurance Corporation; for life insurance companies, from *Statistical Abstracts* of the United States and from *Compendium of Official Life Insurance Reports* (Spectator Company); and for savings and loan associations, from *Trends in the Savings and Loan Field, 1953* (Home Loan Bank Board), Table 1, p. 4, and from *Annual Report, 1927* of the Comptroller of the Currency, p. 126.

(*notes continued on next page*)

Notes to Table 17 (continued)

[a] Figures as of June 30 for commercial and mutual savings banks; as of December 31 for life insurance companies and savings and loan associations.

[b] Represents companies reporting their financial statements to the Spectator Company; the aggregates published yearly in the Spectator Year Book are considered to represent nearly 100 percent of the business of United States legal reserve life companies. Estimates compiled by the Institute of Life Insurance on the number of companies reporting to individual state insurance departments in 1940 and 1950 through mid-1953 are from about one-third to one-half larger than those given by Spectator.

emphasizes the relatively small size of those that are most numerous. Over three-fifths of all institutions have portfolios of less than $250,000, while less than one percent of them have urban mortgage portfolios in excess of $50 million (Table 18). Furthermore, inter-institutional differences in portfolio size are clearly discernible. Commercial banks are the most frequent type of institution in the small size group; savings and loan associations and commercial banks appear with about equal frequency in the middle-sized group; and among the largest lenders insurance companies and mutual savings banks predominate (Table 18).

When the individual agencies in each of the four groups of institutional lenders are classified according to size of urban mortgage holdings, it is seen that about three-fourths of the commercial banks

TABLE 18

Distribution of Number of Lending Institutions, 1946, by Type of Institution within Size Class of Nonfarm Mortgage Portfolio

Type of Lender	*Under $250,000*	*$250,000 to 49.9 Million*	*$50 Million and Over*	*Total*
Mutual savings banks	0.2%	6.4%	32.1%	2.6%
Insured commercial banks[a]	81.2	41.0	9.4	65.6
Life insurance companies[b]	1.0	2.7	56.6	1.8
Savings and loan associations[c]	17.6	49.9	1.9	30.0
Total	100.0%	100.0%	100.0%	100.0%
Distribution by portfolio size	61.4%	38.3%	0.3%	100.0%

Data compiled from records of the Federal Deposit Insurance Corporation, the National Association of Mutual Savings Banks, the Home Loan Bank Board, and the United States Savings and Loan League, and from *Compendium of Official Life Insurance Reports, 1947* (Spectator Company).

[a] Includes banks in continental United States only, as of June 30.

[b] Distribution as of December 31, excluding five companies for which data were not available.

[c] Data as of December 31. Distribution of associations with portfolios of less than $50 million is estimated.

have nonfarm mortgage portfolios of less than $250,000, that mutual savings banks are approximately symmetrically distributed around their most frequent size group ($1 million to $5 million), and that insurance companies, though having nearly the same mode as the distribution of mutual savings banks, reach further into the large size classes (Table 19). No comparable information could be ob-

TABLE 19
Distribution of Number of Lending Institutions, 1946, by Size of Nonfarm Mortgage Loan Portfolio

Nonfarm Mortgage Loan Portfolio	*Mutual Savings Banks*[a]	*Insured Commercial Banks*[b]	*Life Insurance Companies*[c]	*Savings and Loan Associations*[d]
No holdings	..	3.8%	9.7%	..
Under $250,000	3.6%	72.2	24.9	29.4%
$250,000 - 0.9 million	18.3	17.5	15.1	36.2
1 - 4.9 million	45.0	5.7	21.9	27.3
5 - 24.9 million	25.2	0.7	15.7	6.6
25 - 49.9 million	4.7	e	3.2	0.5
50 million and over	3.2	e	8.1	e
Not available	..	..	1.4	..
Total	100.0%	100.0%	100.0%	100.0%

Compiled from records of the National Association of Mutual Savings Banks, and the Federal Deposit Insurance Corporation, and from *Compendium of Official Life Insurance Reports, 1947* (Spectator Company); data for savings and loan associations were prepared by the Operating Analysis Division of the Home Loan Bank Board.

[a] Distribution is by size of total mortgage loan portfolio, as of December 31.

[b] Covers banks in continental United States, as of June 30.

[c] Refers to companies in continental United States, as of December 31.

[d] Distribution is by estimated asset size and covers all associations as of December 31. For percentage of assets consisting of mortgage loans, see Table 22.

[e] Less than 0.05 per cent.

tained for savings and loan associations, but estimates based on asset size rather than on size of mortgage portfolio reveal a rather uniform distribution within a more confined size range: it is known, for example, that more than three-fifths of all savings and loan associations have assets of less than $1 million.

The four types of lender also differ quite clearly when compared with respect to the distribution of the industry's urban loan total among the portfolios of individual lending institutions: most even were the distributions for savings and loan associations and for mutual savings banks; least even, that for the life insurance companies; commercial banks assumed an intermediate position (Chart 5).

This account of the portfolio size pattern of the mortgage lending industry can be supplemented with data for 1951 showing the types

CHART 5

Lorenz Curves of Nonfarm Mortgage Holdings of Institutional Lenders, 1946
(cumulative percentage distribution of number of institutions, and of their nonfarm mortgage holdings, for lenders ranked by size of portfolio)

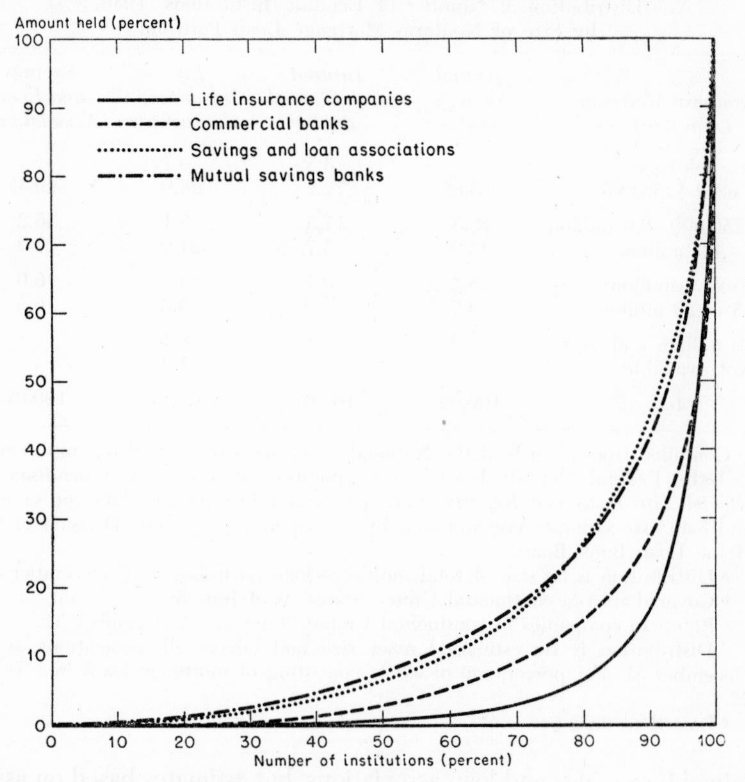

Computed from Table C-4.

of loans which tend to characterize, and to differentiate, the various size groups of lending agencies.[4] It is seen that conventionally financed loans predominate in the holdings of the small lenders, and that the proportion of insured loans increases as the portfolio size of the lender increases (Table 20). Only for insurance com-

[4] In these data the portfolios include farm as well as nonfarm residential mortgage loans.

TABLE 20

Relation between Size of Residential Mortgage Portfolio and Percent of Holdings Government-Insured, 1951

(*percentage distribution of amount outstanding*)

TYPE OF LENDER AND SIZE OF MORTGAGE LOAN PORTFOLIO	INSURED			CONVEN-TIONAL	TOTAL
	FHA	*VA*	*Total*		
Mutual Savings Banks	*28%*	*20%*	*48%*	*52%*	*100%*
Under $25,000	..	..	..	..	..
$25,000 - 99,999	..	..	..	100	100
100,000 - 499,999	11	19	30	70	100
500,000 - 0.9 million	7	16	23	77	100
1 - 4.9 million	5	24	29	71	100
5 - 9.9 million	8	27	35	65	100
10 - 24.9 million	13	28	41	59	100
25 - 49.9 million	27	18	45	55	100
50 million and over	37	15	52	48	100
Commercial Banks	*31*	*23*	*54*	*46*	*100*
Under $25,000	4	10	14	86	100
$25,000 - 99,999	8	13	21	79	100
100,000 - 499,999	12	22	34	66	100
500,000 - 0.9 million	13	25	38	62	100
1 - 4.9 million	19	26	45	55	100
5 - 9.9 million	29	26	55	45	100
10 - 24.9 million	43	22	65	35	100
25 - 49.9 million	52	22	74	26	100
50 million and over	45	22	67	33	100
Insurance Companies[a]	*40*	*21*	*61*	*39*	*100*
Under $25,000	9	4	13	87	100
$25,000 - 99,999	13	2	15	85	100
100,000 - 499,999	17	5	22	78	100
500,000 - 0.9 million	12	7	19	81	100
1 - 4.9 million	28	12	40	60	100
5 - 9.9 million	37	16	53	47	100
10 - 24.9 million	38	12	50	50	100
25 - 49.9 million	35	17	52	48	100
50 million and over	41	23	64	36	100
Savings and Loan Associations	*6*	*22*	*28*	*72*	*100*
Under $25,000	5	3	8	92	100
$25,000 - 99,999	[b]	2	2	98	100
$100,000 - 499,999	1	5	6	94	100
500,000 - 0.9 million	2	11	13	87	100
1 - 4.9 million	3	20	23	77	100
5 - 9.9 million	5	21	26	74	100
10 - 24.9 million	8	25	33	67	100
25 - 49.9 million	9	27	36	64	100
50 million and over	11	28	39	61	100

Based on data as of May 31, 1951 covering residential mortgages (nonfarm and farm) in "Real Estate Loans of Registrants under Regulation X" by Doris P. Warner, *Federal Reserve Bulletin,* June 1952, Table 5, p. 626.

[a] Includes property insurance companies and other types as well as life companies.

[b] Less than 0.5 percent.

panies and commercial banks with total mortgage portfolios of $5 million or more, and for mutual savings banks having portfolios of $50 million or more, do holdings of government-insured loans exceed those that are conventionally financed. Two other facts stand out. First, savings and loan associations in every size group had a smaller proportion of government-insured holdings than did the other types of lender. Second, among lending institutions of different types but comparable in size, differences in the percentage of insured holdings were smallest for the small lenders and largest for the large ones.

The composition of lenders' portfolios according to the type of property being financed is less clearly related to the size of the portfolio than is the insurance status of loans. The data do suggest a tendency for holdings of loans on nonresidential income-producing properties to increase with the size of the lender's total mortgage portfolio.[5] Commercial banks are an exception, however; for them the opposite tendency was observed. Mutual savings banks in all size classes but the very largest had smaller ratios of nonresidential to all nonfarm mortgage loans than the other lenders except savings and loan associations, whose activity in the nonresidential market is negligible.

Relative Importance of Mortgage Investments to Various Institutions

An understanding of the characteristics of mortgage lending institutions requires analysis not only of their portfolio size, but also of the importance of their mortgage holdings as against their other investments. Hence a comparison of urban mortgage investments to total assets for the several types of lender should be helpful in interpreting differences among them.

Measured by their percentage relationship to total assets, urban mortgage investments have by far the greatest importance for savings and loan associations; mutual savings banks are next in this ranking, followed by life insurance companies and finally by commercial banks (Table 21). For savings and loan associations the ratio of urban mortgage investments to total assets has oscillated, since the end of World War I, between about two-thirds and nine-tenths; the range for mutual savings banks has been one-quarter to one-half; for insurance companies, one-eighth to three-tenths; and for commercial banks, one fortieth to one-twelfth.

[5] Doris P. Warner, "Real Estate Loans of Registrants under Regulation X," *Federal Reserve Bulletin*, June 1952, Table 5, p. 626.

TABLE 21
Ratio of Nonfarm Mortgage Holdings to Lender's Total Assets, 1920-53

Year[a]	*Mutual Savings Banks*	*Commercial Banks*	*Life Insurance Companies*	*Savings and Loan Associations*[b]
1920	46.5%	4.8%	16.0%	74.3%
1921	46.0	5.0	17.0	73.9
1922	47.4	5.4	17.6	88.1
1923	48.6	6.1	19.6	88.1
1924	50.9	6.9	22.1	88.1
1925	52.4	7.5	24.0	90.8
1926	54.1	7.7	26.9	90.7
1927	55.3	7.8	27.7	90.2
1928	55.6	8.0	29.2	89.0
1929	57.4	8.2	29.8	87.8
1930	57.3	7.7	29.3	85.7
1931	54.0	7.8	28.2	83.0
1932	53.1	8.7	26.4	79.5
1933	51.9	7.3	24.3	75.3
1934	48.3	6.1	21.1	67.2
1935	45.5	5.9	18.5	63.1
1936	42.3	5.1	16.8	62.6
1937	41.8	5.6	16.5	65.9
1938	41.4	5.8	16.4	68.5
1939	40.6	5.6	16.4	72.1
1940	40.3	5.4	16.5	75.8
1941	40.5	5.4	16.9	78.9
1942	38.6	4.4	16.7	77.4
1943	33.7	3.5	15.5	71.7
1944	29.0	2.9	14.3	66.0
1945	24.6	2.6	13.1	62.5
1946	23.7	4.3	13.2	70.9
1947	24.5	5.5	15.0	76.5
1948	28.2	6.4	17.7	79.7
1949	31.0	6.8	19.7	80.0
1950	36.7	7.5	23.1	81.3
1951	42.1	7.6	26.1	81.4
1952	44.9	7.8	26.6	81.5
1953	47.5	8.1	27.3	82.3

Data on total assets were compiled from *Annual Reports* of the Comptroller of the Currency, from *Life Insurance Fact Book, 1954* (Institute of Life Insurance), p. 60, and from *Trends in the Savings and Loan Field, 1953* (Home Loan Bank Board), Table 1, p. 4. Data for savings and loan associations in 1920 and 1921 were supplied by the United States Savings and Loan League. For amount of lender's nonfarm mortgage loans outstanding, see Table C-1.

[a] Figures for total assets as of December 31, except those for commercial banks and mutual savings banks for 1920-35, which refer to June 30.

[b] Represents net mortgage debt outstanding as a percentage of net total assets of all associations in the United States and its possessions.

Mutual savings banks, commercial banks, and life insurance companies increased the ratio of their urban mortgage holdings to their total assets throughout the expansion of the twenties, but the comparable ratio for savings and loan associations started to decline, though only moderately, in 1926. In 1937, however, the share of savings and loan associations began an increase that continued through 1941, while the ratios for other major private lenders declined or held to a roughly stable level until 1946.

Although the rapidly expanding mortgage activity of the late forties and early fifties brought a reversal of the downward trend in the importance of mortgage holdings within all assets, basic differences among lenders were not affected. Nonfarm mortgage investments remained least important for commercial banks and most important for savings and loan associations. Moreover, none of the lenders reached the point where the ratio of their mortgage holdings to their total assets equaled or exceeded that reached in 1929, though by 1953 commercial banks and life insurance companies were very close to it. The ratio for mutual savings banks, on the other hand, remained well behind the 1929 level.

The foregoing comparisons concern averages for all individual agencies within each of the four types of institutional lender. Additional insight may be gained as to the importance of urban mortgage investments to the various types of lender if individual institutions are grouped, as in the 1946 data of Table 22, according to asset size. These groupings reveal that differences between types of lender, rather than differences in the size of the individual agencies within any given group, account for the institutional differences in the ratio of mortgage holdings to total assets. It should be noted, however, that in the case of life insurance companies the ratio was lowest for companies of largest size, while among commercial banks the lowest ratio was observed among both the largest and the smallest banks. The asset size of mutual savings banks, on the other hand, apparently has no systematic effect on the extent to which resources are invested in urban real estate loans. The high ratios that are special to savings and loan associations are also uniformly characteristic except that there is some tendency for them to taper off for the very large associations.

Here it would be of interest to examine the net income derived by the various lenders from their nonfarm mortgage portfolios. Unfortunately such information is extremely scarce, in particular because of the nearly complete absence of data on portfolio costs;

TABLE 22

Ratio of Nonfarm Mortgage Holdings to Total Assets, 1946, for Lenders Classified by Size of Assets

Asset Size	*Mutual Savings Banks*[a]	*Insured Commercial Banks*	*Life Insurance Companies*	*Savings and Loan Associations*[b]
Under $500,000		2.4%	14.1%	69.1%
$500,000 - 0.9 million	23.0%	3.0		71.3
1 - 2.49 million		3.9	15.2	73.4
2.5 - 9.9 million	23.8	5.4	21.9	72.5
10 - 24.9 million	23.1	5.5	18.1	69.1
25 - 49.9 million	23.0	4.4	26.7	
50 - 99.9 million	23.7	3.9	22.4	68.9
100 - 499.9 million	24.2	2.6	24.6	
500 million and over		2.0	10.4	
Total	23.8%	3.4%	13.2%	71.3%

Compiled from records of the National Association of Mutual Savings Banks and the Federal Deposit Insurance Corporation, and from *Compendium of Official Life Insurance Reports, 1947* (Spectator Company); data for savings and loan associations were prepared by the Operating Analysis Division of the Home Loan Bank Board. Figures as of December 31, with the exception of commercial banks (June 30).

[a] Represents total mortgage debt as a percentage of total assets.

[b] Represents estimated gross mortgage debt (i.e. inclusive of mortgage pledged shares) as a percentage of total assets.

what little evidence exists is not uniform and cannot be used to compare the several types of lending institution. Therefore, and because the best information at present available is on life insurance companies,[6] attention will be limited to the annual portfolio cost and income structure which characterized this one type of lender during the period 1945-53.[7]

The data presented in Table 23 are derived from an annual questionnaire survey conducted by the Life Insurance Association of America. In its survey (which continues a similar survey made by the NBER for the years 1945-47) the Association classifies com-

[6] R. J. Saulnier, *Urban Mortgage Lending by Life Insurance Companies* (National Bureau of Economic Research, Financial Research Program, 1950), Chapter 5; *City Mortgage Lending Income and Costs of Life Insurance Companies, 1945-1948* (Life Insurance Association of America, Investment Bulletin 53, 1950), and similar bulletins for later years (Nos. 75, 125, 173, and 201).

[7] For mutual savings banks see Chapter 11 of *Mutual Savings Banks in the Savings and Mortgage Markets*, by John Lintner (Harvard University, 1948); and for commercial banks see *Commercial Bank Activities in Urban Mortgage Financing*, by Carl F. Behrens (National Bureau of Economic Research, Financial Research Program, 1952), Chapter 5.

panies according to whether they operate branches for originating and servicing mortgages or rely predominantly on loan correspondents, and, within these broad groupings, according to the size of the companies' mortgage loan portfolio. For the present discussion,

TABLE 23

Ratios of Gross and Net Income to Average Urban Mortgage Holdings for Life Insurance Companies, 1945-53, by Size of Investment

YEAR	NONBRANCH COMPANIES WITH PORTFOLIOS OF:			
	Under $5 Million	*5 - 24.9 Million*	*25 - 99.9 Million*	*$100 Million and Over*
		Gross Income		
1945	4.55%	4.62%	4.44%	4.28%
1946	4.40	4.30	4.13	4.16
1947	4.26	4.34	4.09	4.03
1948	4.29	4.23	4.09	4.05
1949	4.34	4.31	4.13	4.09
1950	5.11	4.34	4.14	4.03
1951	4.75	4.45	4.28	4.16
1952	4.81	4.64	4.29	4.20
1953	5.10	4.61	4.40	4.27
		Net Income		
1945	3.46%	3.58%	3.69%	3.77%
1946	3.29	3.01	3.28	3.45
1947	2.74	2.97	3.16	3.16
1948	3.06	2.96	3.18	3.24
1949	3.42	3.35	3.39	3.38
1950	4.30	3.35	3.25	3.29
1951	3.99	3.68	3.52	3.50
1952	4.12	3.83	3.63	3.59
1953	4.34	3.88	3.74	3.66

Data supplied by the Life Insurance Association of America. Income data are expressed as percentages of annual average loan investment, computed for 1945-50 by averaging beginning and end of year holdings of city mortgages and real estate sales contract balances, and for 1951-53 by averaging monthly data. Average ratios are weighted by size of loan investment.

With nonbranch companies are included companies originating or servicing less than 25 percent of their loans through branch offices. Through 1949, companies are classified by portfolio size on the basis of their average holdings in 1946; thereafter classification is determined by current portfolio size. The number of companies varies from year to year.

only the data for companies not operating branches are used, since there are too few companies in the other category to yield representative results; and cost comparisons are limited to companies of different portfolio size within a given year. The refinements that have been made during the course of the survey's history to date in the investment base to which income and costs are related, and in classifying companies by portfolio size, impair year-to-year comparability of the data.[8]

Throughout the period 1945-53, gross income per dollar of average outstanding nonfarm loan balance was lowest for the companies having large portfolios, which is consistent with the fact that government-insured or -guaranteed loans and relatively low-rate conventional loans on commercial properties usually predominate in the large portfolios. Companies in the smallest portfolio-size group (under $5 million) in 1945 and 1947 and those with the largest portfolios ($100 million and over) in 1946 were the only exceptions to the inverse relationship between gross income ratios and portfolio size.

The pattern of change in average net income ratios as portfolio size increases is less regular. Net income per dollar of average loan investment varied directly with portfolio size in 1945 and 1947; although the movement in 1946 and 1948 was erratic, the net income ratios of the largest portfolio companies were higher than those of the smallest portfolio companies. A similar though somewhat more nebulous tendency for net income ratios to be highest for companies having large mortgage holdings was also observed by Saulnier in his analysis of lending costs and returns in 1945-47.[9] On the other hand, the data for 1949 and 1950 and especially those for 1951-53 show an inverse relationship between net income ratios and portfolio size.

A partial explanation of the change, first observable in 1949, in the relationship between net rates of return and portfolio size is found in the behavior of the total cost ratios; that is, in the difference between gross and net yields. Throughout the period, average unit costs, like gross yields, tended to vary inversely with portfolio size. During the years 1945 through 1948 unit costs fell sufficiently with size to offset the decline in gross yields associated with increasing size of operations. Consequently, net income ratios were higher for companies with large portfolios. Beginning with 1949, but especially

[8] Through 1950 the investment base is the average of a company's holdings of city mortgages and real estate sales contracts at the beginning and end of each year. For 1951 through 1953, average loan investment is computed from monthly data. During 1945-49, portfolio-size classification was determined by a company's average holdings as of 1946 or the first year thereafter in which it contributed data; since 1950, companies are classified according to their current portfolio size.

[9] See Saulnier, *op. cit.*, p. 69.

in later years, the differences in the total cost ratios for the various portfolio size groups became much less. Substantial decreases in the cost ratios of small-portfolio companies from their highs of the 1945-48 period largely accounted for this greater uniformity of cost ratios and also for the reversal of the previously more favorable position of the large-portfolio companies with respect to their net income ratios.

The LIAA studies for 1951 and 1952[10] also point toward lower cost ratios for portfolios consisting predominantly of conventionally financed loans than for government-insured portfolios. Since gross yields, on the other hand, were generally smaller on the insured part of the portfolios, a substantial spread resulted between net returns on investment from primarily FHA-insured and from conventionally financed portfolios.

All this suggests that for life insurance companies the relationship between net yields and size of the companies' nonfarm mortgage portfolio may be highly irregular. In periods such as the immediate postwar years when companies with small portfolios were expanding their loan volume at unusually high rates, they were not always successful in maintaining their lending costs at a level such as would enable them to hold the advantage which they enjoyed over the large-portfolio companies with respect to gross income ratios. It should be pointed out, however, that the above evidence may exaggerate to some degree the difference between the large- and the small-portfolio lender. It is not unlikely that underreporting of costs is found more often among small- than among large-portfolio companies and that in some small-portfolio companies accounting records do not permit as decisive an allocation of income and costs to lending operations as is feasible for the larger companies. In addition, the data make no allowance for the risk factor, which may be higher for the smaller-portfolio companies, who may well have been holders of higher risk portfolios. Serious consideration should also be given the possibility that variation in the data may result from the small size of the sample (particularly for the small-portfolio size group), from its changing composition, over the period, and from the changes that have been made in computing the investment base.

[10] *City Mortgage Lending Income and Costs of Life Insurance Companies, 1951*, pp. 4 ff., and *ibid., 1952* (Investment Bulletin 201, 1954), pp. 3 ff.

Geographic Patterns of Institutional Holdings

The markets served by the four principal private mortgage lenders cover the entire United States, but the aggregate portfolios of the four are not equally distributed geographically.

Historical data on location of mortgaged properties are available only for life insurance companies; for other institutions, information is limited to location of lender. However, commercial banks, savings and loan associations, and mutual savings banks are, unlike insurance companies, mainly short-distance lenders, though the savings banks have in recent years appreciably increased their purchases of out-of-state mortgages. Hence location of lender and location of collateral should be highly correlated for all three types of lenders, especially if the geographic grouping is in terms of broad areas such as the census divisions used in the subsequent tables. The geographic scope of commercial bank operations would be revealed as more extensive, certainly so far as the larger money-market institutions affect the aggregate, if the analysis were to include loans for large-scale construction projects and short-term loans for carrying mortgages destined for ultimate sale to long-term investors. These activities are not covered, however, in the present analysis.

Observing the geographic patterns of the various lending institutions (Table 24), we find that mutual savings banks showed the heaviest concentration. Few changes have taken place in this situation since the late twenties: the relative importance of some of the South Atlantic and especially of the West North Central states as mortgage investment outlets for the mutuals has increased since 1928, while the importance of the Pacific and East North Central regions has decreased. In spite of those shifts, only about 2 percent of the urban mortgage debt held by mutual savings banks is held by institutions in the West North Central and South Atlantic regions combined; the overwhelmingly most important market of the mutuals is still, as it was in the late twenties, the northeastern United States. In three of the nine census divisions no mutuals were found at all.

This long-standing pattern of heavy geographic concentration is confirmed by the recently tabulated results of the Survey of Residential Financing of 1950, which do throw some light on geographic location of collateral.[11] Nearly nine-tenths of the mutual savings banks' aggregate portfolio of loans on one- to four-family homes was

[11] Reference is to the *1950 Census of Housing*, Vol. 4, Residential Financing, Part 1, Chapter 2, Table 2, pp. 40 ff. The data are tabulated by type of lender and by actual location of the property.

TABLE 24

Regional Distribution of Nonfarm Mortgage Holdings of Institutional Lenders, 1928-50

Region and Census Division[a]	*1928*	*1933*	*1934*	*1939*	*1946*	*1950*
			Mutual Savings Banks			
North	*97%*	*98%*	*98%*	*98%*	*98%*	*98%*
New England	83	32	31	30	28	26
Middle Atlantic	12	65	65	67	68	70
East North Central	2	1	1	1	1	1
West North Central	..	..	b	b	1	1
South	*1*	*1*	*1*	*1*	*1*	*1*
South Atlantic	1	1	1	1	1	1
East South Central	..	..	..	..	..	..
West South Central	..	..	..	..	..	..
West	*2*	*1*	*1*	*1*	*1*	*1*
Mountain	..	..	..	..	..	..
Pacific	2	1	1	1	1	1
			Commercial Banks			
North	*68%*	*71%*	*66%*	*60%*	*58%*	*58%*
New England	14	12	12	9	7	6
Middle Atlantic	22	41	34	27	21	23
East North Central	30	16	16	19	22	21
West North Central	2	2	4	5	8	8
South	*6*	*6*	*10*	*13*	*16*	*15*
South Atlantic	3	3	6	8	9	9
East South Central	1	1	2	3	3	3
West South Central	2	2	2	2	4	3
West	*26*	*23*	*24*	*27*	*26*	*27*
Mountain	2	1	1	2	3	3
Pacific	24	22	23	25	23	24
			Savings and Loan Associations			
North	*79%*	*79%*	*79%*	*70%*	*66%*	*64%*
New England	8	9	10	12	10	8
Middle Atlantic	35	34	35	23	20	20
East North Central	29	29	28	27	28	28
West North Central	7	7	6	8	8	8
South	*15*	*15*	*15*	*21*	*22*	*22*
South Atlantic	7	7	8	13	14	13
East South Central	2	3	3	3	3	3
West South Central	6	5	4	5	5	6
West	*7*	*6*	*6*	*9*	*12*	*14*
Mountain	2	1	1	2	2	2
Pacific	5	5	5	7	10	12

(continued on next page)

TABLE 24 (continued)

Region and Census Division[a]	*1928*	*1933*	*1934*	*1939*	*1946*	*1950*
			Life Insurance Companies			
North	*73%*	*74%*	*74%*	*74%*	*68%*	*50%*
New England	3	3	3	4	5	3
Middle Atlantic	40	40	41	43	39	23
East North Central	22	24	24	21	19	18
West North Central	8	7	6	6	5	6
South	*18*	*16*	*16*	*17*	*22*	*32*
South Atlantic	10	9	9	10	12	15
East South Central	4	4	3	3	3	5
West South Central	4	4	4	4	7	12
West	*9*	*10*	*10*	*9*	*10*	*18*
Mountain	1	1	1	1	1	3
Pacific	8	9	9	8	9	15

Based on data for mutual savings banks and commercial banks from the *Annual Reports* of the Comptroller of the Currency (as of June 30 for 1928, 1933, and 1934), and for life insurance companies from relevant issues of the *Proceedings of the Annual Meeting of the Life Insurance Association of America*; the latter represent the holdings of 49 companies (in 1928, 52 companies) whose admitted assets accounted for about 90 per cent of the assets of all legal reserve life companies in the United States. For savings and loan associations the 1928-46 figures are based on the distribution of mortgage investments by state given in the *Annals of the United States Savings and Loan League*; regional totals in 1928, where the distribution was incomplete, were adjusted upward by apportioning the amount for "other states" according to the relationship between the components of the "other states" group and their regional totals in 1933. Data for 1950 are from *Trends in the Savings and Loan Field, 1951* (Home Loan Bank Board), Table 7, p. 11.

[a] Refers to location of institution except in the case of life insurance companies, where reference is to the location of the mortgaged properties. For a listing of states included in the census divisions, see Table 3, note a.

[b] Less than 0.5 percent.

secured by collateral located in the Northeast; only 3 percent was located in the two North Central regions combined, and the same small fraction in the whole of the South.

A number of reasons have been advanced to explain the heavy geographic concentration of the mutual savings banks, which distinguishes them sharply from other major types of lending institutions. Of these the most important is probably the early need for thrift institutions to invest the modest but regular savings of urban industrial workers in the New England and Middle Atlantic states, which contrasts markedly with the greater possibilities and greater demands for direct investment by the individual saver in the agricultural areas of the Middle West and the South. By the time the demand for capital in the West had assumed significant proportions, there had already been established a network of commercial banks with the right to accept savings deposits unlimited by the restrictions which surrounded that function in the East.[12]

Commercial banks and savings and loan associations—which, like mutual savings banks, have been primarily short-distance lenders serving a local market—differed from mutual savings banks in their geographic pattern, which was much more diversified. In 1950 about one-quarter of the entire urban mortgage debt held by commercial banks was held by banks located in the Pacific states (Table 24). The relatively large number of big lenders in California—including the largest single urban mortgage lender, the Bank of America—accounts for the fact that the Pacific coast is such an outstanding mortgage market for banks. The industrial Middle Atlantic and the East North Central states follow closely; the South Central and Mountain states are the least important. Since the predepression peak, gradual changes have occurred in this geographic pattern, suggesting a growing interest in the new markets of the South, of the western farm belt (West North Central), and of the Mountain states, at the expense of the traditional investment areas of commercial banks—the East North Central, New England, Pacific, and Middle Atlantic states.

Mortgage holdings of savings and loan associations were more heavily concentrated geographically than those of commercial banks, but less so than the holdings of mutual savings banks. In 1928 nearly three-quarters of the aggregate mortgage holdings of the associations was held by those located in the Northeast and in the midwestern states east of the Mississippi; but the associations' market has been slowly shifting, like the markets of commercial banks, toward the South and the West (Table 24). Thus, while the importance of the East North Central and of the Middle Atlantic states decreased, the newer markets of the South and West have gradually expanded.

Insurance companies showed a different pattern from any of the foregoing three. By their very nature they are long-distance lenders, serving markets far away from their home offices. Since their lending radius is not restricted by legislation comparable to that applying to some of the other lenders, and since in many instances they have created elaborate and far-flung channels for the acquisition of loans, insurance companies have been comparatively free to allocate their funds regionally. The most important regions of urban mortgage

[12] See Lintner, *op. cit.*, Chapter 3 in particular.

investment for insurance companies, as for savings and loan associations, were the Northeast and the part of the Middle West lying east of the Mississippi; in the late twenties and thirties over three-fifths of the entire outstanding urban mortgage debt of insurance companies was secured by properties located in the Middle Atlantic and East North Central states (Table 24). Until the end of 1946 the geographic pattern of the urban mortgage holdings of insurance companies was more stable over time and underwent fewer changes than the distributions for savings and loan associations and, especially, commercial banks. This may be due to the greater stability of insurance companies in the depression of the thirties and to their greater flexibility in the choice of markets, which permitted them to follow a steady policy of gradual diversification. Over the entire period beginning with 1928 and including the depression, the greatest shift was a relative increase for the West South Central states and a corresponding decrease for the Middle Atlantic and East North Central states.

Institutional Participation in Insured Lending

The availability of mortgage loan insurance seems to have been of greatest interest to the lending institutions which in the past have been least heavily committed to the mortgage as a type of investment, and of least interest to those institutions that, by and large, have been most heavily dependent on urban mortgage financing as a channel of investment. Thus, judging by FHA reports of the number of institutions with insured holdings at the end of 1950, nearly all life insurance companies, but less than three-tenths of all savings and loan associations, had then some investment in insured mortgages, despite the fact that mortgage investment has traditionally been the major outlet for the associations' funds. In another manner the same contrast is revealed in figures which show that insurance companies and commercial banks held about three-fourths of all FHA-insured loans on one- to four-family homes in 1950, and that the largest numbers of conventional loans were held by the savings and loan associations and the group labeled "individuals" (Table 25).

A second point of interest in this connection is that, except for the savings and loan associations, the various lenders have tended to make their relatively heaviest use of mortgage loan insurance in the more recently industrializing and more rapidly developing sections of the country. Thus, for life insurance companies the percentage of

TABLE 25

Distribution of Conventional and of Insured Mortgages on Owner-Occupied Homes, 1950, by Type of Mortgage Holder

TYPE OF MORTGAGE HOLDER	INSURED *FHA*	*VA*	*Total*	CONVEN-TIONAL	TOTAL
Commercial banks	34%	31%	33%	17%	22%
Mutual savings banks	10	11	10	8	8
Savings and loan associations	9	31	20	33	29
Life insurance companies	40	14	27	6	12
Mortgage companies	3	1	2	1	1
Federal National Mortgage Association	2	10	6	..	2
Individuals	..	a	a	31	22
Other	2	2	2	4	4
Total	100%	100%	100%	100%	100%

Based on data covering first mortgages on one- to four-family nonfarm homes occupied by owner, from *1950 Census of Housing*, Vol. 4, Residential Financing, Part 1, Chapter 2, Table 2, p. 41.

[a] Less than 0.5 percent.

insured mortgage holdings in 1950 was highest in the South and lowest in the Northeast (Table 26). For commercial banks the percentage was highest in the West, and for mutual savings banks it was high in both the South and the West. By and large, savings and loan associations have made about equal use of the insurance device in all areas of the country.

By way of explanation, it would appear that life insurance companies and mutual savings banks have relied on government loan insurance most heavily in markets that were not their accustomed ones; namely, the insurance companies in the South and the mutual savings banks in the South and West—in the case of the mutuals, particularly because the liberalization of geographic restrictions on their investment in mortgages applied only to FHA and VA loans. With respect to the commercial banks, an explanation of their extensive use of government insurance and guaranty in connection with mortgage lending in the West can probably be found in the lending policies of the largest single mortgage lender serving the markets of the West, the Bank of America, and its favorable attitude toward FHA and VA loans. The over-all effect observable in the data on utilization of government insurance has been toward a greater homogeneity in the markets, both with respect to the participation in mortgage lending by various types of institutional lenders and in mortgage investment in various parts of the country.

TABLE 26

Differences in Extent of Use of Government Home Mortgage Insurance, Regionally and by Type of Lender
(percentage distribution of lender's holdings within region: number of mortgages and amount outstanding, 1950)

REGION AND TYPE OF LOAN	MUTUAL SAVINGS BANKS		COMMERCIAL BANKS		LIFE INSURANCE COMPANIES		SAVINGS AND LOAN ASSOCIATIONS		MORTGAGE COMPANIES	
	No.	*Amt.*	*No.*	*Amt.*	*No.*	*Amt.*	*No.*	*Amt.*	*No.*	*Amt.*
NORTHEAST										
Insured	*33*	*46%*	*41*	*51%*	*41*	*45%*	*21*	*33%*	*68*	*80%*
FHA	14	18	16	16	21	19	2	3	36	37
VA	19	28	25	35	20	26	19	30	32	43
Conventional	*67*	*54*	*59*	*49*	*59*	*55*	*79*	*67*	*32*	*20*
NORTH CENTRAL										
Insured	*39*	*47*	*41*	*56*	*63*	*67*	*21*	*30*	*50*	*62*
FHA	29	32	22	31	47	48	4	6	41	52
VA	10	15	19	25	16	19	17	24	9	10
Conventional	*61*	*53*	*59*	*44*	*37*	*33*	*79*	*70*	*50*	*38*
SOUTH										
Insured	*56*	*67*	*31*	*49*	*71*	*74*	*19*	*28*	*63*	*80*
FHA	42	51	19	29	54	54	7	10	40	47
VA	14	16	12	20	17	20	12	18	23	33
Conventional	*44*	*33*	*69*	*51*	*29*	*26*	*81*	*72*	*37*	*20*
WEST										
Insured	*61*	*67*	*60*	*73*	*64*	*64*	*21*	*31*	*55*	*64*
FHA	46	47	35	38	53	52	10	14	41	44
VA	15	20	25	35	11	12	11	17	14	20
Conventional	*39*	*33*	*40*	*27*	*36*	*36*	*79*	*69*	*45*	*36*
UNITED STATES										
Insured	*35*	*48*	*44*	*59*	*64*	*67*	*20*	*31*	*59*	*73*
FHA	17	21	23	29	48	48	5	7	40	46
VA	18	27	21	30	16	19	15	24	19	27
Conventional	*65*	*52*	*56*	*41*	*36*	*33*	*80*	*69*	*41*	*27*

Based on data covering first mortgages on one- to four-family nonfarm homes occupied by owner, from *1950 Census of Housing*, Vol. 4, Residential Financing, Part 1, Chapter 2, Table 2, pp. 41-57 *passim*. For areas included in each region, see note under Table 9.

The complexities of the mortgage-credit-supplying industry in general, and the differences between the four principal mortgage lenders in particular, are the result of a long list of circumstances, among which are (1) differences in the legal framework within which the various types of lending institution have operated, (2) differences in the types of funds they channeled into the market and in the costs of, and returns from, such operations, and (3) differences in the historical setting within which these institutions developed.

Differences in their policies consequent on those varied circumstances all played an important role. Thus, savings and loan associations—the successors to the early building societies—even today reflect their original preoccupation with the field of housing, although like other lending institutions they have diverted an increasing part of their assets into the government bond market. These associations today, as earlier, are the most uniformly distributed important supplier of the home mortgage markets of the nation. They continue to rely largely on conventional mortgage financing, having made less use of government-sponsored loan insurance than any of the other principal mortgage lenders.

Less heavily involved in the mortgage lending business than the savings and loan associations were the mutual savings banks, and still less so the commercial banks. Mutual savings banks, at one time a close second to the associations, steadily declined after 1920 in their importance among mortgage fund suppliers. Some of the reasons underlying the geographic restriction of these lending institutions to the older markets of the country may also furnish part of the explanation for their relative decline as mortgage fund suppliers. Yet the slowing down of the momentum of residential construction in the old industrial centers of the East cannot sufficiently account for the decline of mutual savings banks. Even in their traditional markets they have fallen behind other mortgage lenders because of a failure to increase their resources as rapidly as other institutions and through a tendency to increase their investment in public securities.

Commercial banks assumed a position of relative importance as direct lenders in the mortgage field before the life insurance companies but later than the savings and loan associations, and the banks' share of the mortgage market has increased more slowly than that of the life companies. This in-between situation of the commercial banks with respect to historical development is matched by their position within the present lending industry's structure: between the small savings and loan association and the large life insurance company, between the specialist in small home loans and the distributor of large mortgages on income-producing property, and between the short-distance, single-outlet dealer and the long-distance, multiple-outlet lending institution.

Last among the four principal lenders to be drawn into the financing of the building boom were the life insurance companies. Whereas associations and banks declined in numbers from the early twenties onward, the life insurance sector of the industry increased, not only in number of lenders but also in its share of the market. This rapid expansion of the nonfarm mortgage portfolios of life insurance companies probably ranks close to the rapid increase in the importance of the government's role in the mortgage markets as an outstanding feature of the structural change that has taken place since the end of World War I. A glance at the structure of mortgage assets and their distribution for various lenders will quickly persuade the observer of the tremendous impact that must be exerted by even a minor change in the portion of investable funds that insurance companies seek to locate in the nation's mortgage markets.

Within the general framework of interlender differences, certain realignments can be discerned; and although the uncertainty of the future trends cautions against overemphasizing them, it may be worth while to point out the presence of elements in today's mortgage lending structure that tend to overshadow some of the time-honored distinctions between the four major types of lending institution.

Overlapping the historical grouping of nonfarm mortgage lenders into savings and loan associations, mutual savings banks, commercial banks, and life insurance companies, new and functionally important differences emerge: the difference between the small and the large mortgage portfolio, between the locally and the nationally oriented lender, between institutions making extensive use of FHA insurance and those relying more heavily on conventional forms of mortgage finance. Though these differences are not independent of the accustomed four-way grouping of lenders, they do point toward new affinities—say, from the point of view of the cost structure—between lenders that resemble one another with respect to size, geographic lending horizon, and the like. Frequently the new affinities are, in turn, closely interrelated. Thus institutions which, because of the amount of funds to be invested, are driven toward large-scale mortgage lending operations are likely also to consider markets beyond the immediate local ones; and to such lenders, since they are engaged in what might be compared to mass production, the lower net returns on FHA-insured loans are not in themselves discouraging. Therefore the large-scale, long-distance lender often will make eager use of government loan insurance in the markets that are unfamiliar to him.

In this connection it should be recalled that the impact of government on the structure of the mortgage industry has by no means been limited to the effects of the insurance and guaranty programs on mortgage characteristics—that is, to direct intervention in the mortgage markets through the FHA and VA. Less direct, though probably more potent in long-range effect on the structure of the lending industry, was the government fiscal program, the consequences of which are only in part reflected in the tables on the preceding pages. At the same time that the government through its mortgage insurance programs furthered a cost and income structure tending to reduce the spread between net returns on mortgages and on government bonds, it also provided a growing demand for funds through its constantly expanding debt. So strong has been the government's influence on the structure of the lending industry, that it seems hardly exaggerated to think of the successful mortgage lender's future policy problems in terms of attempts to anticipate the government's over-all policies rather than of the traditional attempts to evaluate mortgage risks. In conclusion, it might again be pointed out that in effect, though probably not by intention, most of the government's measures in the mortgage field facilitated and hastened a development toward greater uniformity in the markets and in the lending industry.

≺ 4 ≻

CHARACTERISTICS OF OUTSTANDING MORTGAGES

DIFFERENCES among the various types of institutional lender are reflected also by the characteristics of the loans in their portfolios. At the time the National Bureau undertook its studies of urban mortgage lending, the lack of anything but very fragmentary information on the types of loans held by different lending agencies made it impossible to give an adequate account of such differences. In order to overcome the deficiency, a sample of urban real estate loans was drawn in 1947 from the files of selected life insurance companies, commercial banks, and savings and loan associations.[1] For each of the sampled loans, data were transcribed on the salient characteristics of the property being financed and the loan contract entailed.

The general dimensions of the survey, which included both active and inactive loans, were as follows:[2] Of the 300 or so life insurance companies then existing, whose aggregate mortgage holdings were concentrated among a small number of large companies, 24 of the large lending institutions—accounting for roughly two-thirds of the entire urban mortgage debt held by all companies at the end of 1944—furnished a one percent sample, which produced information on approximately 9,000 mortgage loans. Commercial banks and savings and loan associations of all sizes were included in the sample. Ultimately 170 commercial banks, representing about one-third of the commercial banks' total nonfarm mortgage portfolio as of mid-1945, and 202 savings and loan associations, holding an estimated one-fourth or more of the corresponding mortgage debt, responded to the canvass and together produced a total of 15,000 loan cards.

Of about 24,000 loans reported in all, nearly 11,000 were outstand-

[1] Mutual savings banks were excluded because they were under study elsewhere.

For a detailed description of the designing of the sample, and an appraisal of the results, see Appendix A.

[2] The loans have been analyzed separately for the different lenders by R. J. Saulnier in *Urban Mortgage Lending by Life Insurance Companies*, by Carl F. Behrens in *Commercial Bank Activities in Urban Mortgage Financing* (National Bureau of Economic Research, Financial Research Program, 1950 and 1952 respectively), and by Edward E. Edwards in "Urban Real Estate Financing by Savings and Loan Associations" (*id.*, mimeo., December 1950).

ing at the survey date.[3] The different lenders contributed to the current loan sample approximately as follows: life insurance companies, 3,400 loans; commercial banks, 4,600; savings and loan associations, 3,000.

While these materials make possible a more detailed description of the loans held by different types of institutional lender than could ever before be given, the sample is subject to certain very definite and important weaknesses. In the first place, the response to the National Bureau's inquiry, especially by small commercial banks and savings and loan associations, was deficient. Even after several follow-up efforts the deficiency could not be removed. Therefore the sample estimates are subject to a nonresponse bias of unknown magnitude. The seriousness of the nonresponse factor is moderated somewhat by the fact that the characteristics of the loans held by small institutions, where nonresponse was heaviest, appear to be somewhat more uniform than for the sample as a whole. Yet despite this favorable circumstance differences in the distributions shown in the various tables must be interpreted with caution. Accordingly, attention is called in the text only to those features of the tabulations which are so pronounced as hardly to be affected by the bias of nonresponse.

Second, it should be remembered that among the large commercial banks the portfolio of a single west coast lender is of such overwhelming magnitude as to affect heavily the total of the group.

Third, throughout this chapter and the next, one of the major shortcomings of the interpretation, and perhaps more generally of the historical approach, is the difficulty of disentangling the joint effect simultaneously exerted by the many factors affecting mortgage behavior. As so frequently happens, when controlled experiment is impractical reliance must be placed on the analysis of past experience. Only rarely, however, does past experience provide information in such a form that the separate effects of a number of concurrent forces can feasibly be brought under observation. When provision of evidence must be left to the "historical accident" of the mortgage market, the number of cases that would fall in the many cells required by even a modest four-way table could hardly be expected to yield statistically valid results unless a sample of forbidding size

[3] For brevity, 1947 will be given as the date of report, in both text and tables. Life insurance companies reported as of the end of 1946; returns from commercial banks came chiefly in mid-1947 and from savings and loan associations chiefly in the fall of 1947, in both cases continuing into early 1948.

were drawn. This is an additional reason why the subsequent data should be considered as suggestive at best, and certainly not as conclusive.

Type of Property

In terms of the number of mortgages involved, the single most important type of property on which mortgages were held by the various lenders in 1947 was the one- to four-family home (Table 27).

TABLE 27
Distribution of Nonfarm Mortgage Loans Outstanding 1947, by Type of Property

Type of Property	*Life Insurance Companies*	*Commercial Banks*	*Savings and Loan Associations*
		Number of Loans	
1- to 4-Family Homes	*91%*	*89%*	*97%*
1-family	86	80	84
2- to 4-family	5	7	12
1- to 4-family with business use	[a]	2	1
All Other Property	9	*11*	3
Apartments	5	3	1
Stores	3	3	[a]
Other[b]	1	5	2
Total	100%	100%	100%
		Amount Outstanding	
1- to 4-Family Homes	*44%*	*64%*	*94%*
1-family	40	56	78
2- to 4-family	3	6	15
1- to 4-family with business use	[a]	3	1
All Other Property	*56*	*36*	*6*
Apartments	35	7	2
Stores	13	7	[a]
Other[b]	8	22	4
Total	100%	100%	100%

Based on National Bureau of Economic Research survey of urban mortgage lending; for coverage, see text shortly preceding.

[a] Less than 0.5 percent.

[b] Includes office buildings, institutions, and industrial, miscellaneous, and unclassified properties. Also includes a few farm properties for savings and loan associations.

Nine-tenths of all urban real estate loans held by life insurance companies and commercial banks at that time, and 97 percent of those held by savings and loan associations, were secured by small residential properties. Nearly all of the home mortgage loans held by life insurance companies were secured by single family homes, but commercial banks and especially savings and loan associations also held significant percentages of their portfolios in loans secured by two- to four-family residences. Loans on one- to four-family homes with business use, though of negligible importance to all lenders, were found most often in the portfolios of commercial banks; loans on apartments were held most frequently by life insurance companies. In any case, loans on all residential properties, including apartments and properties with only incidental business use, accounted for about 95 percent of the loans in the portfolios of each of the lenders.

Investment in income-producing properties—that is, in all property except one- to four-family residences—was heaviest for life insurance companies; and for them, investment within the category of income-producing properties was heaviest in residential buildings. Commercial banks (and this was particularly true of the medium-sized and small ones) also held substantial portions of their urban real estate investment in the form of loans on income-producing properties; unlike insurance companies, however, they specialized in nonresidential properties—industrial structures, office buildings, and the like.

A comparison of the number of loans with amounts outstanding reveals that the investments of life insurance companies in loans secured by income-producing properties consisted primarily of loans of relatively large outstanding balances. Apartment house loans, for example, accounted for only one-twentieth of the number of loans held by insurance companies but for more than one-third of their outstanding balances. On the other hand, apartment loans were almost as unimportant for savings and loan associations in amount as in number.

Loans secured by stores and by industrial and related properties show a similar pattern of differences among the principal institutional lenders. Such loans comprised only about one-twenty-fifth of the number of loans held by life insurance companies, but over one-fifth of the amount outstanding. The comparable measures for commercial banks are 8 percent and nearly 30 percent.[4] Savings and loan associations held few such loans and these were of relatively small size.

[4] The percentages for commercial bank loans in Table 27 and other tables of this chapter sometimes differ slightly from those given by Behrens (*op. cit.*) because of the adjustment for nonresponse described in Appendix A (page 137).

In summary, savings and loan associations were most narrowly specialized in terms of the major types of property securing their loans, and life insurance companies were the most diversified. Life insurance companies were particularly interested in large income-producing properties; commercial banks were the most active lenders on small and middle-sized income-producing properties; and savings and loan associations were interested almost exclusively in small residential properties.

Insurance Status

Over nine-tenths of the mortgages on income-producing properties held by each of the three types of institution, and from about one-half to three-fourths of those secured by one- to four-family homes, were conventionally financed (Table 28). Most of the conventionally financed home mortgages were fully amortized loans—nearly all of

TABLE 28

Insured Loans and Conventional Amortized Loans as Percents of Nonfarm Mortgages Outstanding 1947

TYPE OF LOAN	1- TO 4-FAMILY HOMES: Life Ins. Cos.	1- TO 4-FAMILY HOMES: Commercial Banks	1- TO 4-FAMILY HOMES: Savings & Loan Assocs.	ALL OTHER PROPERTY: Life Ins. Cos.	ALL OTHER PROPERTY: Commercial Banks	ALL OTHER PROPERTY: Savings & Loan Assocs.
			Number of Loans			
Insured	*55%*	*45%*	*21%*	*4%*	*9%*	*5%*
FHA	51	23	5	3	1	1
VA	4	22	16	1	7	4
All Conventional	*45*	*55*	*79*	*96*	*91*	*95*
Fully amortized	32	34	78[a]	33	48	94[a]
Partially amortized	8	16	..	56	29	..
Nonamortized	5	5	1	7	14	1
			Amount Outstanding			
Insured	*53%*	*53%*	*32%*	*9%*	*2%*	*3%*
FHA	48	19	6	8	b	b
VA	5	34	26	b	2	3
All Conventional	*47*	*47*	*68*	*91*	*98*	*97*
Fully amortized	36	26	67[a]	17	31	96[a]
Partially amortized	6	17	..	68	51	..
Nonamortized	5	4	1	6	16	1

Based on National Bureau of Economic Research survey of urban mortgage lending; for coverage, see the opening of Chapter 4.

[a] Includes the following types of loan: direct reduction, cancel and endorse, and share accumulation plan.

[b] Less than 0.5 percent.

those held by savings and loan associations, approximately seven-tenths of those held by life insurance companies, and six-tenths of those held by commercial banks.

As would be expected, the proportion of fully amortized loans of the conventional type was somewhat smaller among loans secured by income-producing properties than among those secured by homes: about one-third for life insurance companies and over one-half for commercial banks (though much higher for savings and loan associations, where the amount involved was very small). Adding to these the small but not negligible number of partially amortized loans, we see that the nonamortized mortgage had become the exception, representing one-tenth or less of the noninsured home mortgage loans held by leading institutional lenders in 1947.

Contract Length

The contract length of loans in the portfolios of various types of lenders in 1947 also varied according to the type of property which served as collateral. In general, contract lengths were longer for mortgages secured by homes than for those secured by income-producing properties, even among conventional loans, where the effects of government insurance on contract length were not in play (Table 29). Among conventionally financed home mortgages, those held by life insurance companies had the longest terms and those held by commercial banks (especially those with medium-sized portfolios) the shortest. The typical maturities used by insurance companies were fifteen years or longer, whereas most loans of savings and loan associations had terms of from ten to fourteen years; those made by commercial banks were the shortest of all, with typical contract lengths of from five to fourteen years. Finally, it should be observed that in home mortgage lending activities the greatest variety of practice with respect to contract length was shown by commercial banks; in comparison, insurance companies and savings and loan associations followed far more uniform policies.

Because of aforementioned deficiencies in the sample, data on the characteristics of loans secured by income-producing properties are especially weak, and observation should be limited to the most salient features. It is apparent that insurance was of relatively little importance on these loans, and that they were made with much shorter contract maturities than loans secured by one- to four-family homes.

TABLE 29

Contract Lengths of Nonfarm Mortgage Loans Outstanding 1947

(*percentage distribution of lender's holdings*)

CONTRACT LENGTH	1- TO 4-FAMILY HOMES			ALL OTHER PROPERTY		
	Life Ins. Cos.	*Commercial Banks*	*Savings & Loan Assocs.*	*Life Ins. Cos.*	*Commercial Banks*	*Savings & Loan Assocs.*
			Number of Loans			
All Loans						
0 - 4 years	4%	11%	1%	3%	19%	2%
5 - 9	4	24	8	21	43	11
10 - 14	10	23	45	43	34	46
15 - 19	18	12	25	23	2	22
20 and over	63	30	19	10	2	5
Unspecified	[a]	..	2	..	..	14
Conventional						
0 - 4 years	10	19	1	3	20	2
5 - 9	9	42	10	22	46	11
10 - 14	19	32	54	45	32	48
15 - 19	31	6	25	23	1	22
20 and over	31	1	7	7	[a]	2
Unspecified	[a]	..	3	..	..	15
			Amount Outstanding			
All Loans						
0 - 4 years	5%	7%	1%	2%	15%	3%
5 - 9	3	16	4	13	30	7
10 - 14	8	25	33	40	53	34
15 - 19	18	11	32	28	1	25
20 and over	66	41	29	17	1	27
Unspecified	[a]	..	1	..	..	4
Conventional						
0 - 4 years	10	14	1	2	16	3
5 - 9	6	34	6	14	31	7
10 - 14	16	44	44	43	52	35
15 - 19	31	7	36	30	1	25
20 and over	37	1	11	10	[a]	26
Unspecified	[a]	..	2	..	..	4

Based on National Bureau of Economic Research survey of urban mortgage lending; for coverage, see the opening of Chapter 4.

[a] Less than 0.5 percent.

Loan-to-Value Ratios

The uncertainty of the basis on which property valuations are made is such that important reservations must be borne in mind when dealing with loan-to-value ratios; nevertheless data on this point are useful in indicating broad differences in the lending policies of different types of institutional lender. Like the tabulations of length of contract, data on loan-to-value ratios indicate that credit terms have generally been more liberal for mortgages on homes than for those secured by income-producing properties, and more liberal for insured than for conventionally financed mortgage loans. Approximately one-half of the home mortgages held by life insurance companies and one-third of those held by banks had loan-to-value ratios of 80 percent or more; but only about one-eighth and one-twelfth, respectively, of these agencies' loans on income-producing properties exhibited comparably high ratios (Table 30). Tabulations

TABLE 30

Loan-to-Value Ratios for Nonfarm Mortgage Loans Outstanding 1947
(*percentage distribution of lender's holdings*)

LOAN-TO-VALUE RATIO	1- TO 4-FAMILY HOMES			ALL OTHER PROPERTY		
	Life Ins. Cos.	*Commercial Banks*	*Savings & Loan Assocs.*	*Life Ins. Cos.*	*Commercial Banks*	*Savings & Loan Assocs.*
			Number of Loans			
0 - 39%	2%	8%	5%	11%	22%	15%
40 - 59	18	33	16	47	49	29
60 - 79	28	26	55	27	20	31
80 and over	52	32	23	13	8	22
Not available	[a]	1	1	1	1	3
			Amount Outstanding			
0 - 39%	2%	4%	2%	7%	12%	10%
40 - 59	17	26	10	34	37	51
60 - 79	30	27	54	42	21	27
80 and over	51	42	33	15	28	10
Not available	[a]	1	1	2	2	1

Based on National Bureau of Economic Research survey of urban mortgage lending; for coverage, see the opening of Chapter 4.
[a] Less than 0.5 percent.

not reproduced here also show that only one-seventh of the conventional loans held by life insurance companies, and less than one-tenth of those found in the portfolios of savings and loan associations, had such liberal loan-to-value ratios; for commercial banks the fraction was even smaller. As in other respects, the pattern characterizing large commercial banks is similar to that of the life insurance companies, whereas smaller banks more closely resemble savings and loan associations.

Interest Rates

Along with contract lengths and loan-to-value ratios, interest rates serve to illustrate interinstitutional differences in mortgage lending policies. Since the mortgages present in lenders' portfolios in 1947 had been outstanding for a number of years, refinancing and similar contract adjustments could have affected their original contract rates. Consequently, tabulations are given both for current interest rates, i.e. the rates effective under the contracts in 1947, and for the original contract rates.

In the mortgage portfolios of life insurance companies and commercial banks, current interest rates were somewhat lower on loans secured by income-producing properties than on those secured by homes (Table 31). This difference persists after adjusting for the effects of government insurance programs; that is, it reappears when observation is limited to conventionally financed mortgages. For example, one-half of the life insurance company noninsured mortgages on homes, but three-fourths of those on income-producing properties, carried current interest rates of less than 5 percent; the corresponding proportions for commercial banks were one-third and somewhat more than one-half. Mortgage loans held by savings and loan associations showed a low proportion with interest rates under 5 percent, about one-eighth, whether for home loans or for others. The highest interest rates were encountered in the conventional lending of savings and loan associations—where loans are of relatively small size and possibly subject to somewhat higher than average risk[5]—and the lowest on noninsured mortgages in life insurance company portfolios—in considerable part, large mortgages secured by properties of prime quality.

A tendency toward the readjustment of interest rates is clearly recognizable when current interest rates are compared with original contract rates, particularly among the mortgages held by life insurance companies, though less so for those held by commercial banks and savings and loan associations (Tables 31 and 32). For example, nearly one-third of the conventionally financed home mortgages in the portfolios of life insurance companies were written at interest rates in excess of 5 percent, but on over one-half of these

[5] Here, in particular, the third reservation about the sample (page 72) should be remembered. The data do not answer, for instance, the important question whether there are institutional differences in interest rates on loans of the same type, of the same size, on the same type of property, in a city of the same size, and in the same geographic region.

TABLE 31

Current Interest Rates on Nonfarm Mortgage Loans Outstanding 1947
(*percentage distribution of lender's holdings*)

CURRENT INTEREST RATE	1- TO 4-FAMILY HOMES			ALL OTHER PROPERTY		
	Life Ins. Cos.	*Commercial Banks*	*Savings & Loan Assocs.*	*Life Ins. Cos.*	*Commercial Banks*	*Savings & Loan Assocs.*
				Number of Loans		
All Loans						
Under 4.0%	1%	1%	a	8%	5%	..
4.0	13	35	19%	27	37	7%
4.1 - 4.9	60	22	10	42	18	9
5.0	20	26	34	18	30	32
5.1 - 5.9	3	2	8	3	a	9
6.0 and over	3	14	29	2	11	43
Conventional						
Under 4.0%	1	1	a	7	5	..
4.0	18	20	4	26	32	3
4.1 - 4.9	33	13	9	42	19	9
5.0	34	37	41	18	32	33
5.1 - 5.9	8	3	10	4	a	9
6.0 and over	6	25	36	3	12	46
				Amount Outstanding		
All Loans						
Under 4.0%	1%	1%	a	15%	14%	..
4.0	17	49	31%	37	56	29%
4.1 - 4.9	61	21	13	39	12	7
5.0	17	22	35	6	16	40
5.1 - 5.9	2	1	6	1	a	8
6.0 and over	2	6	15	2	2	17
Conventional						
Under 4.0%	2	2	a	9	14	..
4.0	22	29	6	39	55	27
4.1 - 4.9	38	15	13	42	12	7
5.0	29	40	50	6	17	41
5.1 - 5.9	5	1	8	1	a	8
6.0 and over	4	13	23	2	2	17

Based on National Bureau of Economic Research survey of urban mortgage lending; for coverage, see the opening of Chapter 4.
[a] Less than 0.5 percent.

the interest rate was subsequently reduced. For both savings and loan associations and commercial banks about one-seventh of the loan contracts written at more than 5 percent had been altered, after origination, with respect to interest rate.

Because of the trend toward lower interest rates, the above description of loan portfolios in terms of number of mortgages can-

TABLE 32

Contract Interest Rates on Nonfarm Mortgage Loans Outstanding 1947
(*percentage distribution of lender's holdings*)

	1- TO 4-FAMILY HOMES			ALL OTHER PROPERTY		
CONTRACT INTEREST RATE	*Life Ins. Cos.*	*Commercial Banks*	*Savings & Loan Assocs.*	*Life Ins. Cos.*	*Commercial Banks*	*Savings & Loan Assocs.*
			Number of Loans			
All Loans						
Under 4.0%	a	1%	a	5%	4%	..
4.0	11%	33	17%	20	34	9%
4.1 - 4.9	56	22	8	34	16	7
5.0	18	26	32	18	30	28
5.1 - 5.9	5	2	8	11	a	9
6.0 and over	10	16	35	12	16	47
Conventional						
Under 4.0%	1	1	a	5	4	..
4.0	16	19	1	20	29	4
4.1 - 4.9	24	12	6	33	17	8
5.0	28	36	38	18	33	28
5.1 - 5.9	10	3	10	12	a	9
6.0 and over	21	29	45	12	16	50
			Amount Outstanding			
All Loans						
Under 4.0%	a	1%	a	14%	12%	..
4.0	15%	48	28%	26	55	30%
4.1 - 4.9	57	21	11	31	11	6
5.0	17	22	35	15	17	36
5.1 - 5.9	4	1	6	5	a	9
6.0 and over	7	7	20	9	5	19
Conventional						
Under 4.0%	1	2	a	12	12	..
4.0	19	27	2	26	54	28
4.1 - 4.9	29	15	11	31	11	6
5.0	27	39	49	16	17	37
5.1 - 5.9	8	1	9	6	a	10
6.0 and over	16	16	29	9	5	19

Based on National Bureau of Economic Research survey of urban mortgage lending; for coverage, see the opening of Chapter 4.

[a] Less than 0.5 percent.

not be used for inferring differences in lenders' incomes from their outstanding mortgage investments, and comparisons taking account of the amounts involved are needed. Observing, therefore, the distribution of outstanding balances according to current interest rate, we find, for instance, that over six-tenths of the amount outstanding on conventionally financed home loans of life insurance companies, and approximately one-half and one-fifth of the amounts held by commercial banks and savings and loan associations respectively, were earning less than 5 percent in 1947 (Table 31). For home loans that were government-insured, and for loans on income-producing properties generally, the corresponding fractions are much higher. For each lender, average returns were higher on conventionally financed than on government-insured loans, and mortgages on one- to four-family homes brought higher average returns than those on income-producing properties (Table 33).

The differences between interest rates on insured and noninsured loans were large for savings and loan associations but negligible for life insurance companies (Table 33). No consistent interest rate pattern is observable with respect to repayment provision, though nonamortized loans, which were in general the older loans, tended toward higher rates than amortized loans. The highest average rates were found among noninsured mortgages in the portfolios of savings and loan associations: 5.2 percent for home mortgages and 4.9 percent for loans on income-producing properties.

Summarizing, the tabulations of sample data suggest the presence of the following relationships between weighted current interest rates (i.e. current in the 1947 portfolios) and other loan characteristics:

a. An inverse relationship between interest rate and contract length of loans secured by one- to four-family homes, but a less clear pattern among loans secured by income-producing properties (Table 33).
b. Similarly, an inverse relationship between interest rate and loan-to-value ratio in the case of all home loans (Table 33). The relationship is apparently influenced, however, by the presence of government-insured loans in the lenders' portfolios; it largely disappears when the effect of government insurance is eliminated (Table 34).
c. For conventionally financed loans, an inverse relationship between interest rates and original loan amounts (Table 34).

Tabulations of current interest rates by region were also made. It appeared that in 1947 the pattern of regional differences in interest rates for outstanding noninsured home mortgages was characterized by higher rates in the West than in the South, and higher rates in the South than in the North. Interinstitutional differences decreased in the same order: the interest rate structure was con-

TABLE 33

Average Current Interest Rates on Nonfarm Mortgage Loans Outstanding 1947, by Contract Terms

LOAN CHARACTERISTICS	1- TO 4-FAMILY HOMES			ALL OTHER PROPERTY		
	Life Ins. Cos.	*Commercial Banks*	*Savings & Loan Assocs.*	*Life Ins. Cos.*	*Commercial Banks*	*Savings & Loan Assocs.*
TYPE OF LOAN						
Insured	*4.4%*	*4.2%*	*4.1%*	*3.6%*[a]	*4.0%*	b
FHA	4.5	4.5	4.5	b	4.5[a]	b
VA	4.0	4.0	4.0	b	4.0	b
Conventional	*4.6*	*4.7*	*5.2*	*4.2*	*4.2*	*4.9%*
Fully amortized	4.6	4.8	5.2[c]	4.3	4.4	4.9[c]
Partially amortized	4.9	4.6	..	4.2	4.0	..
Nonamortized	4.9	4.9	4.8[a]	4.5[a]	4.1	b
CONTRACT LENGTH						
0 - 4 years	5.0	4.8	4.7[a]	b	4.3	5.4[a] (0 - 9 years)
5 - 9	5.1	4.8	5.4	3.9	4.2	
10 - 14	4.6	4.6	5.2	4.2	4.1	5.3[a]
15 - 19	4.6	4.3	4.8	4.2	4.7[a]	4.5[a] (15 and over)
20 and over	4.5	4.2[a]	4.3	4.1[a]	4.2[a]	
LOAN-TO-VALUE RATIO						
0 - 39%	4.4	5.0	5.2	4.0[a]	4.0	5.6[a]
40 - 59	4.6	4.8	5.1	4.3	4.3	4.6[a]
60 - 79	4.6	4.5	5.1	4.2	4.2	5.2[a]
80 and over	4.5	4.2	4.3	4.1[a]	4.1[a]	4.9[a]
ORIGINAL LOAN AMOUNT[d]						
Under $5,000	4.6	4.7	5.6	b	4.9	5.9[a]
$5,000 - 9,999	4.4	4.3	5.2	4.5[a]	4.5	5.1[a]
10,000 - 19,999	4.6	4.3	4.8	4.4	4.4	5.4[a]
20,000 - 49,999	4.7[a]	4.5[a]	4.6	4.3	4.4	5.3[a]
50,000 - 99,999	..	..	4.5	4.2[a]	4.3[a]	4.7[a] (50,000 and over)
100,000 and over	..	b	4.5	4.1	3.8[a]	
All loans	4.5%	4.4%	4.8%	4.2%	4.1%	4.9%

Based on National Bureau of Economic Research survey of urban mortgage lending; for coverage, see the opening of Chapter 4. Average current interest rates are weighted by the outstanding amounts of the included loans.

[a] Based on less than fifty loans.

[b] Not shown because less than ten loans included.

[c] Includes the following types of loan: direct reduction, cancel and endorse, and share accumulation plan.

[d] Breakdown for loans by savings and loan associations is as follows: under $2,000; $2,000-3,999; $4,000-5,999; $6,000-9,999; and $10,000 and over.

siderably more heterogeneous in the West than in the South and was most uniform in the North. It also was more uniform for the loans held by life insurance companies than for those held by commercial banks.

TABLE 34

Average Current Interest Rates on Conventional Nonfarm Mortgage Loans Outstanding 1947, by Contract Terms

LOAN CHARACTERISTICS	1- TO 4-FAMILY HOMES		ALL OTHER PROPERTY	
	Life Insurance Companies	*Commercial Banks*	*Life Insurance Companies*	*Commercial Banks*
CONTRACT LENGTH				
0 - 4 years	5.0%	4.7%	[a]	4.2%
5 - 9	5.0	4.9	4.0%	4.2
10 - 14	4.7	4.8	4.2	4.0
15 - 19	4.6	4.5	4.2	[a]
20 and over	4.5	4.4[b]	4.5[b]	[a]
LOAN-TO-VALUE RATIO				
0 - 39%	4.4	4.9	4.0[b]	4.0
40 - 59	4.6	4.9	4.3	4.3
60 - 79	4.6	4.8	4.3	4.0
80 and over	4.9	4.3	4.2[b]	4.1[b]
ORIGINAL LOAN AMOUNT				
Less than $5,000	4.8	5.1	4.5[b] (Less than $5,000 and $5,000 - 9,999 combined)	5.2
$5,000 - 9,999	4.6	4.8		4.7
10,000 - 19,999	4.6	4.6	4.4	4.5
20,000 - 49,999	4.7[b]	4.5[b]	4.3	4.7
50,000 - 99,999	..	..	4.2[b]	4.2[b]
100,000 and over	..	[a]	4.2[b]	3.7[b]
All loans	4.6%	4.8%	4.2%	4.1%

Based on National Bureau of Economic Research survey of urban mortgage lending; for coverage, see the opening of Chapter 4. The average current interest rates are weighted by the outstanding amounts of the included loans.

[a] Not shown because less than ten loans included.

[b] Based on less than fifty loans.

Age Distribution of Outstanding Loans

Differences in the age composition of portfolios (Table 35) are suggestive of expected tendencies in portfolio turnover, hence of the varying needs of institutions to acquire new mortgages; yet a distribution of loans according to the year in which they were made is only an indirect means of gauging the life expectancy of outstanding investments. A distribution according to unexpired contract terms, on the other hand, is a more direct (though not conclusive) indication of the life expectancies of loan balances, and thus of the future volume of lending activity required to maintain present portfolio size.

With respect to home mortgages, loans on the books of commercial banks in 1947 had the shortest contract expectancies (unexpired

TABLE 35

Distribution of Nonfarm Mortgage Loans Outstanding 1947, by Period Loan Made

PERIOD MADE	1- TO 4-FAMILY HOMES: *Life Ins. Cos.*	*Commer-cial Banks*	*Savings & Loan Assocs.*	ALL OTHER PROPERTY: *Life Ins. Cos.*	*Commer-cial Banks*	*Savings & Loan Assocs.*
			Number of Loans			
All Loans						
1920-24	1%	1%	1%	3%	a	..
1925-29	5	1	1	13	4%	5%
1930-34	3	1	1	3	1	3
1935-39	15	10	11	20	4	10
1940-44	56	22	31	41	22	37
1945-47[b]	20	65	55	19	69	45
Conventional						
1920-24	2	1	1	3	1	..
1925-29	11	3	2	14	4	6
1930-34	6	2	2	3	1	3
1935-39	22	5	12	20	7	9
1940-44	38	21	36	42	20	39
1945-47[b]	21	68	47	18	67	43
			Amount Outstanding			
All Loans						
1920-24	1%	a	a	2%	a	..
1925-29	4	1%	1%	9	2%	1%
1930-34	3	1	a	1	2	a
1935-39	13	6	6	24	4	6
1940-44	53	15	23	35	17	19
1945-47[b]	26	77	70	29	75	74
Conventional						
1920-24	1	1	a	2	a	..
1925-29	9	2	1	10	2	2
1930-34	6	2	1	1	2	a
1935-39	18	3	6	23	9	5
1940-44	37	15	30	36	12	19
1945-47[b]	29	77	62	28	75	74

Based on National Bureau of Economic Research survey of urban mortgage lending; for coverage, see the opening of Chapter 4.

[a] Less than 0.5 percent.

[b] Includes a few loans made in 1948.

contract terms), and those held by life insurance companies the longest (Table 36). Contract expectancies for commercial banks were more widely spread among different ranges of length than those for savings and loan associations, which were most heavily concentrated in the range of from ten to fourteen years, or those for

TABLE 36

Contract Life Expectancies for Nonfarm Mortgage Loans Outstanding 1947
(*percentage distribution of lender's holdings*)

REMAINING TERM[a]	1- TO 4-FAMILY HOMES			ALL OTHER PROPERTY		
	Life Ins. Cos.	*Commercial Banks*	*Savings & Loan Assocs.*	*Life Ins. Cos.*	*Commercial Banks*	*Savings & Loan Assocs.*
			Number of Loans			
All Loans						
0 - 4 years	4%	21%	9%	18%	39%	14%
5 - 9	7	28	30	23	40	31
10 - 14	22	17	35	23	8	30
15 - 19	26	16	16	8	1	1
20 and over	32	10	6	3	b	1
Expired	9	8	3	25	12	18
Conventional						
0 - 4 years	8	36	12	18	42	15
5 - 9	12	39	36	24	38	31
10 - 14	34	10	38	23	7	32
15 - 19	20	1	9	7	b	3
20 and over	6	b	1	2	..	..
Expired	20	14	4	26	13	19
			Amount Outstanding			
All Loans						
0 - 4 years	2%	13%	3%	12%	33%	8%
5 - 9	5	26	18	32	52	22
10 - 14	22	17	39	17	4	35
15 - 19	28	21	27	11	1	29
20 and over	34	18	12	11	b	1
Expired	8	5	1	17	10	5
Conventional						
0 - 4 years	5	27	4	14	34	8
5 - 9	10	46	25	35	51	22
10 - 14	35	14	48	18	4	36
15 - 19	26	2	17	9	b	29
20 and over	8	1	3	6	..	..
Expired	16	10	3	18	11	5

Based on National Bureau of Economic Research survey of urban mortgage lending; for coverage, see the opening of Chapter 4.

[a] Remaining term equals contract length minus actual length; expired term refers to loans for which actual length exceeds contract length.

[b] Less than 0.5 percent.

life insurance companies, where twenty years and over was the most frequent remaining term.

Excluding government-insured loans and concentrating on conventionally financed home mortgages, we find that the most frequent life expectancies were clearly less than ten years for loans held by commercial banks, five to fourteen years for those held by savings and loan associations, and ten to nineteen years for life insurance company loans (Table 36). Thus even apart from the influence exerted by the longer terms of government-insured loans, the loans of life insurance companies had the longest contract expectancies, and those of commercial banks the shortest. By 1960, for example, if contract terms should be fulfilled, one-third of the conventionally financed home loans in the sample from life insurance companies would be outstanding, but only about 10 percent for savings and loan associations and 1 percent for commercial banks. By 1965, nearly all of the conventional home mortgages which were on the books of commercial banks and savings and loan associations in the National Bureau sample will have reached the end of their contract life, and about 95 percent of those in the portfolios of life insurance companies. Among government-insured home loans, on the other hand, even by 1965 about one-quarter of those held in 1947 by commercial banks and savings and loan associations, and more than one-half of those held by insurance companies, would still be outstanding.

Contract life expectancies were generally shorter for loans on income-producing properties than for those on homes. With the exception of the loans held by life insurance companies, which were the most evenly distributed as to remaining term, few of the sample loans on commercial and multifamily properties had contract expectancies of more than fourteen years, and most of them had much shorter ones.

From the pattern of differences among the many loans which comprise the nation's outstanding nonfarm mortgage debt as represented by the foregoing sample results, it would seem that some of the observed variations are due to interlender differences in policy, others to genuine differences between markets. Thus, the differences in the characteristics of mortgages held by different types of lending institutions—differences in average size of loan, in risk, and in length of term—as far as they are clearly observable at all may be only indirectly related to the type of lender. Conversely, since most loan applicants finally place their mortgages with one or another kind of lender, the question may be raised whether there is a division of labor in the mortgage market, and if so, how far such functional specialization reaches.

The preceding description suggests that such functional specialization does exist. There are the savings and loan associations operating in the local market, with their tendency to make loans on modestly valued properties, at somewhat higher rates and at terms otherwise somewhat more liberal than the competing institutional lenders do. There are the large life insurance companies, the typical long-distance lenders, whose mortgage portfolios are spread over a wide national market, whose loans are frequently government-insured and made at lower rates than the average gross yields of the small lenders' portfolios, and with average maturities nevertheless exceeding those typical for commercial banks.

Here, however, as in other parts of the financial structure, a tendency toward declining specialization is noticeable. Geographic as well as functional differentiation has been generally diminishing, not only in the areas of consumer and of business credit,[6] but also in nonfarm mortgage finance.

[6] With respect to consumer lending, see *Industrial Banking Companies and Their Credit Practices*, by R. J. Saulnier (National Bureau of Economic Research, Financial Research Program, 1940).

5

LENDING EXPERIENCE

DATA on the characteristics of mortgages that have been extinguished are even scarcer and more deficient than data on loans still outstanding. This paucity of evidence on past lending practices and lending experience is the more surprising as such information is essential to the exploration of some of the most important problems confronting individual lending institutions and the agencies responsible for policy on a national level in the vast field of housing and housing credit. An attempt was made, therefore, as part of the National Bureau's survey of urban mortgage finance, to obtain data on extinct loans through a sampling of lenders' files, in the hope that —with data on active loans reported by the same institutions— representative information on nonfarm mortgage loans made since 1920, and on the outcome of such of the transactions as had been completed, would be at hand.

Sampling the inactive files of lenders is, of course, a more difficult and complex task than canvassing the files of active loans. The historical information kept varies greatly from institution to institution in amount and in kind, and is generally much less complete than information available for current loans. For these and related reasons the limitations of the historical part of the National Bureau's sample are considerably greater than those affecting its sample of active loans.[1] In addition to the fact that nonresponse by commercial banks and savings and loan associations was heavier in connection with past than with current loans, the historical part of the sample suffers from the incompleteness of the original population from which it was drawn. A good many small lending institutions had been wiped out as a consequence of the depression; it is not improbable that their mortgage lending experience was worse than average and that their exclusion from the sample has introduced some bias. Since the extent of the bias is unknown, no correction for it can be offered.

All 24 of the life insurance companies cooperating in the survey supplied information on inactive as well as active loans; of the other lenders, 116 commercial banks and 92 savings and loan associations responded to the historical part of the questionnaire. The resulting

[1] See Appendix A, especially pages 126 ff. and 137.

sample covers some 20,000 mortgage loans made during 1920-47, of which about two-thirds were completed transactions and one-third still outstanding at the survey date.[2] The primary objective of the present chapter is to reconstruct the pattern of changing lending practices and lending experience as reflected in the sample of mortgage loans made since 1920 by the responding institutional lenders.

Trends in Loan Characteristics since 1920

A sustained upward movement in loan-to-value ratios and in contract lengths and a downward movement in contract interest rates have been the outstanding features of lending patterns since 1920 for the life insurance companies, commercial banks, and savings and loan associations included in the historical part of the loan sample (Charts 6 and 7). These tendencies appear more uniform for loans on one- to four-family homes than for loans on income-producing properties, though the smallness of the sample of loans of the latter type may account in part for their more erratic behavior. The relative decline in interest rates on home mortgage loans over the period beginning with 1920 was about the same for all three lenders. Throughout, these rates were lowest on the loans made by life insurance companies, slightly higher on commercial bank loans, and highest for those made by savings and loan associations. Toward the end of the period, however, the rate structure had become more uniform: absolute interlender variability of rates had declined, primarily because of the sharp fall in interest rates on loans made by savings and loan associations from over 7 percent in 1920 to less than 5 percent in 1946. Loans on income-producing properties in the sample tended toward slightly lower rates, with the loans of commercial banks showing the sharpest decline—from over 6 to about 4 percent (Chart 7).

Both contract lengths and loan-to-value ratios increased perceptibly for all three lenders, and for loans on homes and on income-producing properties as well. For home mortgage loans the interlender variability both of contract lengths and of loan-to-value ratios was less at the end of the period than at the beginning. For contract

[2] The cut-off date varied somewhat for the different lenders; see Chapter 4, footnote 3. Appendix Tables A-9 through A-14 show the composition of the historical part of the sample in detail.

A sample of mortgage loans made since 1918 by mutual savings banks has been analyzed by John Lintner in *Mutual Savings Banks in the Savings and Mortgage Markets* (Harvard University, 1948), to which reference will be made in connection with foreclosure experience.

CHART 6

Contract Terms of Straight Mortgage Loans Made on Nonfarm Homes 1921-47

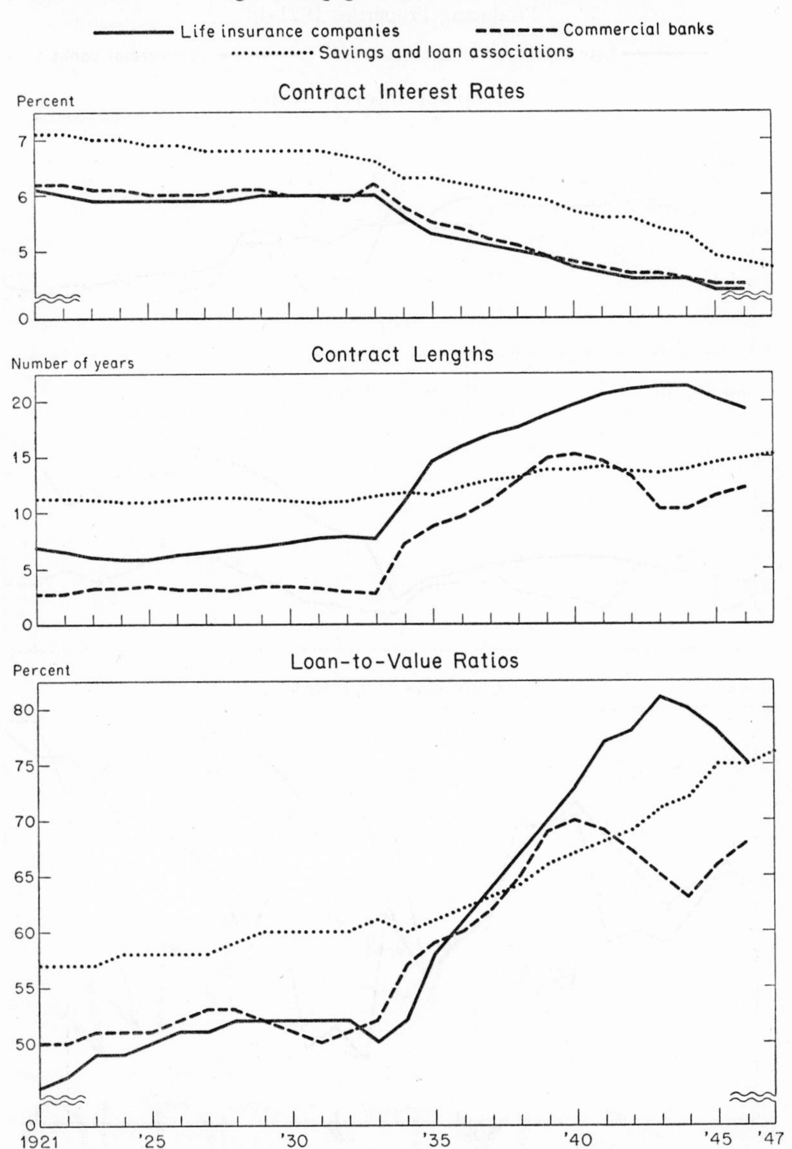

Three-year moving averages of interest rates, contract lengths, and loan-to-value ratios, weighted by three-year moving averages of original loan amounts. Based on sample data in Tables C-5 through C-7; refers to loans secured by one- to four-family homes.

CHART 7

Contract Terms of Straight Mortgage Loans Made on Nonfarm Income-Producing Properties 1921-46

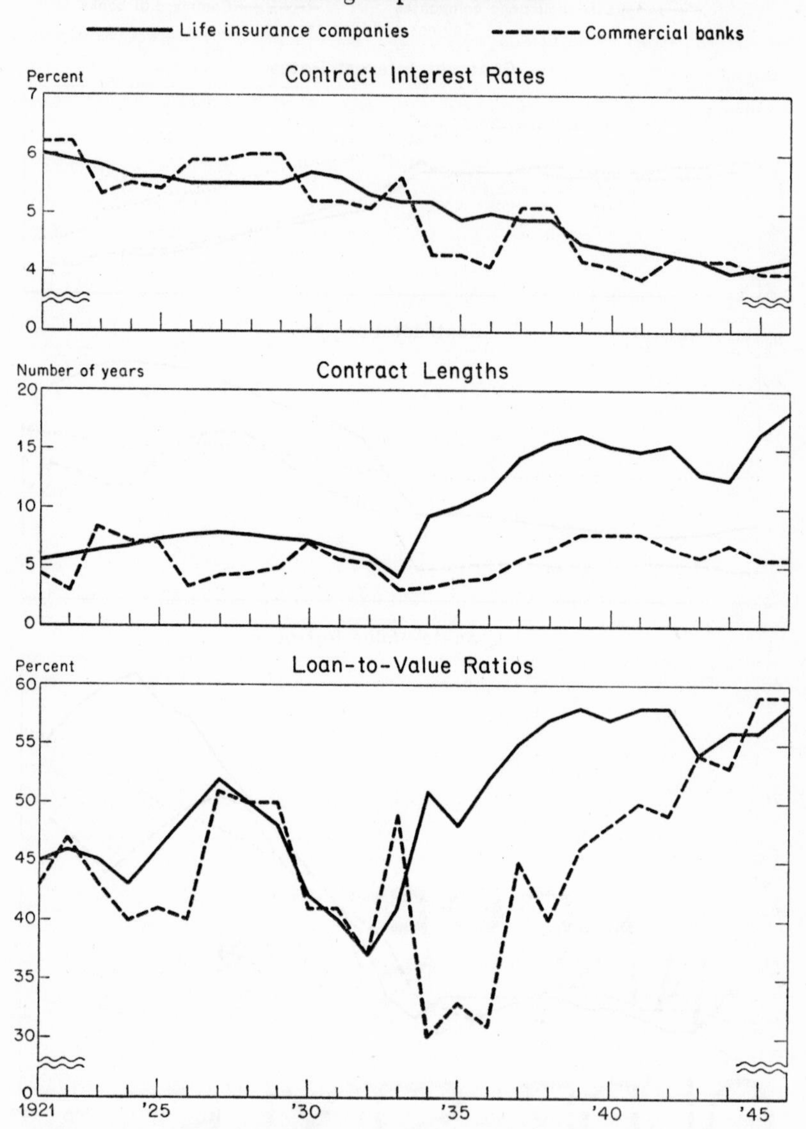

Three-year moving averages of interest rates, contract lengths, and loan-to-value ratios, weighted by three-year moving averages of original loan amounts. Based on sample data in Tables C-8 through C-10; refers to loans secured by properties other than one- to four-family homes.

length of loans on income-producing properties, however, the opposite was found, a fact which appears attributable to the proportionately greater absorption of FHA-insured loans into the portfolios of life insurance companies than of commercial banks. To the extent that high loan-to-value ratios and long contract terms are indicative of liberality of credit, savings and loan associations appear to have been the most liberal home mortgage lender at the beginning of the period. At the end of the period, however, life insurance company home loans showed loan-to-value ratios equal with, and average contract lengths far exceeding, those of savings and loan associations. By the same criteria, commercial banks were least liberal almost throughout, and at the end of the period life insurance companies had become the most liberal lender in the home mortgage market. Again, this reflects the fact that life insurance companies utilized government insurance or guaranty in a larger proportion of their home mortgage lending than other lenders did.

Among loans secured by income-producing properties (a field in which savings and loan associations participated very little) the lengthening of contract terms proceeded much more rapidly in the case of life insurance companies than of commercial banks. Thus the sample reflects a division of the market into a large-property sector mainly consisting of government-insured mortgages and served by life insurance companies, and a small-property sector mainly consisting of conventionally financed nonresidential properties and served by commercial banks (Chart 7).

Changes in the average size of loans made by the various types of lender confirm the main tendencies already observed. Throughout the period beginning with 1920 and ending with 1947, home mortgage loans of life insurance companies averaged larger than those of commercial banks, and very much larger than those of savings and loan associations (Table 37). Over the period as a whole, and for all three lenders, there was a pronounced tendency toward higher original loan amounts. This rising tendency in mortgage size was steepest for savings and loan associations; next came commercial banks, and last life insurance companies—again a development resulting in greater uniformity among the different types of institutional lender at the end of the period than at its beginning.

For mortgages on income-producing properties, however, differences in loan size as between the several types of lender were larger, at the beginning of the period, than for home mortgages; and the differences increased over time (Table 37). The average size of all

TABLE 37

Average Size of Nonfarm Mortgage Loans 1920-47, by Period Loan Made

(dollar figures in thousands)

PERIOD MADE	1- TO 4-FAMILY HOMES						ALL OTHER PROPERTY					
	Life Insurance Companies		*Commercial Banks*[a]		*Savings & Loan Associations*		*Life Insurance Companies*		*Commercial Banks*[a]		*Savings & Loan Associations*	
	No. of Loans	*Av. Size*	*No. of Loans*	*Av. Size*	*No. of Loans*	*Av. Size*	*No. of Loans*	*Av. Size*	*No. of Loans*	*Av. Size*	*No. of Loans*	*Av. Size*
1920-24	851	$4.4	714	$3.9	551	$2.7	118	$47.5	86	$33.7	67	$ 4.4
1925-29	2,061	5.4	1,097	4.6	859	3.0	239	70.1	160	20.4	86	4.9
1930-34	809	5.5	408	4.3	386	2.8	54	49.8	69	38.3	25	4.4
1935-39	1,177	5.5	1,012	3.7	755	2.6	139	64.5	124	22.3	26	5.6
1940-47	3,243	5.1	2,388	4.5	1,937	3.7	224	70.2	304	32.6	51	10.5
1920-47[b]	8,157	$5.2	5,626	$4.3	4,492	$3.2	774	$64.3	744	$28.9	255	$ 5.9

Based on National Bureau of Economic Research surveys of urban mortgage lending; for coverage, see the opening of Chapter 5.

[a] Based on original sample returns without adjustment for nonresponse.

[b] Includes 28 loans for which year made was not available: 16 loans made by insurance companies, 8 loans by banks, and 4 loans by associations.

such loans made by life insurance companies from 1920 through 1946 was over twice that of similar loans made by commercial banks; and in turn, the average size of commercial bank loans on income-producing properties was five times that of similar loans made by savings and loan associations.

Over-All Foreclosure Record

The most dramatic and painful aspects of the lending experience of all types of lender were brought about by the repercussions of the Great Depression on the mortgage markets. While the effects of the depression permeated all sectors of the mortgage market, their force varied from lender to lender. First of all, foreclosure experience varied with the type of housing involved and with the general economic characteristics of different areas. Thus the estimated number of nonfarm foreclosures occurring annually after 1933[3] was highest in the heavily industrialized Middle Atlantic, East North Central, and New England states; and annual rates of foreclosure declined more slowly in the Middle Atlantic states than elsewhere (Chart 8). Similarly, the impact of foreclosures was considerably heavier on large communities than on small ones. Foreclosure relatives—expressing estimated foreclosures on all nonfarm properties annually during 1934-41 as percentages of the number of nonfarm residential structures in 1940—show up always higher the larger the community size group, being nearly 2 percent for the largest urban centers in 1934 and 1935 (Table 38).[4] Throughout the post-depression period foreclosure relatives were higher than the national average in places with 20,000 residential structures or more—heavily urban areas—and less than the average for the rest. However, annual foreclosure relatives declined more rapidly for large than for small communities. Consistent with the record is the fact that the National Bureau's sample shows foreclosure rates to have been highest for life insurance companies and large commercial banks, both of which held a substantial proportion of their mortgages on properties in

[3] Breakdowns of Home Loan Bank Board foreclosure estimates by location of loss are available only from 1934 on.

[4] Being based on estimates of foreclosures on nonfarm properties of all types, of which about one-seventh are commercial rather than home properties, the relatives in Table 38 somewhat exceed the true foreclosure ratios for home mortgages. But the contrast between the mid-thirties and the later years is by no means exaggerated. Since the 1940 inventory was taken as the basis throughout, the high foreclosure ratios of the early years are probably understated in comparison with the others.

CHART 8

Foreclosures on Nonfarm Properties of All Types, by Region, 1934-47

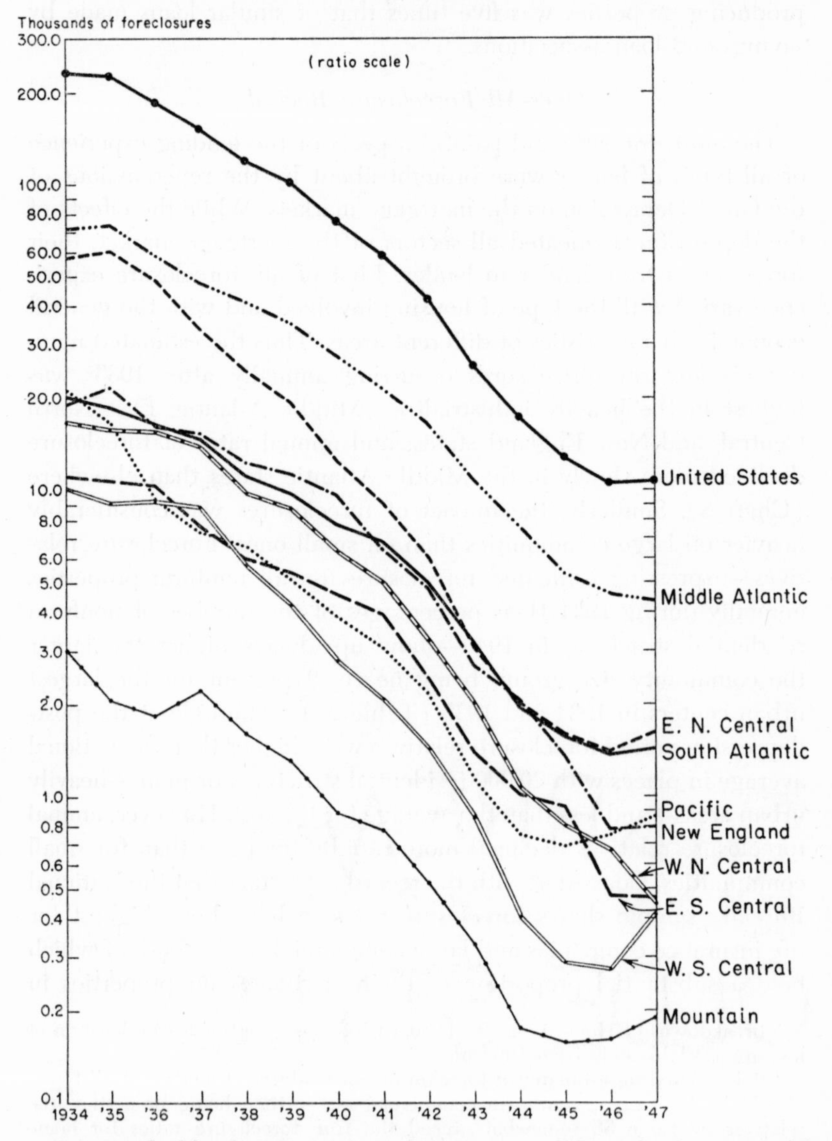

Data supplied by the Operating Analysis Division of the Federal Savings and Loan Insurance Corporation.

large places and in the heavily industrialized parts of the country. For example, two-thirds of the home mortgage loans made by life insurance companies before the depression, and an even larger proportion of loans on income-producing properties, were on collateral located in metropolitan districts with more than one-quarter

TABLE 38

Foreclosures on Nonfarm Properties of All Types, Annually 1934-41, per Hundred Nonfarm Homes in 1940, by Size of Community

Year	*Under 5,000*	*5,000-19,999*	*20,000-59,999*	*60,000 & over*	*Total*
1934	0.41	0.57	1.16	1.73	1.06
1935	0.39	0.56	1.15	1.74	1.06
1936	0.40	0.49	0.99	1.31	0.86
1937	0.37	0.47	0.83	0.99	0.70
1938	0.28	0.36	0.60	0.79	0.54
1939	0.24	0.27	0.50	0.71	0.46
1940	0.18	0.20	0.38	0.53	0.35
1941	0.15	0.16	0.30	0.39	0.27

Compiled from *Nonfarm Real Estate Foreclosures* (monthly reports of the Federal Home Loan Bank Board), and from data supplied by the Federal Savings and Loan Insurance Corporation on the number of nonfarm homes within each size group in 1940.

Size classification of communities is by number of nonfarm homes.

million inhabitants. The corresponding foreclosure rates were substantially higher than for smaller metropolitan districts and for nonmetropolitan areas.[5] Similarly, for sample loans by life insurance companies on properties in the Middle Atlantic and the East North Central states foreclosure rates were substantially higher than in the rest of the country.

For small commercial banks and savings and loan associations, which as a rule catered to a market more diversified geographically and by size of community than that of the larger institutions, foreclosure experience appears to have been more favorable. However, it should be remembered that the high mortality rate among small lending institutions during the depression may have introduced a

[5] R. J. Saulnier, *Urban Mortgage Lending by Life Insurance Companies* (National Bureau of Economic Research, Financial Research Program, 1950), Table 25, p. 87.

For commercial banks and savings and loan associations the bias of nonresponse in the historical part of the sample was too pronounced to permit construction of estimates for geographic distributions.

downward bias in the foreclosure estimates based on their loan samples.

Aside from the record of foreclosures, there are no aggregate data pertinent to an analysis of lenders' experience by type of institution and by loan characteristics. In the sections to follow, based entirely on sample material, the limitations mentioned earlier should be kept in mind. The survey results, especially where they refer to commercial banks and savings and loan associations, should be considered suggestive rather than conclusive. Although tabulations will usually cover the full time span, the findings on which the discussion is based are derived chiefly from the characteristics of loans made before 1930, since for later years the proportion of uncompleted transactions grows higher, and the sample accordingly thinner from the standpoint of an experience study.

Determinants of Foreclosure

Before the depression, the year a loan was made appears to have been one of the most outstanding determinants of the outcome of lending operations. For all three lenders included in the survey, foreclosure rates increased rapidly as the year in which the loan was made approached the peak of the mortgage financing boom in 1929 (Chart 9).[6] Moreover, for each lender annual average foreclosure rates reached or exceeded the average for the entire period 1920 to 1947 as early as 1924 and remained above it until 1933 (Table 39). Thus the entire period 1925-32 was one of substantially higher than average foreclosure rates. However, the sustained and rapid increases of these rates during the years 1926-29 suggest that the factors most directly and uniformly associated with waves of foreclosures were those which usually appear during a boom—namely, high real estate values, high incomes, and a large volume of credit.

With respect to type of property, foreclosure experience was more favorable with mortgages on one- to four-family homes than on income-producing properties (Tables 39 and 40). For loans made during the five-year period before 1930, commercial banks, in particular, fared twice as badly with loans on income-producing properties as with loans secured by homes. The experience of savings and

[6] The same general pattern emerges if we confine the tabulations to loans outstanding at the beginning of the depression in 1930 (Table C-12). As would be expected, individual foreclosure rates are then uniformly higher, since the preponderantly good loans extinguished before 1930 have been excluded.

loan associations with home loans made during 1925-29 closely resembled that of commercial banks. Life insurance companies experienced substantially higher foreclosure rates than other lenders,

CHART 9

Foreclosure Rates by Year Loan Made: Nonfarm Home Mortgage Loans, 1920-47

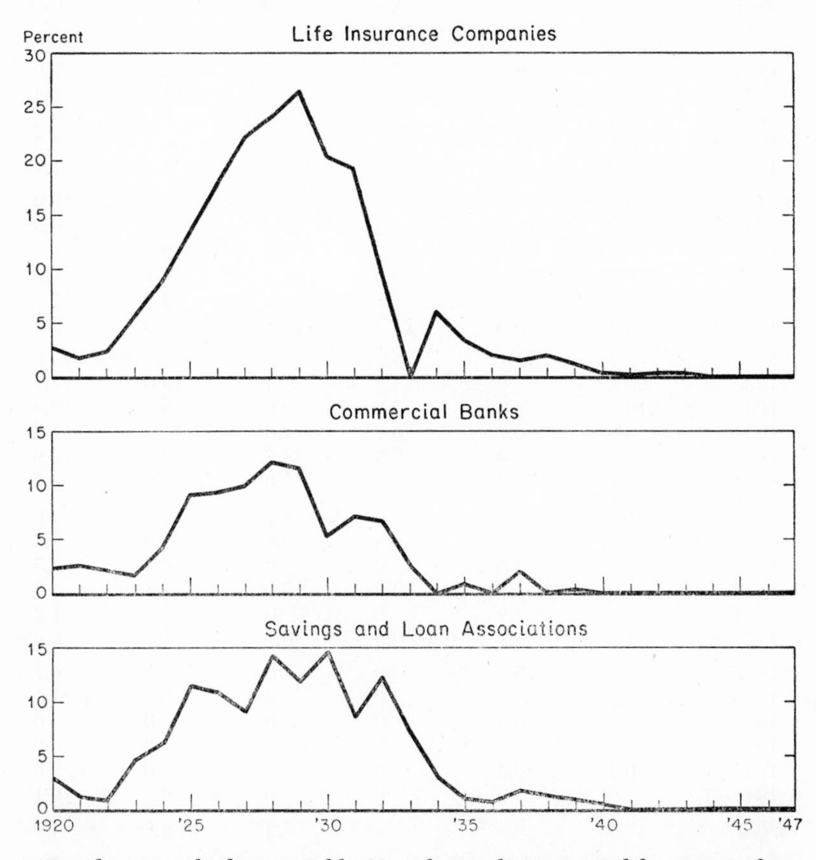

Based on sample data in Table 39; refers to loans secured by one- to four-family homes. Foreclosure rate is the percentage ratio of the number of loans made in a given year and foreclosed by date of report (1947) to all loans made in that year.

especially with loans on one- to four-family homes, and the same is true for one group among the commercial banks—the medium-sized institutions, with portfolios of $2 million to $7.8 million. In the case of life insurance companies, experience appears to have been par-

TABLE 39

Foreclosure Rates for Mortgage Loans on Nonfarm Homes, 1920-47, by Year Loan Made

PERIOD AND YEAR MADE	LIFE INSURANCE COMPANIES		COMMERCIAL BANKS		SAVINGS & LOAN ASSOCIATIONS	
	No.	*Amt.*	*No.*	*Amt.*	*No.*	*Amt.*
1920-24	*5.3%*	*8.0%*	*2.7%*	*3.4%*	*3.4%*	*4.1%*
1920	2.7	6.2	2.2	2.1	2.9	4.0
1921	1.7	4.9	2.5	2.3	1.2	1.4
1922	2.4	3.2	2.1	2.0	0.9	0.3
1923	5.7	7.9	1.6	2.5	4.7	5.3
1924	8.9	12.0	4.2	5.6	6.1	7.1
1925-29	*20.9*	*23.0*	*10.3*	*11.5*	*11.6*	*12.9*
1925	13.4	15.0	9.2	10.6	11.5	9.5
1926	18.0	19.6	9.3	8.9	10.9	11.0
1927	22.2	21.8	9.9	11.1	9.1	9.0
1928	24.1	28.5	12.1	14.1	14.3	15.1
1929	26.4	29.6	11.5	13.7	11.9	19.2
1930-34	*17.4*	*21.1*	*5.1*	*6.4*	*10.4*	*14.0*
1930	20.4	22.0	5.2	6.4	14.6	17.7
1931	19.3	23.9	7.1	9.0	8.5	12.0
1932	9.7	16.7	6.7	4.6	12.2	11.3
1933	0	0	2.5	2.5	7.1	12.2
1934	6.1	5.2	0	0	3.0	9.7
1935-39	*1.8*	*2.0*	*0.6*	*1.1*	*1.2*	*2.0*
1935	3.4	3.4	0.8	0.8	1.0	1.2
1936	2.0	2.5	0	0	0.8	3.5
1937	1.6	1.8	2.0	5.0	1.8	3.8
1938	2.0	1.7	0	0	1.3	1.2
1939	1.2	1.9	0.3	0.1	1.0	0.6
1940-47	*0.2*	*0.2*	*0*	*0*	*0.1*	*0.1*
1940	0.4	0.4	0	0	0.5	1.1
1941	0.2	0.1	0	0	0	0
1942	0.4	0.3	0	0	0	0
1943	0.4	0.4	0	0	0	0
1944-47	0	0	0	0	0.1	0.1
1920-47	7.9%	9.3%	2.8%	3.4%	3.8%	4.2%

Based on National Bureau of Economic Research survey of urban mortgage lending; for coverage see the opening of Chapter 5. Refers to loans secured by one- to four-family homes. Foreclosure rate is the number or original amount of loans made in a given year and foreclosed before date of report (1947) as a percentage of all loans made in that year. For number and original amount of sampled loans, see Table A-9.

TABLE 40
Foreclosure Rates for Mortgage Loans on Nonfarm Income-Producing Properties, 1920-47, by Period Loan Made

PERIOD MADE	LIFE INSURANCE COMPANIES		COMMERCIAL BANKS		SAVINGS & LOAN ASSOCIATIONS	
	No.	*Amt.*	*No.*	*Amt.*	*No.*	*Amt.*
1920-24	9.3%	7.6%	2.3%	0.2%	1.5%	1.1%
1925-29	26.8	34.7	16.9	19.8	17.4	10.1
1930-34	14.8	8.8	7.2	2.2	0	0
1935-39	0.7	0.4	6.5	7.3	0	0
1940-47	0.9	0.1	0.3	a	0	0
1920-47	11.1%	13.1%	5.8%	4.2%	6.3%	3.0%

Based on National Bureau of Economic Research survey of urban mortgage lending; for coverage, see the opening of Chapter 5. Refers to loans secured by properties other than one- to four-family homes. Foreclosure rate is the number or original amount of loans made in a given period and foreclosed before date of report (1947) as a percentage of all loans made in that period. For number and original amount of sampled loans, see Table A-10.

[a] Less than 0.05 percent.

ticularly bad with the two- to four-family homes and with apartment buildings.[7]

In general, foreclosure experience with loans on income-producing properties was slightly more uniform among the different types of lender than experience with loans on homes (Tables 39 and 40). Also, a comparison of foreclosure rates based on number of loans with rates based on original amounts of loans reveals that the loans made from 1925 through 1929 on income-producing properties and later foreclosed were substantially larger than average loans; and that they were larger for life insurance companies than for commercial banks. Foreclosed loans on one- to four-family homes were also larger than the average loan made during 1925-29, but only slightly so, and with greater uniformity among the three lenders. The home loan market suffered less from the adverse effects of the depression than the market for loans on income-producing properties. Tabulations not reproduced here show that among surviving institutions the savings and loan associations and the smaller commercial banks had a somewhat less unfavorable experience than their larger competitors.

Among the factors other than the location of a property and the year in which the loan was originated that affect foreclosure experi-

[7] *Ibid.*, Table 24, p. 86.

ence, amortization and the loan-to-value ratio seem to have been most important. Foreclosure indexes[8] show that fully amortized home loans were better risks in terms of foreclosure experience than other mortgages (Table 41). For the sample of life insurance companies, however, a breakdown of the period 1920-29 into two subperiods indicates that the advantage of the fully amortized type of loan diminished during the later phases of the expansion.[9] This suggests that amortization was a protective device primarily for seasoned loans, but that it had little effect where loans encountered difficulties early in their contract life. The impression is reinforced by the fact that the sample loans made during 1925-29 by savings and loan associations and commercial banks on income-producing properties—that is, the typical short-lived loans—performed worse than their loans as a whole (Tables 39 and 40). In general, loans of relatively small size as compared with the appraised values of the underlying properties showed better foreclosure experience than loans with high loan-to-value ratios (Table 41). Differentiation in that respect among loans made by commercial banks was especially pronounced, suggesting that these institutions were able to acquire high quality loans with low loan-to-value ratios.

Small loans, of less than $5,000, performed better than average, though less well than mortgages of all sizes for which the loan-to-value ratio was low. Thus, the data would imply that loans of large original amount, in particular those with high loan-to-value ratios, and on which repayment had been relatively small at the time of foreclosure, presented the greatest foreclosure risks.

The above tendencies are revealed more explicitly if we observe some of the effects of age, size, amortization provision, and loan-to-value ratio on the foreclosure experience reflected by the most uniform and best part of the National Bureau's sample, i.e. the data on mortgage loans made by large life insurance companies in the twenties and still outstanding in 1930 that were secured by single family owner-occupied homes (Table 42). In particular the tabulation shows that the relative frequency of foreclosures varied directly with size of loan for all observed years for both of the loan-to-value classes examined; similarly, that foreclosure rates during each period

[8] See Table 41 for definition of the measure used. The indexes measure relative risk of foreclosure for subcategories of loans within each lender group, 100 being the average for the group or for a subperiod within it.

[9] The same conclusions can be drawn if the analysis is limited to loans that were outstanding in 1930.

TABLE 41

Foreclosure Indexes for Mortgage Loans Made on Nonfarm Homes, 1920-29, by Contract Terms

Loan Characteristics	*Life Insurance Companies*	*Commercial Banks*	*Savings and Loan Associations*[a]
TYPE OF LOAN			
1920-24			
Fully amortized	23	102	b
Partial or no amortization	131	100	b
1925-29			
Fully amortized	51	86	b
Partial or no amortization	113	103	b
1920-29			
Fully amortized	44	90	103
Partial or no amortization	117	102	51
CONTRACT INTEREST RATE			
5.0 - 5.9%	76	89	26
6.0 - 6.9	107	111	83
7.0 and over	76	49	117
CONTRACT LENGTH[c]			
0 - 4 years	135	107	40
5 - 14	89	86	101
15 and over	178	47	260
LOAN-TO-VALUE RATIO			
Less than 40%	49	35	38
40 and over	106	114	113
ORIGINAL LOAN AMOUNT			
Less than $5,000	71	b	97
$5,000 - 9,999	155	b	122
10,000 - 19,999	165	b	44 (10,000 and over)
20,000 and over	135	b	

Based on National Bureau of Economic Research survey of urban mortgage lending; for coverage, see the opening of Chapter 5. Refers to loans secured by one- to four-family homes; for number of sampled loans, see Tables A-11 and A-12.

The foreclosure index is defined as

$$100 \frac{f_i}{g_i} \frac{\Sigma_i g_i}{\Sigma_i f_i}$$

where f_i is the number of foreclosed loans, and g_i the number of good loans (i.e. nonforeclosed loans) in the ith subgroup of the variable, and where the summation extends over all subgroups included: e.g. all loans—with full, or partial, or no amortization—made in a given period by a given type of lender.

[a] Loans secured by all types of property are included, 95 percent being loans on one- to four-family homes.

[b] Not available.

[c] Excludes loans with indefinite maturities, e.g. share accumulation plan loans made by savings and loan associations.

TABLE 42

Foreclosure Rates on Life Insurance Company Home Loans Made 1920-29 and Outstanding January 1, 1930, by Amortization Provision and Size of Loan within Loan-to-Value Ratio

TYPE OF LOAN AND ORIGINAL LOAN AMOUNT	LOAN-TO-VALUE RATIO		
	Under 50%	*50% & Over*	TOTAL
TYPE OF LOAN			
1920-24	*6.1%*	*23.8%*	*14.4%*
Fully amortized	a	18.2[b]	10.0[b]
Partially amortized	5.8	20.4	11.4
Nonamortized	10.5[b]	30.5[b]	23.6
1925-27	*15.7*	*24.2*	*20.9*
Fully amortized	4.5[b]	17.3	13.5
Partially amortized	16.6	23.4	20.3
Nonamortized	16.1	27.5	24.6
1928-29	*10.5*	*29.5*	*23.4*
Fully amortized	0[b]	16.1[b]	10.6[b]
Partially amortized	10.4	29.3	22.9
Nonamortized	16.7[b]	34.8	30.2
1920-29	*12.4*	*26.2*	*20.9*
Fully amortized	2.1[b]	17.0	12.0
Partially amortized	12.7	25.8	20.1
Nonamortized	15.3	30.0	26.1
ORIGINAL LOAN AMOUNT			
1920-25	*10.5%*	*19.9%*	*15.2%*
Under $5,000	9.3	18.0	13.7
$5,000 and over	13.5	24.6	19.2
1926-27	*15.6*	*26.5*	*22.5*
Under $5,000	12.1	22.7	18.8
$5,000 and over	21.4	32.5	28.5
1928-29	*10.5*	*29.5*	*23.4*
Under $5,000	6.4	27.6	20.7
$5,000 and over	17.1	32.2	37.5
1920-29	*12.4*	*26.2*	*20.9*
Under $5,000	9.5	23.3	17.9
$5,000 and over	17.6	31.1	26.2

Based on National Bureau of Economic Research survey of urban mortgage lending; for coverage, see the opening of Chapter 5. Refers to life company loans made in the twenties that were secured by one- to four-family homes. Foreclosure rate is the number of loans foreclosed during 1930-47 as a percentage of all loans outstanding at the beginning of 1930.

[a] Not shown because less than ten loans included.

[b] Based on less than fifty loans.

varied directly with loan-to-value ratios within each size class of loans; and that foreclosure rates varied inversely with age of loan, and inversely with degree of amortization. It also points to the tendency for the highest foreclosure rates to concentrate in groups of loans that exceeded $5,000, had loan-to-value ratios of 50 percent or more, and were made during the latter part of the twenties (Table 42).

Insurance companies had better than average foreclosure experience with loans on which interest rates ranged from 5 to 5.9 percent; high interest rate loans—that is, those carrying rates of 7 percent or over—were the best foreclosure risk group for commercial banks, but the worst for savings and loan associations (Table 41). This suggests that in the market for high risk home mortgages commercial banks absorbed the best loans, and that at least some of the savings and loan associations may have absorbed the worst.

Foreclosure experience on long-term mortgages, those with contract terms of fifteen years or longer, was worse than average for life insurance companies and especially poor for savings and loan associations (Table 41); but the entire sample of home mortgage loans made before 1930 included only 132 with such long terms. With mortgages having contract lengths of less than fifteen years, for two of the three lenders good foreclosure experience did not coincide with the contract lengths they typically used. Thus, commercial banks, which during the twenties had specialized in short-term loans, fared worst on loans with contract lengths of less than five years; and savings and loan associations had their best foreclosure experience with such loans, though terms of more than ten years were predominant in their lending. Not only with contract lengths but in general, a comparison of foreclosure indexes for the various loan categories with the frequency distributions of loans made by each lender within those categories suggests that lending institutions were frequently more selective, or at any rate more successful, with respect to mortgage transactions lying outside their established lending spheres than with mortgages conforming more closely to their established policies.[10] It also appears—always in terms of foreclosure experience with home mortgage loans made before 1930—that the different loan characteristics were of varying usefulness in discriminating between good and bad loans. In general, most of the characteristics examined were less effective discriminators for loans made by life insurance companies than by commercial banks or, especially, by savings and loan associations. This would suggest that commercial banks and savings and loan associations had more nearly uniform lending habits and policies than insurance companies as a group.

[10] See Table A-12.

The foreclosure experience of life insurance companies was most sensitive to amortization provision, size of loan, and loan-to-value ratio; that of commercial banks and savings and loan associations to the usual contract terms—loan-to-value ratio, interest rate, and contract length. By and large, the characteristics examined are more effective in screening out good than bad loans. This, of course, is not necessarily an attribute of the selected characteristic but may also be due to the particular scale used; that is, to the boundaries set in grouping the loans. However, the sample data more or less suggest that it is easier to recognize a good loan than a bad one. To signalize the latter, much more efficient indicators would be needed, quite possibly involving many other factors and their complex interactions. Thus analysis of foreclosure rates,[11] rather than directly assisting in the rejection of bad loans, would seem to be more helpful in pointing out the limitations—at least for the period under study—of some of the time-honored lending criteria.

Many of the observations made with respect to the foreclosure experience of life insurance companies, commercial banks, and savings and loan associations are confirmed for mutual savings banks by Lintner's study of sample loans made in Massachusetts.[12] For mutual savings banks, too, considering loans made before 1932, experience was far better with mortgages on residential property, especially on single family owner-occupied homes, than with those on income-producing properties. With respect to the year a loan was made, foreclosure rates for the mutuals also increased during the period leading up to the depression and reached their peak for loans made during the immediate predepression years 1927-29. Foreclosure frequency varied directly with size of loan, and—as in the case of mortgage lending by the other three lenders—amortized loans performed better than others; likewise, the foreclosure rate varied directly with loan-to-value ratios.

In addition, the data for mutual savings banks throw some light on the effect of two geographic characteristics: community size, and distance of lender from the mortgaged property. For mortgages on single family homes foreclosure experience was worse the larger the

[11] For additional material on foreclosures, see Appendix Tables C-11 and C-12.

[12] John Lintner, *Mutual Savings Banks in the Savings and Mortgage Markets* (Harvard University, 1948). The sample, drawn at approximately the same time as the National Bureau's and covering loans made from January 1, 1918 to October 31, 1945, is described in pages 440ff., and the findings summarized here are developed in pages 359-439.

community. With respect to distance, experience was better the closer the lender to the mortgaged collateral. These findings are based, of course, on experience with uninsured loans only. To what extent the insurance feature of loans made under FHA protection would have weakened the effect of city size and of distance cannot be ascertained from present sources. The point gains added interest when it is recalled that long-distance lenders—for example, the large life insurance companies—made use of FHA insurance earlier and more freely than some of the other lenders.

Among factors other than those already discussed, borrower characteristics and socio-economic aspects of the locality and the neighborhood of the property would seem to be of particular interest in an analysis of foreclosure rates. Unfortunately, the requisite data are for all practical purposes nonexistent. It is, of course, extremely difficult to obtain historical information on borrower characteristics from any lender; and it proved impossible to reconstruct lending experience in terms of comparable borrower characteristics for an adequate loan sample from the past records of a representative group of lending institutions. It was possible, however, to obtain data for a limited group of loans indicative of foreclosure experience during the depression in one particular sector of the home mortgage market—namely, for loans acquired by the Home Owners' Loan Corporation, chiefly in 1934. These loans came from the portfolios of a great many different lenders and therefore provide adequate coverage with respect to type of lender. Two important limitations attach to them as a source of information on borrower characteristics. Since the loans refinanced by the HOLC, though not the worst, were likely to be poorer than average risks, they are not representative of all home mortgage loans outstanding during the early thirties. Moreover, the National Bureau's sample of HOLC loans is geographically limited, being restricted to loans made in Connecticut, New Jersey, and New York. The fact that nearly four-tenths of the sample loans were still outstanding at the time of the survey (1947) hardly affects the basic conclusions with respect to foreclosure experience, since only a negligible number of foreclosures occurred from 1947 until the liquidation of the HOLC in May 1951.

Accordingly, the HOLC sample can be used for the reconstruction of experience with probably worse than average risks among home mortgages made before the depression or during its early phases by a variety of lending institutions in parts of the highly industrial Northeast.[13]

In the HOLC data, foreclosure rates are closely related to size of loan. A classification of loans by size (six groups at $2,000 intervals) within family income shows a tendency at all income levels toward worse experience the larger the loan. But eliminating the effect of loan size shows that borrower's income was also an important factor in the outcome of the lending operation.[14] Within nearly all loan size groups a tendency was observed for foreclosure rates to decrease with increasing income, though less so in the highest income groups.[15]

Both the very young borrowers (under thirty years at the time the loan was refinanced) and the older ones (fifty years and over) were less successful in avoiding foreclosure of their homes than the middle-aged group; nearly one-half of the sampled loans to mortgagors under thirty years were foreclosed.[16] Thus economic pressure on borrowers at an early stage of their earning careers and on those at a late stage had a clear effect on the outcome of the lending operation.

The ratio of borrower's estimated equity in the mortgaged property to the original amount of the loan was inversely associated with foreclosure rates for all but the smallest and the very large mortgages; in other words, relatively large equity apparently was effective in avoiding default by a borrower, though even here the influence exerted by the absolute size of the economic burden—that is, the size of the loan—was more pronounced and decisive.[17]

In the low income group of mortgagors large families (seven dependents and more) were the best foreclosure risks, but the absolutely best risks with respect to family size in the entire sample were the small families (no dependents) in the high income brackets.[18]

Thus, the socio-economic status of the borrower as reflected by income, age, and size of family, and the relative financial importance

[13] For detailed tabulation and analysis of foreclosure experience, see *History and Policies of the Home Owners' Loan Corporation*, by C. Lowell Harriss (National Bureau of Economic Research, Financial Research Program, 1951), pp. 87-100. The sample is described on pages 49f.

[14] *Ibid.*, Table 23, p. 89.

[15] The income figures used were family income at the time the loan was refinanced, mainly 1934.

[16] Harriss, *op. cit.*, Table 24, p. 90.

[17] *Ibid.*, Table 30, p. 98.

[18] *Ibid.*, Table 23, p. 89.

of the property to the borrower—the latter as expressed by the ratio of equity to original loan amount—were all more or less effective elements in loan experience. The most obvious element, however—borrower's income—only proved to be a satisfactory discriminator between good and bad loans for the larger mortgages ($4,000 or more); that is, for loans that were generally poorer than average risks. For smaller loans the borrower's family income at the time the loan was acquired by the HOLC was not significantly associated with loan experience; other characteristics must have accounted for the defaults of these mortgages.[19] Although over-all experience does suggest that the middle income brackets were somewhat better foreclosure risks than either the high or the low income groups, this result was due apparently to the particular shape of the joint distribution of incomes and loan sizes prevailing at that time.[20]

Loss Experience

The possibility that a loan may default is only one of several considerations that enter into a lender's appraisal of risks. More important to him than the mere fact of foreclosure is the gravity of the default as indicated by the ultimate financial outcome of the loan transaction. The financial outcome of an unsuccessful mortgage transaction is determined by happenings not only during the life of the loan but also throughout the subsequent period during which the property acquired is part of the lender's owned real estate account. For this reason, a description of a lender's experience that seeks to gauge the amount of risk, rather than its mere frequency, will have to consider the combined outcome of both phases of a mortgage transaction: experience with the loan while it is active and, if the loan resulted in foreclosure, experience with the acquired collateral until the lender has disposed of it.

In order to compare differentials in the loss experience of various lenders on defaulted loans in the National Bureau's sample, the estimated net proceeds of all operations subsequent to foreclosure

[19] In connection with other factors that may influence experience, an HOLC tabulation of reasons for foreclosure, covering foreclosures in all regions of the country up to mid-1944, is of interest. The agency found that only one-sixth of the foreclosures were attributable to "total inability to pay," a slightly smaller proportion to "abandonment of property," "death of borrower," or "legal complications," and two-thirds to "noncooperation of borrower" and "obstinate refusal to pay" (Harriss, *op. cit.*, Table 21, p. 80).

[20] The same result was observed for a roughly comparable exposure period with respect to FHA loans. See *Foreclosure Experience with Insured Mortgages*, by Mortimer Kaplan (Federal Housing Administration, ms., 1941), pp. 217ff.

were subtracted from an estimate of the lender's investment at time of foreclosure for each completed transaction. The resulting loss figure was then related to the original amount of the loan, and to the lender's investment at the time of foreclosure.

It appears that the average loss ratios on all loans made after 1920 and foreclosed by 1947 were highest for commercial banks and lowest for life insurance companies. This was true both for loans secured by homes and for those secured by income-producing properties (Table 43). Thus, for commercial banks, losses on foreclosed loans on one- to four-family homes were about one-fourth of the original loan amount, and on income-producing properties, over one-third. Even life insurance companies, which according to the sample fared best, had substantial average loss ratios—in the neighborhood of one-tenth. Comparing loss experience with the foreclosure rates and foreclosure indexes discussed earlier, it would appear that commercial banks and savings and loan associations were more successful than life insurance companies in selecting good risks in the sense of loans that did not default, but that the savings and loan associations and especially the commercial banks were much less successful than the life insurance companies in their handling of acquired properties. An explanation of these differences between institutions might be found in the possible advantages of large-scale operation with respect to property management and sale, and of small-scale, local operations with respect to loan selection and servicing. Differences in the cost of foreclosure to the lender and in the proceeds of deficiency judgments may also have contributed to the differences in loss experience.

For each type of lender, and for each major property type, loans made after 1925 and subsequently foreclosed had higher loss ratios the longer the property was outstanding and the later it was sold, which suggests that easily disposable properties did not remain long in the owned real estate accounts but that less attractive collateral did.

Similarly, the difference between loss as a percent of original loan amount and the (smaller) rate of loss as a percent of the lender's investment at foreclosure was highest for loans on properties sold after 1935. Since the difference between the two ratios varies directly with foreclosure expenses (including noncapitalized delinquent interest and taxes paid by lender at the time of foreclosure, etc.), and inversely with borrowers' repayments up to time of foreclosure, it would appear that lenders found it generally difficult or

TABLE 43
Liquidation Experience on Foreclosed Nonfarm Mortgage Loans by Period of Property Disposal within Period Loan Made, 1920-47

		1- TO 4-FAMILY HOMES			ALL OTHER PROPERTY		
PERIOD LOAN MADE	PERIOD OF PROPERTY DISPOSAL	*Life Ins. Cos.*	*Commercial Banks*	*Savings & Loan Assocs.*	*Life Ins. Cos.*	*Commercial Banks*	*Savings & Loan Assocs.*
				Loss as Percent of Original Loan Amount			
1920-24	*1930-47*	*4%*	*19%*	*23%*	*23%*	a	a
	1930-34	12	..	a	..	..	..
	1935-39	5	19	26	a	a	a
	1940-47	2	20	a	57	..	..
1925-29	*1925-47*	*9*	*24*	*10*	*14*	*34%*	*26%*
	1925-29	a	a	a	..	..	a
	1930-34	4	10	7	a	a	a
	1935-39	7	24	9	17	29	24
	1940-47	12	37	14	24	40	..
1930-34	*1930-47*	*12*[b]	*28*	*22*	*−13*	*22*	..
	1930-34	−2	a	13	..	a	..
	1935-39	11	17	23	a	a	..
	1940-47	15	a	32	−20	a	..
1935-39	*1935-47*	*8*	*15*	*14*	a	*48*	..
	1935-39	a	..	a	..	a	..
	1940-47	8	15	a	a	51	..
1940-47	*1940-47*	*6*	..	a	a	a	..
	Total	9%	24%	14%	13%	36%	27%
				Loss as Percent of Lender's Investment			
1920-24	*1930-47*	*5%*	*19%*	*19%*	*16%*	a	a
	1930-34	11	..	a	..	..	..
	1935-39	6	16	23	a	a	a
	1940-47	2	21	a	44	..	..
1925-29	*1925-47*	*9*	*21*	*9*	*13*	*31%*	*25%*
	1925-29	a	a	a	..	..	a
	1930-34	4	10	7	a	a	a
	1935-39	7	20	9	−17	29	23
	1940-47	11	32	12	22	36	..
1930-34	*1930-47*	*11*[b]	*23*	*20*	*−11*	*10*	..
	1930-34	−2	a	12	..	a	..
	1935-39	9	14	21	a	a	..
	1940-47	13	a	31	−17	a	..
1935-39	*1935-47*	*8*	*16*	*13*	a	*55*	..
	1935-39	a	..	a	..	a	..
	1940-47	8	16	a	a	77	..
1940-47	*1940-47*	*5*	..	a	a	a	..
	Total	9%	21%	13%	12%	33%	26%

Based on National Bureau of Economic Research survey of urban mortgage lending; for coverage, see the opening of Chapter 5. For number of foreclosed loans, original amount, and lender's investment, see Table C-13. Negative loss ratios indicate gains.

[a] Not shown because less than five loans included.

[b] Includes one loan for which period of property disposal was not available.

unattractive to part with real estate acquired through foreclosure of mortgages with high unpaid balances. This tendency was more pronounced for commercial banks than for life insurance companies, which reflects probable differences in policy between the large and the small lenders, and the presence of a higher proportion of not fully amortized and of delinquent loans in the portfolios of commercial banks than of insurance companies.

Investor Returns in Urban Mortgage Lending

The loss ratios considered so far pertained to experience with foreclosed mortgages only. A convenient and summary means for analyzing over-all investment experience is the average return actually realized by various types of lender on different groups of loans that include successful and unsuccessful transactions. In addition, the amount by which the rate of realized return falls short of what is termed here the expected yield, and which would have been realized if the terms promised in the original contract had been fulfilled, serves as an approximate measure of the per annum loss rate: that is, the rate at which reserves should have been accumulated to have offset the full amount of losses incurred. Thus interlender variations in loss rates according to the various characteristics of the loan contracts, the types of properties securing them, or the periods in which the loans were made summarize in a simple and compact way the risk differentials associated with different types of loan investment.

The actual measurement of return on investment, however, presents numerous and difficult problems. Since comparison within the lending experience reflected by thousands of sample loans was the primary purpose of the National Bureau survey, it seemed appropriate to sacrifice conceptual refinement to the exigencies of mass survey operations. In view of the information available and the different accounting and record-keeping practices of lenders, measures of return were computed for sample loans originated and extinguished during 1920-47 as follows: (1) The contract interest rate, weighted, in averaging, by the original amounts of the included loans, gave an estimate of expected yield in the sense indicated above. (2) The realized yield was assumed equal to the expected yield for fully paid mortgages, except if the original contract rate was later modified.[21] For foreclosed mortgages, the realized yield

[21] In such instances the last interest rate weighted by the original amount of the loan was used. For details of the techniques used in calculating the realized

was computed as the ratio of the lender's estimated net return to his investment in the foreclosed loan, including in the transaction the weighted financial experience both with the active loan and with the foreclosed property while carried in the owned real estate account.

Though these measures are only rough approximations to accurate and conceptually refined accounting ratios, they are useful for the comparison of broad lender groups and major types of loans. In particular the loss rates—the excess of the expected over the realized yield for various categories of loans—are suggestive of differences in financial experience, even though their absolute values may suffer from many technical shortcomings.

The realized yields on sample loans made from 1920 through 1929 (Tables 44 and 45) were generally higher for loans on homes than on income-producing properties and generally higher for fully amortized than for other mortgages. Since interest rates followed a similar pattern, the expected yields are also indicated in most cases as lower for mortgages on income-producing properties, and lower for nonamortized loans, than for others. Comparing realized yields as well as loss rates for the two types of lender whose experience data suffice (Tables 44 and 45), we find that commercial banks fared better than life insurance companies, especially with respect to mortgages on homes.

As to contract length, both life insurance companies and commercial banks had more satisfactory returns on investment with home mortgages in the ten- to fourteen-year contract length group than with other loans (Table 46). In general, loan categories for which the average expected yield was comparatively high fared better than others with respect to both realized yields and loss rates (Table 46). Since foreclosure experience (Tables 41 and C-12) did not follow the same pattern, this would suggest that, as a group, loans with interest rates at 6 to 6.9 percent, though frequently displaying higher foreclosure rates, produced better returns on investment than loans with either low or very high interest rates.[22]

---

yields, see *Urban Mortgage Lending by Life Insurance Companies*, by R. J. Saulnier, pp. 96ff.

[22] Similarly, realized yields and loss rates indicate that the financial experience of life insurance companies was less satisfactory with loans having low loan-to-value ratios than with others, though in terms of foreclosure rates alone the reverse is found.

TABLE 44

Yields and Loss Rates for Mortgage Loans on Nonfarm Homes, 1920-47, by Period Loan Made and Amortization or Insurance Provision

PERIOD MADE AND TYPE OF LOAN	LIFE INSURANCE COMPANIES			COMMERCIAL BANKS		
	Exp. Yield	*Real. Yield*	*Loss Rate*	*Exp. Yield*	*Real. Yield*	*Loss Rate*
1920-24	*5.99%*	*5.81%*	*0.18%*	*6.14%*	*5.99%*	*0.15%*
Fully amortized	6.04	6.01	0.03	6.17	6.06	0.11
Partially amortized	5.97	5.81	0.16	6.03	5.84	0.19
Nonamortized	5.96	5.55	0.41	6.26	6.13	0.13
1925-29	*5.89*	*5.03*	*0.86*	*6.04*	*5.37*	*0.67*
Fully amortized	6.01	5.44	0.57	6.31	6.17	0.14
Partially amortized	5.88	5.05	0.83	6.04	5.38	0.66
Nonamortized	5.86	4.68	1.18	5.99	5.18	0.81
1930-34	*5.98*	*4.79*	*1.19*	*6.13*	*5.53*	*0.60*
Fully amortized	5.97	4.89	1.08	6.36	6.00	0.36
Partially amortized	6.02	5.08	0.94	6.05	5.46	0.59
Nonamortized	5.87	4.07	1.80	6.13	5.41	0.72
1935-39	*5.21*	*4.97*	*0.24*	*5.21*	*5.10*	*0.11*
Fully amortized	5.25	5.15	0.10	5.42	5.42	0
Partially amortized	5.38	4.76	0.62	5.30	4.87	0.43
Nonamortized	5.37[a]	4.86[a]	0.51[a]	5.69	5.66	0.03
FHA	4.97	4.86	0.11	4.90	4.88	0.02
1940-47	*4.60*	*4.57*	*0.03*	*4.69*	*4.68*	*0.01*
Fully amortized	4.69	4.62	0.07	4.77	4.76	0.01
Partially amortized	4.74[a]	4.73[a]	0.01[a]	4.88	4.88	0
Nonamortized	[b]	[b]	[b]	5.19	5.12	0.07
FHA[c]	4.52	4.50	0.02	4.48	4.48	0
1920-47	*5.59*	*5.01*	*0.58*	*5.58*	*5.27*	*0.31*
Fully amortized	5.51	5.15	0.36	5.51	5.43	0.08
Partially amortized	5.86	5.17	0.69	5.75	5.35	0.40
Nonamortized	5.84	4.76	1.08	6.01	5.46	0.55
FHA[c]	4.64	4.60	0.04	4.65	4.65	0

Exp. = expected. Real. = realized.

Based on National Bureau of Economic Research survey of urban mortgage lending; for coverage, see the opening of Chapter 5. Refers to loans secured by one- to four-family homes, exclusive of loans and properties still on the books in 1947. Average yields and loss rates are weighted by the original amounts of the included loans.

[a] Based on less than fifty loans.

[b] Not shown because less than ten loans included.

[c] Includes a few VA-guaranteed loans.

TABLE 45

Yields and Loss Rates for Mortgage Loans on Nonfarm Income-Producing Properties, 1920-47, by Period Loan Made and Amortization or Insurance Provision

PERIOD MADE AND TYPE OF LOAN	LIFE INSURANCE COMPANIES			COMMERCIAL BANKS		
	Exp. Yield	*Real. Yield*	*Loss Rate*	*Exp. Yield*	*Real. Yield*	*Loss Rate*
1920-24	*5.89%*	*5.58%*	*0.31%*	*5.38%*	*5.35%*	*0.03%*
Fully amortized / Partially amortized	5.92	5.64	0.28	6.09[a]	6.17[a]	–0.08[a]
Nonamortized	5.79[a]	5.40[a]	0.39[a]	5.28[a]	5.25[a]	0.03[a]
1925-29	*5.51*	*3.81*	*1.70*	*5.96*	*4.94*	*1.02*
Fully amortized	5.80[a]	5.78[a]	0.02[a]	5.47[a]	4.98[a]	0.49[a]
Partially amortized	5.59	3.54	2.05	6.15	4.20	1.95
Nonamortized	5.30	4.20	1.10	5.91	5.42	0.49
1930-34	*5.51[a]*	*5.06[a]*	*0.45[a]*	*5.71*	*4.44*	*1.27*
Fully amortized / Partially amortized	5.80[a]	5.06[a]	0.74[a]	5.80[a]	4.57[a]	1.23[a]
Nonamortized	5.19[a]	5.06[a]	0.13[a]	5.65[a]	4.29[a]	1.36[a]
1935-39	*4.78*	*4.67*	*0.11*	*4.27*	*3.59*	*0.68*
Fully amortized	4.80[a]	4.73[a]	0.07[a]	5.12[a]	4.58[a]	0.54[a]
Partially amortized	4.76	4.67	0.09	4.46[a]	2.00[a]	2.46[a]
Nonamortized	b	b	b	3.88[a]	4.08[a]	–0.20[a]
FHA	b	b	b	b	b	b
1940-47	*4.33[a]*	*4.31[a]*	*0.02[a]*	*4.26*	*4.23*	*0.03*
Fully amortized	4.33[a]	4.34[a]	–0.01[a]	4.54	4.53	0.01
Partially amortized	4.33[a]	4.18[a]	0.15[a]	3.93[a]	3.88[a]	0.05[a]
Nonamortized	b	b	b	4.79[a]	4.68[a]	0.11[a]
FHA	b	b	b	b	b	b
1920-47	*5.31*	*4.41*	*0.90*	*5.18*	*4.57*	*0.61*
Fully amortized	4.58	4.56	0.02	5.03	4.78	0.25
Partially amortized	5.49	4.29	1.20	5.18	3.85	1.33
Nonamortized	5.37	4.61	0.76	5.21	4.87	0.34
FHA	b	b	b	b	b	b

Exp. = expected. Real. = realized.

Based on National Bureau of Economic Research survey of urban mortgage lending; for coverage, see the opening of Chapter 5. Refers to loans secured by properties other than one- to four-family homes, exclusive of loans and properties still on the books in 1947. Average yields and loss rates are weighted by the original amounts of the included loans. Negative loss rates indicate gains.

[a] Based on less than fifty loans.

[b] Not shown because less than ten loans included.

TABLE 46

Yields and Loss Rates for Nonfarm Mortgage Loans Made 1920-29, by Loan-to-Value Ratio and Contract Length

CONTRACT TERMS	LIFE INSURANCE COMPANIES			COMMERCIAL BANKS		
	Exp. Yield	*Real. Yield*	*Loss Rate*	*Exp. Yield*	*Real. Yield*	*Loss Rate*
			One- to Four-Family Homes			
LOAN-TO-VALUE RATIO						
0 - 39%	5.96%	5.09%	0.87%	6.35%	6.11%	0.24%
40 - 79[a]	5.90	5.19	0.71	6.04	5.52	0.52
CONTRACT LENGTH						
0 - 4 years	5.89	5.02	0.87	6.14	5.57	0.57
5 - 9	5.89	5.24	0.65	5.94	5.55	0.39
10 - 14	5.99	5.48	0.51	6.18	5.95	0.23
15 - 19[b]	5.97	4.74	1.23	6.10	5.98	0.12
Total	5.92%	5.24%	0.68%	6.08%	5.60%	0.48%
			All Other Property			
LOAN-TO-VALUE RATIO						
0 - 39%	5.55%	5.24%	0.31%	6.04%	5.11%	0.93%
40 - 79[c]	5.63	4.07	1.56	5.57	5.11	0.46
CONTRACT LENGTH						
0 - 4 years	5.30	4.76	0.54	6.08	5.62	0.46
5 - 9	5.75	3.95	1.80	6.15	3.89	2.26
10 - 14	5.52	4.56	0.96	5.10	5.05	0.05
15 - 19[d]	5.72	5.16	0.56	e	e	e
Total	5.61%	4.29%	1.32%	5.67%	5.14%	0.53%

Exp. = expected. Real. = realized.

Based on National Bureau of Economic Research survey of urban mortgage lending; for coverage, see the opening of Chapter 5. Includes loans made during 1920-29 that were extinguished by 1947. Average yields and loss rates are weighted by the original amounts of the included loans. For number and original amount of sampled loans, see Table A-14.

[a] Includes 10 loans with loan-to-value ratios of 80 percent and over.
[b] Includes 21 loans with contract lengths of twenty years and over.
[c] Includes 6 loans with loan-to-value ratios of 80 percent and over.
[d] Includes 8 loans with contract lengths of twenty years and over.
[e] Not shown because less than ten loans included.

Actual versus Contract Length in Mortgage Lending

Less dramatic than foreclosure rates and loss ratios but quite important as an experience factor is the duration of the investment; that is, the number of years a mortgage remains on the lender's books. Interlender differences in average length of investment are helpful in interpreting yield and loss differentials. Comparisons between average contract and average actual length of loan—each weighted by original loan amounts—are also suggestive of discrepancies between a lender's "expectations" and actual loan performance.

For sample loans made and extinguished during 1920-47 the discrepancy between actual and contract term was considerable for each of the lenders. Relatively few loans were extinguished within a year of contract maturity. In the part of the sample where completed experience records are reasonably numerous—namely, among loans made from 1920 through 1934—a substantial proportion were extinguished either before or after having reached contract maturity (Table 47). Although average actual lengths of loans varied from lender to lender, the variations were much smaller than those observed with respect to average contract lengths. Thus for savings and loan associations, whose contract lengths averaged substantially longer than those of the other two lenders, actual duration of investment fell short of contract length. For life insurance companies, on the other hand, and still more for commercial banks, the opposite was observed—average actual duration of loan exceeded average contract length (Table 48).

A similar pattern of difference among types of lender as to the relationship of contract length and actual loan performance is evident when the sample loans are classified by contract maturity. Because of the limitations of the sample no firm conclusions can be drawn with respect to the behavior of the small subcategories by period of origin. Among loans made during the fifteen years 1920-34 it appears that for commercial banks and life insurance companies about one-tenth of those with short contract maturities (five years and less), one-half of the middle group (six to ten years), and three-quarters of the loans with longer maturities (eleven to fifteen years) were paid off before having reached contract maturity (Table 47).[23] For savings and loan associations, however, the corresponding ratios generally exceeded those for the other two lenders, and among the associations' loans with contract lengths of six years and over about 70 percent were repaid before having reached their expected maturity.

Looking back over the data presented, it can be seen that most of them point toward a broad similarity in the experience of all principal lenders; certainly they reveal no striking differences among

[23] Heavy pay-offs are also indicated for loans with contract terms in excess of fifteen years; but the evidence is too scanty to permit comparison with other groups.

TABLE 47

Relationship of Actual to Contract Length for Nonfarm Mortgage Loans Made 1920-34, by Contract Length and Period Loan Made

(percentage distribution of number of loans within period)

PERIOD MADE AND RELATIONSHIP OF ACTUAL TO CONTRACT LENGTH[a]	CONTRACT LENGTH: 1 - 5 Years			6 - 10 Years			11 - 15 Years			16 Years and Over		
	Life Ins. Cos.	*Commercial Banks*	*Savings & Loan Assocs.*	*Life Ins. Cos.*	*Commercial Banks*	*Savings & Loan Assocs.*	*Life Ins. Cos.*	*Commercial Banks*	*Savings & Loan Assocs.*	*Life Ins. Cos.*	*Commercial Banks*	*Savings & Loan Assocs.*
1920-24												
Under contract length	15%	9%	27%	69%	73%	63%	78%	57%	73%	..	100%	50%
Equals contract length	45	30	44	18	10	25	16	14	12	..	..	..
Over contract length	40	61	29	13	17	12	6	29	15	..	..	50
1925-29												
Under contract length	9	7	26	41	46	70	66	84	68	48%	94	75
Equals contract length	26	21	38	26	26	17	22	5	15	23	6	25
Over contract length	65	72	36	33	28	14	12	11	17	29	..	..
1930-34												
Under contract length	10	5	25	54	44	76	84	70	69	100	100	100
Equals contract length	27	24	58	22	37	14	12	30	18	..	..	..
Over contract length	63	71	17	24	19	11	4	..	13	..	..	..
1920-34												
Under contract length	10	7	26	52	54	69	74	75	70	70	97	75
Equals contract length	31	24	44	23	23	18	18	14	15	13	3	6
Over contract length	59	68	30	25	23	13	9	11	15	17	..	19

Based on National Bureau of Economic Research survey of urban mortgage lending; for coverage see the opening of Chapter 5. Refers to loans made during 1920-34 that were extinguished by 1947.

[a] To compensate for possible time bias due to the manner of compiling data from the loan schedules, loans repaid within one year before or one year after contract maturity were classified with loans for which actual length equaled contract length.

TABLE 48

Average Contract and Realized Maturities for Nonfarm Mortgage Loans Made 1920-39, by Period Loan Made

PERIOD MADE	LIFE INSURANCE COMPANIES		COMMERCIAL BANKS		SAVINGS & LOAN ASSOCIATIONS	
	Contract Maturity	*Realized Maturity*	*Contract Maturity*	*Realized Maturity*	*Contract Maturity*	*Realized Maturity*
1920-24	6.1 yrs.	7.9 yrs.	3.2 yrs.	7.5 yrs.	10.6 yrs.	6.9 yrs.
1925-29	6.7	10.8	3.7	8.8	10.7	6.8
1930-34	7.5	8.6	3.4	9.0	10.7	6.0
1935-39	11.3	4.8	9.0	4.7	14.7	5.5

Based on National Bureau of Economic Research survey of urban mortgage lending; for coverage, see the opening of Chapter 5. Refers to loans made during 1920-39 that were extinguished by 1947. Average maturities are weighted by the original amounts of the included loans.

lenders in the major characteristics of their lending patterns.[24] The more subtle variations in lending experience from lender to lender are difficult to identify because of deficiencies in the size and nature of the sample of loans on which much of the analysis is based, and also because of the considerable conceptual complexities involved.

All things considered, it appears that the overwhelming force exerted by the depression of the thirties, and the widely pervasive effects of the preceding building boom, resulted in a more or less uniform experience pattern among all of the major types of mortgage lending institution. There are indications, also, that factors more directly associated with the lending operations, uniformly reflected in the experience of the most diverse lenders, contributed to the similarity in outcome. However, one must not read more into the evidence than is warranted by its quality and by its purely empirical and historical nature. The materials of this chapter have been offered as merely suggestive; as inviting speculation rather than leading to inferences, in the strict sense of the word. Viewed thus, the observed pattern of mortgage lending experience may be thought of as resulting from the joint impact exerted by changing over-all economic forces, and from differences in the aspects of particular loan trans-

[24] This statement should perhaps be qualified by pointing out that the long-distance lender, by and large, was more likely to foreclose than the local lending institution, though no corresponding difference in loss experience was observable once the property was foreclosed. The slightly deviating behavior of the banks may suggest a real difference or may reflect a bias due to the heavy nonresponse in that part of the National Bureau's sample.

actions customarily referred to as borrower, property, and loan characteristics.

Indicative of the impact of the general economic climate on lending experience is the clearly recognizable effect that the year a loan was made had on the outcome of the lending transaction. For the period under consideration, it may well have been that the outstanding factor affecting lending experience was the effect of the cycle time or cycle phase on the value and appraisal of the properties involved, on the borrowers' income expectations, on the lenders' willingness to lend and propensity to foreclose, and on the decisions of mortgage institutions to dispose of acquired properties.

Within the general economic context, and closely interwoven with each other, operated the factors which characterized particular loan transactions and resulted in minor differentials in lending experience as between different groups of loans. Concerning the effects of various economic characteristics of the property, the borrower, and the loan, the data reveal that comparatively favorable experience was associated with relatively small loans secured by modestly priced properties and extended to middle income borrowers; experience was also better with loans on owner-occupied homes and other small residential properties than on large residential structures and income-producing properties in general; and amortized loans performed better than nonamortized loans. Lower ratios of loan amount to appraised value of property, shorter contract maturities, and tighter credit terms in general tended to be inversely associated with relatively bad experience. To go much further toward general and far-reaching conclusions is not warranted by the information now available.

It would, of course, be tempting to ask how the selection of mortgage risks could be improved, and how risks associated with differences in quality among potential mortgage loans could be reduced by appropriately varying lending standards. Quite obviously, however, this problem transcends the straightforward application of actuarial concepts and techniques: experience data, by their very nature, pertain to a particular situation or historical phase of a process and are therefore of limited application where rapid and unexpected changes may take place; moreover, such data are necessarily confined to loans that were actually made, i.e. loans already selected from a much larger number of potential transactions with characteristics that probably differed from those of transactions actually closed. Because of these limitations and of the observed tendency toward greater uniformity of credit terms and loan characteristics generally, it appears unlikely that future lending activity will produce experience data that could make it materially easier to discriminate safely, yet in sufficient detail, between potential loans of different quality.

On the other hand, there seems little doubt that experience information of a better and more reliable kind is genuinely needed. It could be made particularly useful to the lending officer if careful foreclosure analysis and current analysis of serious delinquencies and of prepayments were to become a matter of course. Such an intensive approach seems the more promising as many of the relevant experience factors (for example, neighborhood change) do not lend themselves easily to inclusion in the more extensive, actuarial type of analysis. Moreover, the evidence suggests that for the improvement of lending policies increased importance must be attributed to the correct observation and analysis of conditions in the economy as a whole: to factors affecting loan experience that extend far beyond the horizon of individual mortgage transactions.

APPENDIXES

APPENDIX A

NATIONAL BUREAU SAMPLE OF URBAN MORTGAGES

At the time the National Bureau's Urban Real Estate Project was being planned information on nonfarm mortgage investment was limited, for all practical purposes, to aggregative data, and little was known about the characteristics of individual mortgages.[1] Some of the major private lenders had made studies of their nonfarm mortgage portfolios, but only a few of these provided data on individual assets. Among the public agencies the Federal Housing Administration had given considerable attention to lending experience with individual mortgages, but its data were limited to insured loans. Thus information on the characteristics of current mortgage loans, as well as on the experience with paid-out loans, was limited to a few descriptions of the case study type,[2] whose analytical usefulness from the standpoint of developing a general account of the mortgage market was seriously restricted by their limited representativeness.

Accordingly it was decided to attempt a mortgage survey on a national basis with the hope that it would fill the principal gaps, at least in our information on mortgage loan characteristics. The primary objectives of the survey were a more detailed description of mortgage markets than was then available, and a description of completed loan transactions which would reveal relationships between loan characteristics and the outcome of particular transactions.

[1] Since the conclusion of the National Bureau's survey, however, the Bureau of the Census has completed and published its Survey of Residential Financing.

[2] For example, see the following:

American Bankers Association, *Owned Real Estate and Mortgage Amortization.*

Roy J. Burroughs, *Study of Urban Real Estate Mortgage Delinquency* (unpublished Ph.D. thesis, Michigan State College, 1933).

Federal Housing Administration, *Technique for a Mortgage Experience Study* (November 1, 1937).

Richard W. Hill, Jr., *Lending Experience Studies as an Aid in Determining Credit Policy* (American Institute of Banking, 1940).

Mortimer Kaplan, *Foreclosure Experience with Insured Mortgages: A Report of the First Five Years of Operation of the Mutual Mortgage Insurance Program* (Federal Housing Administration, unpublished ms., 1941), and "A Method of Analyzing the Elements of Foreclosure Risk," *Journal of the American Statistical Association,* Vol. 37, No. 218 (June 1942), pp. 247-55.

Edgar A. Lodge, *A Mortgage Analysis: A Twenty-eight-Year Record of the Mortgages of Home Title Insurance Company, 1906-1934* (Home Title Guaranty Company, New York, 1935).

David Thomas Rowlands, *Two Decades of Building and Loan Associations in Pennsylvania* (unpublished Ph.D. thesis, University of Pennsylvania, 1940).

The problems of survey design would have been simplified if the survey had had but a single purpose, though such investigations are rare exceptions in economic studies. As it was, the present survey was addressed to two major complexes of questions: (1) What are the characteristics of the nonfarm mortgage loans currently held by major institutional lenders? (2) What has been the lenders' experience with such mortgages made since 1920? The first problem calls for cross-section analysis, whereas the second involves changes over time; the first could be approached on the basis of current materials, whereas the second required evidence which might have become unavailable as a particular lending institution went out of business, or for other reasons.

A spot check on a number of filing systems showed that access to paid-out loan dockets would be considerably more difficult and time-consuming than access to the files of current loans, and also that the amount and comparability of data diminish as one goes from present to past records. In particular it was found that although the large life insurance companies and the very large commercial banks were usually able to furnish experience data in addition to information on current loans, small and middle-sized commercial banks and savings and loan associations were much less able to do so.

Since the survey had to rely on voluntary cooperation, estimated dollar expense as well as the psychological cost of difficult-to-furnish answers had to be considered. Thus, three criteria offered themselves for the selection of an optimum design: a survey design best suited to the reconstruction of (i) experience data, (ii) current loan characteristics, or (iii) a combination of the two. The last possibility, though intuitively appealing, appeared on closer inspection the least desirable; it would have led to sacrificing good information on current loans for the sake of only a slight improvement in the evidence on past loan performance. Therefore, the immediate problem was one of choosing between alternatives (i) and (ii).

For life insurance companies the choice was relatively easy. In view of the heavy concentration of lending activity among the large institutions, and the comparative stability of this distribution since 1920, the large life insurance companies were a promising source of information on both paid-out and current loans. Commercial banks and savings and loan associations, on the other hand, presented a far more difficult problem. They are much more numerous and more diversified geographically than insurance companies, and their size distribution is much less concentrated. Furthermore, they have been subject to marked changes since 1920 resulting in material shifts in their size distribution as mortgage holders; and they experienced a serious mortality wave in the early thirties. These two circumstances have produced a highly variable population of establishments. As for mutual savings banks—mostly located in the northeastern part of the United States—a parallel study of Massachusetts mutual savings banks by Lintner[3] was counted upon to provide the essential information.

Consideration of the special problems involved in obtaining data from each of the three types of lender led to the decision to base the sampling plan primarily on the requirements of a canvass of current loan characteristics, but to use the same survey for gathering historical information. This decision, together with the need for estimates pertaining to each type of institution—life insurance companies, commercial banks, and savings and loan associations—suggested an "establishment" rather than a "population" type of sample,[4] designed to reveal the characteristics of current nonfarm mortgage portfolios separately for the three lenders and also to shed light on their past lending experience.

Specification of the Population

Correspondingly, the populations to be sampled were tentatively defined as all nonfarm mortgages made since 1920 by life insurance companies, by commercial banks, and by savings and loan associations. Since a complete enumeration of all lenders and of each lender's loan files was impractical, the sampling plan involved two stages: the population was imagined as consisting of loan clusters—one nonfarm mortgage portfolio for each lending establishment—and the clusters, in turn, as consisting of individual mortgages—nonfarm loans outstanding on the survey date in the portfolio of a particular lender.[5] Clearly, while this model was adequate to describe the population of active loans, it gave only a rough approximation of the population of loans made since 1920.

In accordance with the two-stage design, the loan sample was drawn in two steps: a sample of portfolios (primary sampling units) was selected from each of the three populations, and then a sub-

[3] John Lintner, *Mutual Savings Banks in the Savings and Mortgage Markets* (Harvard University, 1948).

[4] The Survey of Residential Financing undertaken by the Bureau of the Census in 1950 is a population type of sample.

[5] Branch bank systems, such as the Bank of America, were considered as forming one cluster.

sample of mortgages (sampling elements) was drawn from each of the primary sampling units. The unit of inquiry, or sampling element, was an urban mortgage loan. To define such a loan for the purposes of the survey meant to find a concept which would be meaningful in terms of both analytical and operational requirements. Thus, the definition had to consider how to relate the concept of a mortgage to the idea of such a financial transaction as held by lender, borrower, or lawyer. As a result of exploring the record-keeping systems used by institutional lenders through spot check and questionnaire, and because the primary goal of the study was the analysis of lender rather than borrower experience, the sampling element was identified as one loan, or a series of loans, made by a given lender upon the security of a particular nonfarm property and covering one complete mortgage cycle. In other words it was defined as a financial transaction that began with the making of a loan, lasted through subsequent modifications, recastings, and extensions, and terminated, if not still active at the survey date, either when the loan was repaid or when the underlying property acquired through foreclosure or voluntary transfer was sold.[6] A schedule was drafted so that one card could be completed by the respondent for each sampled mortgage transaction as just defined.[7]

Selection of Primary Sampling Units

The choice of a selection principle was based on the following considerations: nonsampling as well as sampling errors should be kept reasonably small, and administrative requirements should be given high priority. Both considerations suggested the selection of primary sampling units for the large and highly variable populations of commercial banks and savings and loan associations with probability of selection proportionate to size. It was expected that of the nonsampling errors the most serious would be nonresponse—an expectation that, unfortunately, was confirmed by experience—and a selection of respondents on the basis of size was expected to

[6] That the matter of definition is far from trivial can be seen if a hypothetical example is viewed under alternative definitions. A mortgage transaction may be defined in strictly contractual terms, in which case a particular transaction is terminated as soon as the original loan term expires; on the other hand, a mortgage transaction may be defined as continuing through successive recastings of the loan. Thus, a loan which was written for one year, renewed for another year nineteen times, and then foreclosed would produce a foreclosure rate of 0.05 under the first definition, and of 1.00 under the second.

[7] Appendix B shows the preliminary questionnaires sent to sampled institutions in advance of the survey, and the data transcription card and instructions.

minimize that risk. Also, administrative considerations made it appear advantageous to avail ourselves fully of the cooperation of the large lending institutions, since they held a considerable proportion of the entire outstanding nonfarm mortgage debt. Finally, a sample based on selection with probability proportionate to size suggested itself in a two-stage sample, such as the present one, for purely statistical reasons, as likely to yield more precise estimates than a sample based on alternative principles of selection.

The next problem, therefore, was to find a measure of size which could be statistically efficient and on which sufficient and valid information could be obtained for all lending institutions in the populations to be sampled. Of the two most obvious choices—number of loans in, or dollar amount of, a lender's nonfarm mortgage portfolio—only the latter was available. Since composition of portfolio as well as average loan balance varied from institution to institution, the choice of a measure of size was not an indifferent one, and perhaps for some of the estimates a measure other than the amount of a lender's portfolio would have resulted in smaller sampling variances. On the other hand, since no single allocation principle and no single measure of size can assure minimum variances for each and every estimate in a multivariable, multipurpose survey, the importance of any particular measure or criterion should not be exaggerated.[8]

After a complete listing and the necessary supporting information had been obtained for the three populations, the samples of primary units were drawn as follows.[9] For life insurance companies the extremely high concentration of outstanding balances among a relatively small number of large companies suggested the use of a simple cut-off procedure: the thirty largest institutions (by size of nonfarm mortgage portfolio), representing 85 percent of the nonfarm mortgage debt held by life insurance companies at the end of 1944, were selected.

[8] For example, no single and simple measure will properly weigh an institution's importance as a lender in both the past and the present.

[9] Data for insurance companies as of December 31, 1944 were taken from *The Spectator Insurance Year Book, 1945*. Data on commercial banks as of June 30, 1945 were secured for state member banks from the Board of Governors of the Federal Reserve System, for insured state nonmember banks from the Federal Deposit Insurance Corporation, and for national banks from the Comptroller of the Currency. Information on savings and loan associations as of December 31, 1945 was obtained from the Home Loan Bank Board for associations which were members of the Federal Home Loan Bank System. For the associations, data on total assets were used to measure size.

For commercial banks the picture was vastly more complex. There were over 13,000 commercial banks in 1945 as compared with less than 400 life insurance companies; the banks differed widely in size and other characteristics, and they were much less heavily concentrated than insurance companies with respect to nonfarm mortgage holdings. A similar situation prevailed with savings and loan associations. Therefore a simple cut-off seemed impractical and inefficient, and a sample of primary units (individual institutions) to be selected with probability proportionate to their 1945 nonfarm mortgage portfolio seemed appropriate. Administrative considerations pointed toward a sample of 500 commercial banks as an upper limit.[10] As soon as a complete listing was obtained, a sampling interval (S) was determined by dividing the combined amount of the nonfarm mortgage portfolios of all commercial banks in 1945 (ΣP_i) by the number of primary sampling units to be selected (m). All institutions (m_I) whose portfolios exceeded the sampling interval—that is, institutions for which

$$P_i > \frac{\Sigma P_i}{500}$$

were selected to form the first stratum.

Next, the combined amount of the portfolios of the remaining institutions was divided by the number of remaining primary sampling units yet to be selected ($m - m_I$) in order to determine a new sampling interval (S'); all institutions for which $P_i > S'$ were selected and added to the first stratum. The procedure was repeated until none of the remaining institutions' measure of size exceeded the corresponding sampling interval. In the present sample, only two steps were needed to reach that point.

The remaining part of the population, from which a sample of primary sampling units with varying probabilities—all less than one—was to be drawn, was first stratified geographically by state of location of head office and ranked within the forty-eight geographic strata by asset size.[11]

For these lists of commercial banks, measure of size (that is, 1945 nonfarm mortgage portfolio) was cumulated within each of the forty-eight strata; a different random start—a random number smaller than the last sampling interval—was then chosen for each

[10] The final sample consisted of 496 banks, since 4 were later found to have been misclassified as commercial banks.

[11] In fact this was an additional stratification—by size of institution—to safeguard representativeness by type of bank as reflected by total assets.

of the forty-eight lists, to which the sampling interval was added in succession until the sum of the ranked portfolios in a particular stratum was reached. A list of the numbers obtained by successive addition was prepared for each of the forty-eight states and compared with the list of cumulated portfolios. As soon as the cumulated portfolios reached an entry on the list of numbers, the corresponding institution was selected.

With savings and loan associations the procedure was similar. For lack of information on size of mortgage loan portfolio, total assets were used as the measure of size. Three steps were required to complete the selection of the first stratum. The arrangement of the remaining primary sampling units was by FHLB district and type of association (that is, federal, insured state-chartered, and noninsured state-chartered); and within type, alphabetically by state and city.

Selection of Subsampling Elements

The main considerations in drawing subsamples from the selected primary sampling units were, again, administrative feasibility and avoidance of nonsampling as well as sampling errors. It was important to keep the processing simple and to a minimum, particularly in the case of the very large lenders. Since the purpose of the sample was a reconstruction of the universe of mortgages and not of the population of lenders (that is, portfolios), the subsampling plan that suggested itself because of its relative efficiency was a self-weighting design. Therefore, a subsampling procedure was used in which the product of the probability of selecting a primary sampling unit and the (conditional) probability of obtaining a mortgage from a selected primary sampling unit would be constant within a few broad layers of the population.[12] After obtaining subsampling intervals for each of the selected primary sampling units (portfolios), a random start was assigned to each selected institution and the sub-

[12] Thus, using a systematic random model for the subsampling of the selected primary sampling units (i.e. assuming equal probability of selection for any mortgage regardless of size or other characteristics), the design called for subsampling intervals that would satisfy the simple equality

$$\frac{n_i P_i}{N_i S} = t$$

where n_i refers to number of nonfarm mortgages in the subsample from the ith portfolio and N_i to the size of the ith portfolio in terms of number of nonfarm mortgages, and where t is the over-all sampling rate for the particular population layer (e.g. t equaled 0.01 for first stratum commercial banks and 0.005 for all other banks); P_i and S have the same meaning as before.

sample of mortgages was selected by drawing the mortgage corresponding to a random start, to the random start plus once, plus twice, . . . plus k times the subsampling interval until the entire file was exhausted.[13] Depending on the particular filing system, the subsamples were either systematic random or unrestricted random samples.[14]

In drawing the subsamples several pitfalls had to be avoided; for instance, in the spot checks preceding the survey it was found that in some filing systems more than one loan card had been used for a loan. Though that presented no problem where the selection of subsamples was by loan number, it proved to be a complication where cards had to be hand counted to arrive at the sample cases. Since the number of cards per loan was often inversely associated with the quality of a loan, disregard of the possible effect of multiple cards on the selection of the subsample would have introduced a not negligible systematic bias.[15] Therefore, actual cases (that is, loans), instead of cards, had to be counted. A similar problem arose in connection with the occasional practice of assigning a new case number and preparing a new docket for a recast loan. Thus two or more "cases" in the file may have referred to one and the same loan cycle; that is, to the same mortgage as defined for purposes of our study.

Therefore, in drawing the subsamples, loans which turned out to be successor loans were rejected without replacement.[16] On the other hand, where a loan was selected which was later recast, and for which a new loan record was set up at that time, it was necessary to trace the particular transaction forward, often through several loan "cases." Where loan chains occurred frequently, as for some savings and loan associations, it was important to see that the entire

[13] See sampling instructions in Appendix B for greater detail.

[14] Samples were systematic random in the many instances in which the loans were numbered in sequence, usually by date of origination, or unrestricted random where the dockets were filed in alphabetical order and the sampling intervals had to be counted off. In a few instances both selection principles were combined, the first being used for the active and the second for the inactive file. In general, the first procedure was chosen wherever possible because it provided an easier means of checking the selection process and because it assured a better representation in terms of age of loan and therefore in terms of the many other variables which had been changing systematically with time, such as interest rates.

[15] For example, there were more cards in the file for frequently delinquent or modified loans than for good loans.

[16] Assuming randomness of the distribution over the entire file for loan chains involving more than one docket or card, this method produces no bias.

subsample was assembled before engaging in forward tracing of the cases; the opposite method—immediate tracing of successor loans currently with the selection of the "first" loans and their removal from the file—would have introduced a systematic bias, since it would have resulted in a cumulative shortening of the subsampling interval as more and more successor loans had to be removed from the file.

The Biases of the Sample

Ideally, the results from a sample should be such that any discrepancy between the sample estimates and the true but unknown population values is due to the vagaries of sampling fluctuations only. In actual practice, however, there is hardly ever a sample that is entirely free from bias, despite the amount of care expended.

The following are four major types of bias which may have invaded the present sample.

I. BIAS RESULTING FROM THE WAY IN WHICH PRIMARY SAMPLING UNITS WERE SELECTED

The actually sampled universe of institutional lenders differed from the ideal one, as defined for the purposes of the study, because:

(a) Some institutions operating in the urban real estate market after 1920, especially commercial banks and savings and loan associations, became extinct before 1945, the benchmark year.

(b) The estimates for both commercial banks and savings and loan associations were affected by the fact that some institutions, although still in existence, had no urban real estate loans in their portfolios in 1945.

(c) Some institutions formed mergers after 1920 but before 1945, and since the probability weights are derived from the portfolios of the merged institutions, which were probably heavier than those of their earlier components, a bias is introduced in favor of selecting merged institutions. This bias, which primarily affects savings and loan associations, is disturbing to the extent that the mortgage experience of merged institutions might have differed from that of unmerged ones.

II. BIAS RESULTING FROM THE METHOD OF SELECTING INDIVIDUAL MORTGAGES

(a) It was not always possible to trace the history of a transaction through a complete mortgage cycle. Where the forward tracing of a loan through its successor loans was incomplete, a downward bias resulted in the estimated average length of loan and in the related foreclosure rates. Where backward tracing was unsuccessful—that is, where a selected loan was not recognized as a successor loan, hence not rejected—a downward bias in the estimate of average loan length may have occurred.

By and large, these biases were negligible for large commercial banks and life insurance companies but they may have been substantial in the sample from small commercial banks and from savings and loan associations. Although great care was taken to advise the respondent on handling the tracing problem, instances were found where forward tracing was physically impossible.

(b) Subsampling intervals were not always counted off properly. Since the respondents furnished an estimate of the number of loans made since 1920 it was possible to check for the presence of systematic over- or undercounting. Most respondents used numerical files, so that subsampling was based on predetermined lists of loan numbers, which eliminated the possibility of error in the counting of sampling elements.

(c) The suspicion was voiced that a lender might suppress part of his unfavorable lending experience by substituting a successful for a foreclosed loan. Little could be done to check on this kind of bias; but with the exception of the sample from the small commercial banks there is no reason to believe that it has crept into the selection process. Foreclosure rates for small banks appear to be surprisingly low, but it was impossible to ascertain whether this was so because surviving institutions perhaps had better than average experience, or because commercial banks as a group had a more favorable experience than, say, insurance companies, or because there was underreporting of foreclosures by small and middle-sized commercial banks.

III. BIAS RESULTING FROM ERRORS IN ANSWERS TO QUESTIONS ON THE NATIONAL BUREAU'S LOAN CARD

Errors in the report of a particular transaction should be expected on two levels: those that crept into the original mortgage document, and those that occurred in filling out the National Bureau's loan card. Here the limited validity of appraised value figures, loan-to-value ratios, and similar quantities should be kept in mind. Although no corrections can be offered to the user of the data, he can readily make assumptions necessary to gauge the direction of the bias. It was apparent from the first pretests that the accounting data required for completing the information on the financial outcome of the lending operation might not always be readily available to the respondent or strictly comparable from company to company.[17] In an effort to avoid bias on that account, respondents were advised on how to build up the final loss or profit figures step by step in a way best adapted to their accounting practices.[18] To minimize errors due to misunderstanding a question or to clerical mistakes, all cards were checked for internal consistency.

IV. BIAS DUE TO NONRESPONSE

The most annoying bias, and by far the most troublesome in the outcome of the survey, is that resulting from nonresponse to the National Bureau's inquiry. Such bias was expected on four levels, from:

(a) noncooperation in the survey by institutions selected in the sample of primary sampling units,
(b) failure to supply information on inactive loans,
(c) exclusion of a particular loan (sampling element) drawn in the subsample of loans from a selected institution, and
(d) failure to answer a particular question on a loan card returned by the respondent.

With respect to (c), the difficulty of determining how carefully respondents followed the subsampling instructions has already been mentioned. For several large lenders spot checks on the basis of loan numbers revealed that sampling instructions were closely followed; however, for small lenders—especially for commercial banks and some savings and loan associations—there was indirect indication of an occasional substitution.

Nonresponse of type (d) occurred infrequently, generally among the smaller institutions. Approximately 3 percent of the current-loan cards returned by all commercial banks and about 4 percent of the returns from banks sampling both current and paid-out loans were affected by item nonresponse. Among the larger institutions, inadequate reporting was present in slightly over 1 percent of the returns

[17] For example, foreclosure costs may not be allocated to an individual asset in the same way by a large institution with its own legal department as by a small lender using the services of a law firm; recoveries from deficiency judgments may be credited to a profit and loss account or they may be deducted from the loan balance; the cost of recovery judgments may be frequently but not always excluded from "proceeds from deficiency judgments"; and so on.

[18] See the loan card and transcription instructions in Appendix B.

from the large (first stratum) banks and only in a very small number of loans from life insurance companies. Thus, bias resulting from item nonresponse may have been negligible for all but the older loans made by small lenders.

The most serious form of nonresponse bias occurred in connection with (a) and stemmed from the reluctance or inability of a respondent to participate in the survey. Among the thirty sampled life insurance companies, which held about 85 percent of the outstanding nonfarm mortgage debt, six failed to cooperate (Table A-1). The resulting nonresponse accounted for about 25 percent of the sample in terms of nonfarm mortgage balances outstanding, and for about 15 percent in terms of expected sample take in number of loans. One of the six nonrespondents was among the largest lenders; the other five represented only about 5 percent of the sample.

Whereas the survey of life insurance companies resembled an interview survey, since contacts were established by personal visit, the survey of commercial banks and savings and loan associations relied almost entirely on contacts by mail. Consequently the response by these two lenders was small, and remained so despite the fact that considerable effort was expended by the National Bureau, with the support of trade organizations and others, to effect better cooperation (Tables A-2 and A-8).[19]

A tabulation of commercial bank returns according to the date the loan cards were received would seem to indicate that responsiveness to the survey varied with size of institution. Large banks answered quickly; the very small banks, rather slowly (Table A-3).[20] In terms of number of respondents the ratio of follow-up to original response, which might be suggestive of the degree of initial reluctance on the part of respondents, was higher for the smaller (third and fourth stratum) banks than for the larger ones, and in that sense follow-up was more successful with the smaller respondents (Table

[19] For example, commercial banks that had not responded to the National Bureau's inquiry were approached a second time by letter. The remaining nonresponse was then divided into two groups by size of bank. The large member banks and a 25 percent subsample of all small member banks (with nonfarm mortgage portfolios of less than $2 million) were approached by their respective Federal Reserve banks. Nonmember banks were grouped similarly and contacted by the National Bureau.

[20] Although each commercial bank was selected with its own probability (proportionate to the size of its nonfarm mortgage portfolio), the sampled banks were later grouped into four strata in order to present the results for more nearly homogeneous subgroups, since the high rate of nonresponse made it impossible to prepare probability estimates proper.

A-4).[21] Even after follow-up efforts were exhausted, there remained a final nonresponse which increased sharply as size of lender decreased: in terms of nonfarm mortgage holdings, from 20 percent for the large (first stratum) banks to 70 percent for the smallest (fourth stratum) banks. Concerning the type of bank, response by nonmember banks of all sizes was generally poorer than response by national and state member banks (Tables A-4 and A-5).

In view of the heavy remaining nonresponse it seemed inappropriate to prepare probability estimates. However, certain adjustments of the data on current loans did seem advisable to assist the reader in combining the estimates for the various strata of commercial banks. Adjusted totals were derived as ratio estimates in terms of the aggregate nonfarm mortgage portfolios of the various population strata; appropriate inflators were applied to the combined original and follow-up responses to arrive at frequency distributions of outstanding loans.[22]

With savings and loan associations the survey experience was similar to that with commercial banks (Tables A-6 through A-8). Here, too, the nonresponse was unusually heavy: 60 percent in terms of number of associations, and 50 percent in terms of measure of size (total assets).

In the historical part of the inquiry, coverage for life insurance companies was the same as for current loans, and the results for the 24 companies responding closely approximated a one percent sample of loans made during 1920-46. Nonresponse of type (b) was heavy for the other lenders. Only 116 commercial banks (68 percent of all those participating in the survey) and 92 savings and loan associations (46 percent of those participating) were able to report on inactive as well as active loans. With the historical data no attempt was made to adjust for institutional nonresponse or to estimate totals (as was done with current loans of commercial banks); instead, summaries of the composition of the historical part of the sample are presented in Tables A-9 through A-14.

[21] Nearly 50 percent of the recontacted banks in the fourth stratum responded to the follow-up request.

[22] For the fourth stratum, where the largest inflation factors were applied, a comparison was made between data obtained from banks in the original response group and data obtained from banks in the follow-up group with respect to two variables—original loan size and size of outstanding balance. No significant difference was found, which probably reflects the facts, shown elsewhere, that small commercial banks had relatively few loans on income-producing properties and that mortgages on single family homes were more or less uniform with respect to many of their characteristics.

The details of the response composition and its relation to the original population from which the sample was drawn which have been presented in Tables A-1 through A-8 reveal differences in the response pattern that should be useful both for the interpretation of the sample results and for the planning of other canvasses similar to the National Bureau's mortgage survey. In summary, it should be admitted that the very substantial amount of nonresponse—substantial in a sampling sense—has introduced a bias of an unknown though possibly serious nature, affecting especially the information pertaining to the small institutions, both commercial banks and savings and loan associations. On the other hand, it would appear that other sources of bias did not contribute a large amount of error and that the quality of the information furnished was generally satisfactory and reliable. Hence, it seems entirely feasible to produce reasonably good and complete documentation on mortgage characteristics from an establishment sample (that is, a sample of lending institutions), provided the reluctance to answer such an inquiry can be overcome. Considering both the remarkable effort made by the many institutions that responded to the survey at the outset, and the very substantial proportion of lenders, varied as to type and size, that answered follow-up requests, there is every indication that the survey method is by no means impractical in obtaining the kind of data essential for the improvement of our knowledge of mortgage markets and lending experience.

TABLE A-1

Composition of NBER Sample of Life Insurance Companies
by Size of Nonfarm Mortgage Loan Portfolio
(*dollar figures in millions*)

NONFARM MORTGAGE LOAN PORTFOLIO	ALL COMPANIES		COMPANIES IN NBER SAMPLE			SAMPLE RESPONSE					
									Response Ratio[b]		
	No.	*Amt. Held*	*No.*	*Amt. Held*	*Coverage*[a]	*No.*	*Amt. Held*	*Coverage*[a]	*No.*	*Amt.*	*Sample Take*[c]
Less than $100,000	52	$ 1	..	..	..	..	..	..	..	..	..
$100,000 - 499,999	49	11	..	..	..	..	..	..	..	..	..
500,000 - 0.9 million	28	15	..	..	..	..	..	..	..	..	..
1 - 9.9 million	104	331	..	..	..	..	..	..	..	..	..
10 - 99.9 million	48	1,367	15	$ 940	69%	11	$ 662	48%	73%	70%	94%
100 million and over	17	4,151	15	3,975	96	13	3,043	73	76	77	70
Total	298	$5,876	30	$4,915	84%	24	$3,705	63%	80%	75%	73%

Data on nonfarm mortgage holdings of life insurance companies as of December 31, 1944 were compiled from *The Spectator Insurance Yearbook, 1945*. Of the 305 legal reserve companies then existing, 7 are excluded for which data were not available.

[a] Nonfarm mortgage holdings of sampled companies as a percentage of nonfarm mortgage holdings of all companies.

[b] Number and nonfarm mortgage holdings of responding companies as a percentage of the number and nonfarm mortgage holdings of sampled companies.

[c] Number of loan schedules returned by responding companies as a percentage of the number of returns expected from them. A total of 8,931 loans made during 1920-46 were reported on, of which 3,390 were still outstanding at the beginning of 1947.

TABLE A-2

Composition of NBER Sample of Commercial Banks by Size of Nonfarm Mortgage Loan Portfolio and Region

(*dollar figures in millions*)

CENSUS DIVISION[a]	UNDER $2 MILLION		2 - 3.9 MILLION		4 - 7.8 MILLION		$7.9 MILLION AND OVER[b]		TOTAL	
	No. of Banks	*Amt. Held*	*No. of Banks*	*Amt. Held*	*No. of Banks*	*Amt. Held*	*No. of Banks*	*Amt. Held*	*No. of Banks*	*Amt. Held*
					All Commercial Banks					
New England	456	$ 161.2	18	$ 47.8	7	$ 36.5	2	$ 37.7	483	$ 283.3
Middle Atlantic	1,967	605.4	45	124.5	22	122.2	6	77.7	2,040	929.7
East North Central	2,859	476.2	43	110.5	12	63.3	10	199.1	2,924	849.0
West North Central	2,885	192.1	11	28.8	7	37.1	3	43.0	2,906	301.0
South Atlantic	1,485	238.8	14	40.4	6	34.4	1	7.9	1,506	321.4
East South Central	1,052	73.5	4	10.2	1	5.7	..	..	1,057	89.4
West South Central	1,520	81.2	1	2.4	2	10.0	..	..	1,523	93.7
Mountain	448	45.7	9	24.3	4	23.2	..	..	461	93.3
Pacific	348	65.0	11	32.0	8	42.2	12	814.3	379	953.5
United States	13,020	$1,939.1	156	$420.9	69	$374.6	34	$1,179.6	13,279	$3,914.2
					NBER Sample					
New England	26	$ 23.6	8	$ 22.0	7	$ 36.5	2	$ 37.7	43	$ 119.8
Middle Atlantic	108	86.6	16	47.1	19	107.2	6	77.7	149	318.6
East North Central	78	50.8	22	60.0	11	57.8	10	199.1	121	367.7
West North Central	34	16.5	3	8.7	6	32.6	3	43.0	46	100.8
South Atlantic	42	28.4	8	23.1	4	25.3	1	7.9	55	84.7
East South Central	12	7.0	2	5.8	1	5.7	..	..	15	18.5
West South Central	14	9.0	..	..	2	10.0	..	..	16	19.1
Mountain	9	3.4	3	8.3	4	23.2	..	..	16	34.9
Pacific	9	6.4	6	17.8	8	42.2	12	814.3	35	880.7
United States	332	$231.8	68	$192.8	62	$340.6	34	$1,179.6	496	$1,944.8

(continued on next page)

TABLE A-2 (continued)
(dollar figures in millions)

CENSUS DIVISION[a]	UNDER $2 MILLION		2 - 3.9 MILLION		4 - 7.8 MILLION		$7.9 MILLION AND OVER[b]		TOTAL	
	No. of Banks	*Amt. Held*	*No. of Banks*	*Amt. Held*	*No. of Banks*	*Amt. Held*	*No. of Banks*	*Amt. Held*	*No. of Banks*	*Amt. Held*
					Sample Response[c]					
New England	3	$ 3.3	3	$ 8.8	2	$ 10.2	2	$ 37.7	10	$ 60.0
Middle Atlantic	31	28.5	8	23.7	14	80.4	5	57.0	58	189.6
East North Central	15	12.7	6	18.0	5	26.5	8	163.3	34	220.5
West North Central	10	6.3	2	6.3	5	26.7	2	26.2	19	65.5
South Atlantic	10	10.2	8	23.1	2	11.2	1	7.9	21	52.4
East South Central	2	2.2	1	2.4	..	..	..	..	3	4.6
West South Central	3	4.1	..	..	2	10.0	..	..	5	14.1
Mountain	..	..	..	..	3	17.7	..	..	3	17.7
Pacific	3	2.8	5	15.3	2	10.7	7	662.5	17	691.3
United States	77	$70.1	33	$97.6	35	$193.4	25	$954.6	170	$1,315.7

Compiled from data supplied by the Office of the Comptroller of the Currency, the Board of Governors of the Federal Reserve System, and the Federal Deposit Insurance Corporation. Amounts will not always add to totals because of rounding. Classification by size of nonfarm mortgage loan portfolio is as of June 30, 1945.

[a] Refers to location of bank.

[b] The exact range is $7,860,000 and over.

[c] Refers to banks reporting on loans current at the survey date (1947). Amounts refer to nonfarm mortgage holdings as of June 30, 1945.

TABLE A-3
Response of Commercial Banks by Date of Return and Size of Nonfarm Mortgage Loan Portfolio
(*cumulative percentage of number of responding banks*)

Date of Return	*Under $2 Million*	*2 - 3.9 Million*	*4 - 7.8 Million*	*$7.9 Million and Over*[a]	*Total*
			Original Response		
1947—February	..	..	..	15%	3%
March	..	..	..	35	6
April	..	..	..	70	13
May	49%	44%	40%	80	52
June	83	89	76	90	84
July	85	94	88	..	88
August	91	100%	96	..	94
September	96	..	100%	..	96
October	..	..	..	..	..
November	..	..	..	..	..
December	..	..	..	..	..
1948—January	98	..	..	95	98
February	..	..	..	..	..
March	..	..	..	..	..
April	100%	..	..	100%	100%
Banks responding	47	18	25	20	110
			Follow-up Response		
1947—September	3%	..	..	20%	3%
October	23	..	..	..	13
November	47	..	10%	40	28
December	73	73%	60	80	72
1948—January	83	80	80	..	82
February	90	87	90	100%	90
March	100%	100%	100%	..	100%
Banks responding	30	15	10	5	60
			Total Response		
1947—February	..	..	..	12%	2%
March	..	..	..	28	4
April	..	..	..	56	8
May	30%	24%	29%	64	34
June	51	48	54	72	54
July	52	52	63	..	57
August	56	55	69	..	61
September	60	..	71	76	64
October	68	..	..	..	67
November	77	..	74	80	72
December	87	88	89	88	88
1948—January	92	91	94	92	92
February	95	94	97	96	95
March	99	100%	100%	..	99
April	100%	..	..	100%	100%
Banks responding	77	33	35	25	170

Classification by size of nonfarm mortgage loan portfolio is as of June 30, 1945.

[a] The exact range is $7,860,000 and over.

TABLE A-4

Original and Follow-up Response of Commercial Banks by Size of Nonfarm Mortgage Loan Portfolio and Type of Bank
(*dollar figures in millions*)

NONFARM MORTGAGE LOAN PORTFOLIO AND TYPE OF BANK	ORIGINAL RESPONSE		FOLLOW-UP RESPONSE			TOTAL RESPONSE				
	No. of Banks	*Amt. Held*	*No. of Banks*	*As % of Original Response*	*Amt. Held*	*As % of Original Response*	*No. of Banks*	*As % of Total Sample*	*Amt. Held*	*As % of Total Sample*
Under $2 Million	*47*	*$ 40.6*	*30*	*64%*	*$ 29.5*	*73%*	*77*	*23%*	*$ 70.1*	*30%*
National	28	24.1	12	43	11.1	46	40	28	35.2	35
State member	10	10.1	13	130	15.1	151	23	34	25.2	40
State nonmember	9	6.4	5	56	3.3	52	14	11	9.7	14
2 - 3.9 Million	*18*	*53.1*	*15*	*83*	*44.5*	*84*	*33*	*49*	*97.6*	*51*
National	8	24.6	9	113	25.9	105	17	63	50.5	65
State member	6	17.7	6	100	18.6	105	12	43	36.3	45
State nonmember	4	10.8	..	0	..	0	4	31	10.8	31
4 - 7.8 Million	*25*	*140.8*	*10*	*40*	*52.6*	*37*	*35*	*56*	*193.4*	*57*
National	11	59.8	4	36	23.1	38	15	56	82.9	56
State member	12	69.0	6	50	29.5	43	18	64	98.5	65
State nonmember	2	12.0	..	0	..	0	2	29	12.0	29
7.9 Million & Over[a]	*20*	*888.4*	*5*	*25*	*66.2*	*7*	*25*	*74*	*954.6*	*81*
National	10	627.4	3	30	39.3	6	13	76	666.7	92
State member	9	249.8	2	22	26.9	11	11	100	276.7	100
State nonmember	1	11.2	..	0	..	0	1	17	11.2	6
All Portfolio Sizes	*110*	*1,122.9*	*60*	*55*	*192.8*	*17*	*170*	*34*	*1,315.7*	*68*
National	57	735.9	28	49	99.4	13	85	40	835.3	79
State member	37	346.6	27	73	90.1	26	64	48	436.7	76
State nonmember	16	40.4	5	31	3.3	8	21	14	43.7	14

Data on amounts of nonfarm mortgage debt held as of June 30, 1945 were compiled from records of the Office of the Comptroller of the Currency, the Board of Governors of the Federal Reserve System, and the Federal Deposit Insurance Corporation.

[a] The exact range is $7,860,000 and over.

TABLE A-5

Number of Loans Reported on by Responding Commercial Banks, by Region, Size of Nonfarm Mortgage Portfolio, and Type of Bank

Nonfarm Mortgage Loan Portfolio and Type of Bank	*New England*	*Middle Atlantic*	*East North Central*	*West North Central*	*South Atlantic*	*East South Central*	*West South Central*	*Mountain*	*Pacific*	*Total*
Under $2 Million	*55*	*723*	*428*	*267*	*160*	*48*	*78*	..	*63*	*1,822*
National	24	326	158	180	60	..	31	..	38	817
State member	..	274	120	61	100	25	47	..	25	652
State nonmember	31	123	150	26	..	23	..	..	..	353
2 - 7.8 Million	*80*	*403*	*207*	*124*	*237*	*11*	*56*	*95*	*167*	*1,380*
National	9	147	67	72	97	..	56	95	71	614
State member	51	226	130	52	35	11	..	..	96	601
State nonmember	20	30	10	..	105	..	..	..	..	165
7.9 Million & Over[a]	*90*	*115*	*1,989*	*108*	*24*	..	..	..	*3,043*	*5,369*
National	41	..	587	58	24	..	..	..	2,399	3,109
State member	49	67	1,402	50	..	..	..	..	644	2,212
State nonmember	..	48	..	..	..	..	..	..	..	48
All Portfolio Sizes	*225*	*1,241*	*2,624*	*499*	*421*	*59*	*134*	*95*	*3,273*	*8,571*
National	74	473	812	310	181	..	87	95	2,508	4,540
State member	100	567	1,652	163	135	36	47	..	765	3,465
State nonmember	51	201	160	26	105	23	..	..	..	566

Loans sampled are those made during 1920-47; both loans still outstanding at the survey date and inactive loans are included. Classification by size of portfolio is as of June 30, 1945. Regional breakdown refers to location of bank.

[a] The exact range is $7,860,000 and over.

TABLE A-6

Response of Savings and Loan Associations by Date of Return and Size of Assets (*cumulative percentage of responding associations*)

Date of Return	*$14 Million and Over*[a]	*Under $14 Million*	*Total*
1947—July	3%	..	1%
August	21	30%	28
September	47	52	51
October	76	74	75
November	85	86	86
December	88	89	89
1948—January	94	..	90
February	97	100%	99
March	100%	..	100%
Associations responding	34	168	202

Based on NBER survey of 500 associations, among which were included all Federal Home Loan Bank member associations whose assets were larger than the sampling interval.

[a] The exact range is $14,044,328 and over.

TABLE A-7

Number of Loans Reported on by Responding Savings and Loan Associations, by Size of Assets and Federal Home Loan Bank District

FHLB District	*$14 Million and Over*[a]	*Under $14 Million*	*Total*
Boston	186	355	541
New York	164	480	644
Pittsburgh	..	186	186
Winston-Salem	86	173	259
Cincinnati	310	693	1,003
Indianapolis	204	456	660
Chicago	91	332	423
Des Moines	70	439	509
Little Rock	..	84	84
Topeka	148	351	499
San Francisco	74	807	881
Total	1,333	4,356	5,689

Loans sampled are those made during 1920-47; both loans still outstanding at the survey date and inactive loans are included. Classification by size of assets is as of December 31, 1945, from data supplied by the Federal Home Loan Bank System. Classification by district refers to location of institution.

[a] The exact range is $14,044,328 and over.

TABLE A-8

Composition of NBER Sample of Savings and Loan Associations by Size of Assets and Federal Home Loan Bank District

(*dollar figures in millions*)

TOTAL ASSET SIZE & FHLB DISTRICT	ALL MEMBER ASSOCIATIONS[a]		ASSOCIATIONS IN NBER SAMPLE			SAMPLE RESPONSE[c]				
									Response Ratio[d]	
	No.	*Total Assets*	*No.*	*Total Assets*	*Coverage*[b]	*No.*	*Total Assets*	*Coverage*[b]	*No.*	*Assets*
ASSET SIZE										
Stratum One	*63*	*$1,542*	*63*	*$1,542*	*100%*	*34*	*$902*	*58%*	*54%*	*59%*
$25 million and over	24	861	24	861	100	18	621	72	75	72
14 - 24.9 million[e]	39	681	39	681	100	16	281	41	41	41
Stratum Two	*3,596*	*6,137*	*437*	*1,981*	*32*	*168*	*874*	*14*	*38*	*44*
5 - 14 million	273	2,125	151	1,281	60	72	610	29	48	48
1 - 4.9 million	1,410	3,212	229	667	21	86	258	8	38	39
$250,000 - 999,999	1,267	701	52	32	5	9	6	1	17	16
Less than $250,000	646	99	5	1	1	1	[f]	[g]	20	20
FEDERAL HOME LOAN BANK DISTRICT										
Boston	220	766	47	413	54	20	252	33	43	61
New York	359	845	55	412	49	31	252	30	56	61
Pittsburgh	433	469	35	93	20	8	29	6	23	31
Winston-Salem	406	894	54	433	48	14	151	17	26	35
Cincinnati	562	1,439	96	716	50	29	256	18	30	36
Indianapolis	217	491	32	231	47	14	128	26	44	55
Chicago	458	763	50	304	40	18	175	23	36	58
Des Moines	236	419	25	202	48	21	165	39	84	82
Little Rock	269	327	24	86	26	2	8	2	8	9
Topeka	207	270	18	95	35	12	74	27	67	78
San Francisco	292	996	64	539	54	33	286	29	52	53
Total	3,659	$7,679	500	$3,523	46%	202	$1,776	23%	40%	50%

[a] Data supplied by the Federal Home Loan Bank System for all member associations as of December 31, 1945.

[b] Total assets of sampled associations as a percentage of total assets of all member associations.

[c] Refers to associations reporting on loans current at the survey date (1947). Total assets are given as of December 31, 1945.

[d] Number and total assets of responding associations as percentages of the number and total assets of sampled associations.

[e] The exact lower limit is $14,044,328.

[f] Less than $1 million.

[g] Less than 0.5 percent.

TABLE A-9
Number and Original Amount of Sampled Nonfarm Home Mortgage Loans, 1920-47, by Year Loan Made
(dollar figures in thousands)

YEAR MADE	LIFE INSURANCE COMPANIES		COMMERCIAL BANKS BY NONFARM MORTGAGE LOAN PORTFOLIO SIZE[a]								SAVINGS & LOAN ASSOCIATIONS	
			$7.9 Million and Over[b]		*2 - 7.8 Million*		*Under $2 Million*		*Total*			
	No.	*Amt.*	*No.*	*Amt.*	*No.*	*Amt.*	*No.*	*Amt.*	*No.*	*Amt.*	*No.*	*Amt.*
1920-24	*851*	*$ 3,781*	*479*	*$1,869*	*70*	*$ 314*	*165*	*$ 599*	*714*	*$2,781*	*551*	*$1,495*
1920	73	382	62	191	7	28	24	70	93	289	103	242
1921	119	451	55	173	3	11	21	74	79	258	83	198
1922	170	656	103	385	12	43	26	70	141	498	106	275
1923	209	1,001	125	535	16	56	45	159	186	750	127	394
1924	280	1,291	134	585	32	176	49	226	215	987	132	386
1925-29	*2,061*	*11,069*	*569*	*2,442*	*185*	*1,114*	*343*	*1,505*	*1,097*	*5,060*	*859*	*2,614*
1925	359	1,832	138	582	26	113	87	374	251	1,068	174	538
1926	479	2,510	116	537	40	419	60	262	216	1,218	156	448
1927	414	2,445	118	503	42	205	73	303	233	1,010	164	505
1928	411	2,165	114	481	42	198	67	251	223	929	189	578
1929	398	2,117	83	340	35	179	56	316	174	835	176	545
1930-34	*809*	*4,447*	*249*	*876*	*59*	*461*	*100*	*412*	*408*	*1,749*	*386*	*1,094*
1930	348	1,884	80	304	21	109	34	141	135	555	157	477
1931	301	1,792	81	257	20	287	40	179	141	723	71	195
1932	103	512	31	118	6	29	8	33	45	180	49	167
1933	24	105	25	88	6	10	9	40	40	139	42	91
1934	33	154	32	109	6	26	9	19	47	153	67	164

(continued on next page)

TABLE A-9 (continued)
(*dollar figures in thousands*)

YEAR MADE	LIFE INSURANCE COMPANIES		COMMERCIAL BANKS BY NONFARM MORTGAGE LOAN PORTFOLIO SIZE[a]								SAVINGS & LOAN ASSOCIATIONS	
			$7.9 Million and Over[b]		*2 - 7.8 Million*		*Under $2 Million*		*Total*			
	No.	*Amt.*	*No.*	*Amt.*	*No.*	*Amt.*	*No.*	*Amt.*	*No.*	*Amt.*	*No.*	*Amt.*
1935-39	*1,177*	*$ 6,525*	*553*	*$ 2,119*	*152*	*$ 621*	*307*	*$1,054*	*1,012*	*$ 3,794*	*755*	*$ 1,989*
1935	88	468	65	236	21	65	42	119	128	419	100	248
1936	202	1,080	85	341	24	82	42	149	151	572	129	316
1937	252	1,432	111	437	29	145	60	174	200	756	164	463
1938	298	1,730	130	469	25	87	58	239	213	795	159	417
1939	337	1,815	162	637	53	243	105	374	320	1,253	203	545
1940-47	*3,243*	*16,492*	*1,125*	*5,067*	*425*	*2,424*	*838*	*3,308*	*2,388*	*10,799*	*1,937*	*7,125*
1940	447	2,246	175	690	64	281	104	347	343	1,319	201	592
1941	647	3,338	158	656	53	220	100	390	311	1,266	232	677
1942	670	3,228	131	537	56	239	84	293	271	1,069	167	536
1943	508	2,342	119	448	34	139	68	238	221	825	185	564
1944	325	1,651	108	481	34	177	83	328	225	985	246	826
1945	254	1,349	131	588	39	226	93	370	263	1,184	274	975
1946	320	1,965	254	1,380	114	959	247	1,007	615	3,345	379	1,718
1947	72	373	49	287	31	184	59	336	139	806	253[c]	1,237[c]
1920-47[d]	8,157	$42,388	2,980	$12,389	892	$4,944	1,754	$6,880	5,626	$24,213	4,492	$14,329

Based on NBER survey of urban mortgage lending; refers to loans secured by one- to four-family homes. For number of companies reporting, see note under Table A-11. Amounts do not always add to totals because of rounding.

[a] Based on original sample returns without adjustment for nonresponse.

[b] The exact range is $7,860,000 and over.

[c] Includes one loan made in 1948.

[d] Includes 27 loans for which year made was not available: 16 insurance company loans, 7 bank loans, and 4 association loans.

TABLE A-10

Number and Original Amount of Sampled Mortgage Loans on Nonfarm Income-Producing Properties, 1920-47, by Period Loan Made

(dollar figures in thousands)

PERIOD MADE	LIFE INSURANCE COMPANIES		COMMERCIAL BANKS BY NONFARM MORTGAGE LOAN PORTFOLIO SIZE[a]								SAVINGS & LOAN ASSOCIATIONS	
			$7.9 Million and Over[b]		*2 - 7.8 Million*		*Under $2 Million*		*Total*			
	No.	*Amt.*	*No.*	*Amt.*	*No.*	*Amt.*	*No.*	*Amt.*	*No.*	*Amt.*	*No.*	*Amt.*
1920-24	118	$ 5,602	59	$2,576	16	$ 231	11	$ 88	86	$ 2,896	67	$ 298
1925-29	239	16,760	96	1,303	38	1,512	26	450	160	3,265	86	424
1930-34	54	2,689	43	694	14	1,773	12	176	69	2,643	25	110
1935-39	139	8,968	58	640	37	1,878	29	248	124	2,766	26	146
1940-47	224	15,734	155	3,676	61	5,078	88	1,144	304	9,898	51	536
1920-47[c]	774	$49,753	412	$8,924	166	$10,472	166	$2,106	744	$21,502	255	$1,514

Based on NBER survey of urban mortgage lending; refers to loans secured by properties other than one- to four-family homes. For number of companies reporting, see note under Table A-11. Amounts do not always add to totals because of rounding.

[a] Based on original sample returns without adjustment for nonresponse.

[b] The exact range is $7,860,000 and over.

[c] Includes one commercial bank loan for which period made was not available.

TABLE A-11

Number and Original Amount of Sampled Nonfarm Mortgage Loans, 1920-47, by Period Loan Made and by Amortization or Insurance Provision

(dollar figures in thousands)

PERIOD MADE AND TYPE OF LOAN	1- TO 4-FAMILY HOMES						ALL OTHER PROPERTY			
	Life Insurance Companies		*Commercial Banks*[a]		*Savings and Loan Associations*[b]		*Life Insurance Companies*		*Commercial Banks*[a]	
	No.	*Amt.*	*No.*	*Amt.*	*No.*	*Amt.*	*No.*	*Amt.*	*No.*	*Amt.*
1920-24	*851*	*$ 3,781*	*714*	*$2,781*	..	..	*118*	*$ 5,602*	*86*	*$2,896*
Fully amortized	234	807	110	407	..	..	2	33	5	68
Partially amortized	478	2,222	300	1,210	..	..	90	4,198	35	267
Nonamortized	138	745	298	1,127	..	..	24	1,350	46	2,560
Not available	1	7	6	37	..	..	2	20	..	..
1925-29	*2,061*	*11,069*	*1,097*	*5,060*	*1,563*	*$4,830*	*239*	*16,760*	*160*	*3,265*
Fully amortized	390	1,587	176	515	1,471[c]	4,570[c]	15	1,043	17	244
Partially amortized	1,212	6,808	412	1,938	..	..	158	10,737	69	1,268
Nonamortized	457	2,667	500	2,549	88	248	66	4,980	73	1,747
Not available	2	7	9	59	4	12	..	..	1	6
1930-34	*809*	*4,447*	*408*	*1,749*	*411*	*1,204*	*54*	*2,689*	*69*	*2,643*
Fully amortized	270	1,176	69	235	386[c]	1,121[c]	2	22	7	126
Partially amortized	407	2,347	154	617	..	..	37	1,433	27	1,192
Nonamortized	131	894	181	878	24	81	14	1,229	34	1,260
FHA	..	..	1	3	1	2	..	..	..	..
Not available	1	30	3	18	..	..	1	6	1	65

(continued on next page)

TABLE A-11 (continued)
(*dollar figures in thousands*)

PERIOD MADE AND TYPE OF LOAN	1- TO 4-FAMILY HOMES						ALL OTHER PROPERTY			
	Life Insurance Companies		*Commercial Banks*[a]		*Savings and Loan Associations*[b]		*Life Insurance Companies*		*Commercial Banks*[a]	
	No.	*Amt.*	*No.*	*Amt.*	*No.*	*Amt.*	*No.*	*Amt.*	*No.*	*Amt.*
1935-39	*1,177*	*$ 6,525*	*1,012*	*$ 3,794*	*1,221*	*$ 3,442*	*139*	*$ 8,968*	*124*	*$ 2,766*
Fully amortized	529	3,080	250	769	1,140[c]	3,129[c]	31	819	44	382
Partially amortized	244	1,371	209	786	..	..	95	6,609	45	869
Nonamortized	20	141	128	391	3	10	7	218	27	1,431
FHA	383	1,927	423	1,842	60	247	5	1,072	5	21
Not available	1	6	2	6	18	57	1	250	3	63
1940-47	*3,243*	*16,492*	*2,388*	*10,800*	*1,548*[d]	*6,355*[d]	*224*	*15,734*	*304*	9,898
Fully amortized	1,028	6,103	676	2,674	1,267[c]	4,755[c]	112	6,049	149	2,509
Partially amortized	95	572	572	2,721	..	..	93	8,144	107	5,843
Nonamortized	12	141	136	404	3	29	6	395	31	1,358
FHA	1,984	8,906	740	3,447	45	233	7	1,095	4	97
VA	116	733	259	1,515	222	1,286	2	13	9	67
Not available	8	37	5	39	11	53	4	39	4	25
1920-47[e]	8,157	$42,388	5,626	$24,213	4,747	$15,843	774	$49,753	744	$21,502

Based on NBER survey of urban mortgage lending. Respondents reporting on inactive as well as active loans included 24 leading life insurance companies, 116 commercial banks, and 92 savings and loan associations. Amounts do not always add to totals because of rounding.

[a] Based on original sample returns without adjustment for nonresponse.

[b] Includes 81 loans on income-producing properties, 43 on farm properties, and 131 for which type of property was not available. Loans are classified by the following periods: 1920-29, 1930-34, 1935-41, and 1942-47.

[c] Includes the following types of loan: direct reduction, cancel and endorse, and share accumulation plan.

[d] Includes one loan made in 1948.

[e] Includes 28 loans for which period made was not available: 16 insurance company loans, 8 bank loans, and 4 association loans.

TABLE A-12
Number and Original Amount of Sampled Nonfarm Home Mortgage Loans Made 1920-29, by Contract Terms
(*dollar figures in thousands*)

LOAN CHARACTERISTICS	LIFE INSURANCE COMPANIES		COMMERCIAL BANKS[a]		SAVINGS & LOAN ASSOCIATIONS[b]	
	No.	*Amt.*	*No.*	*Amt.*	*No.*	*Amt.*
CONTRACT INTEREST RATE						
5.0 - 5.9%	578	$ 3,698	61	$ 578	43	$ 188
6.0 - 6.9	2,253	10,811	1,452	6,405	628	2,372
7.0 - 7.9	} 77	} 323	284	833	548	1,525
8.0 - 8.9			14	26	119	253
9.0 and over			..	..	170	307
Not available	4	17	c	c	55	184
CONTRACT LENGTH						
0 - 4 years	580	3,247	1,232	5,029	54	159
5 - 9	1,486	7,767	424	2,192	249	464
10 - 14	754	3,316	127	481	1,064	3,432
15 - 19	83	458	8	45	13	47
20 and over	6	47	20	95	2	20
Share accumulation plan, demand, etc.	} 3	} 15	c	c	170	673
Not available			c	c	11	35
LOAN-TO-VALUE RATIO						
0 - 39%	242	1,170	292	781	168	220
40 - 79	2,255	12,219	1,437	6,741	851	2,877
80 and over	3	22	8	39	30	127
Not available	412	1,438	74	281	514	1,605
Total	2,912	$14,849	1,811	$7,842	1,563	$4,830
ORIGINAL LOAN AMOUNT						
Less than $5,000	1,825	5,877	d	d	1,297	2,881
$5,000 - 9,999	863	5,624	d	d	241	1,502
10,000 - 19,999	201	2,420	d	d	21	251
20,000 - 49,999	17	408	d	d	3	85
50,000 - 99,999	4	270	d	d	..	..
100,000 and over	2	250	d	d	1	111

Based on NBER survey of urban mortgage lending; refers to loans secured by one- to four-family homes, except as noted below. For number of companies reporting, see Table A-11. Amounts do not always add to totals because of rounding.

[a] Based on original sample returns without adjustment for nonresponse.

[b] Includes 33 loans secured by income-producing properties, 12 by farm properties, and 108 for which type of property was not available.

[c] Excluded from tabulations.

[d] Not available.

TABLE A-13
Number and Original Amount of Sampled Nonfarm Mortgage Loans Made and Extinguished 1920-47, by Type of Property
(*dollar figures in thousands*)

TYPE OF PROPERTY	LIFE INSURANCE COMPANIES		COMMERCIAL BANKS[a]	
	No.	*Amt.*	*No.*	*Amt.*
1- to 4-Family Homes	*5,035*	*$25,753*	*3,860*	*$15,324*
1-family	4,627	22,243	3,198	12,182
2- to 4-family	371	2,783	555	2,452
1- to 4-family with business use	37	727	107	690
All Other Property	*481*	*29,066*	*515*	*12,001*
Apartments	250	12,998	108	1,904
Stores	145	8,310	82	2,558
Other	86	7,758	325	7,539
Total	5,516	$54,819	4,375	$27,325

Based on NBER survey of urban mortgage lending. Excludes loans for which data necessary for the calculation of yields were inadequate. For number of companies reporting, see Table A-11.

[a] Based on original sample returns without adjustment for nonresponse.

TABLE A-14

Number and Original Amount of Sampled Nonfarm Mortgage Loans Made 1920-29 and Extinguished by 1947, by Loan-to-Value Ratio and Contract Length

(dollar figures in thousands)

CONTRACT TERMS	LIFE INSURANCE COMPANIES		COMMERCIAL BANKS BY NONFARM MORTGAGE LOAN PORTFOLIO SIZE[a]							
			$7.9 Million and Over[b]		*2 - 7.8 Million*		*Under $2 Million*		*Total*	
	No.	*Amt.*	*No.*	*Amt.*	*No.*	*Amt.*	*No.*	*Amt.*	*No.*	*Amt.*
					One- to Four-Family Homes					
LOAN-TO-VALUE RATIO										
0 - 39%	234	$ 1,112	183	$ 480	22	$ 42	80	$ 220	285	$ 741
40 - 79	2,064	11,022	792	3,458	149	1,009	404	1,795	1,345	6,262
80 and over	3	22	5	27	2	9	..	..	7	37
Not available	410	1,429	20	87	31	94	21	82	72	263
CONTRACT LENGTH										
0 - 4 years	492	2,711	832	3,367	136	658	167	485	1,135	4,509
5 - 9	1,413	7,314	56	245	38	390	329	1,542	423	2,177
10 - 14	724	3,127	93	353	22	62	8	35	123	449
15 - 19	78	409	..	..	8	45	..	..	8	45
20 and over	2	12	19	88	..	..	..	..	19	88
Not available	2	12	..	..	..	..	1	35	1	35
Total	2,711	$13,585	1,000	$4,052	204	$1,154	505	$2,097	1,709	$7,303

(continued on next page)

TABLE A-14 (continued)
(*dollar figures in thousands*)

CONTRACT TERMS	LIFE INSURANCE COMPANIES		COMMERCIAL BANKS BY NONFARM MORTGAGE LOAN PORTFOLIO SIZE[a]							
			$7.9 Million and Over[b]		*2 - 7.8 Million*		*Under $2 Million*		*Total*	
	No.	*Amt.*	*No.*	*Amt.*	*No.*	*Amt.*	*No.*	*Amt.*	*No.*	*Amt.*
					All Other Property					
LOAN-TO-VALUE RATIO										
0 - 39%	62	$ 3,421	42	$ 281	7	$ 730	6	$ 40	55	$1,050
40 - 79	240	15,115	96	3,423	29	658	25	444	150	4,525
80 and over	4	154	1	15	1	8	..	..	2	23
Not available	..	..	7	76	9	53	2	10	18	139
CONTRACT LENGTH										
0 - 4 years	42	3,181	123	1,251	28	1,006	13	145	164	2,402
5 - 9	188	9,947	12	319	14	262	16	232	42	813
10 - 14	64	4,950	4	2,113	4	181	4	117	12	2,411
15 - 19	9	260	..	..	..	..	..	..	..	..
20 and over	1	330	7	111	..	..	..	..	7	111
Not available	2	22	..	..	..	..	..	..	..	..
Total	306	$18,690	146	$3,794	46	$1,449	33	$494	225	$5,737

Based on NBER survey of urban mortgage lending. Excludes loans for which data necessary for the calculation of yields were inadequate. Amounts do not always add to totals because of rounding.

[a] Based on original sample returns without adjustment for nonresponse.

[b] The exact range is $7,860,000 and over.

APPENDIX B

PRELIMINARY QUESTIONNAIRES AND LOAN EXPERIENCE CARD AND INSTRUCTIONS

Exhibit 1 of this appendix is the preliminary questionnaire sent to a sample of commercial banks to obtain information from which to compute subsampling ratios. Comparable information for savings and loan associations was obtained through the questionnaire presented as Exhibit 2.

Instructions for the selection of sample loans were sent to each of the institutions selected for inclusion in the sample. A copy of the instructions for life insurance companies is reproduced as Exhibit 3. The instructions for commercial banks and savings and loan associations were substantially the same as those for insurance companies, but certain differences should be noted.

(a) Each life insurance company was requested to sample every 100th loan made after January 1, 1920, whereas commercial banks and savings and loan associations were assigned different subsampling intervals computed separately for each institution (see Appendix A, page 131f.). Regardless of the filing system used, commercial banks and savings and loan associations were instructed to begin by selecting the first loan made after January 1, 1920 and every n^{th} loan thereafter.

(b) Commercial banks were requested to sample only those loans held for their own accounts, exclusive of trust department mortgage holdings. Banks using a filing system similar to that identified as Method B in Exhibit 3 were instructed to start at the beginning of their files of inactive mortgage loans. If their mortgage loans were interfiled with other types of loans, the sample banks were requested to select the first loan (regardless of type) made after January 1, 1920 and every n^{th} loan thereafter, and upon completion of the sampling process to reject from the group of selected loans all those that were not urban mortgage loans (besides rejecting the successor loans described in the instructions for insurance companies). If a loan originally selected turned out to have been canceled before disbursement of funds, banks were instructed to substitute the next loan in the file. The instruction relating to a subsequent increase in the value of the property securing a loan, given on page 161, did not apply to the loans selected by banks.

(c) Savings and loan associations were divided into two groups: those sampling current loans only and those sampling all loans made after January 1, 1920. Separate instructions were prepared for each group. For associations reporting all loans the instructions were similar to those followed by commercial banks, except that associations included loans secured by farm properties in their samples. Associations not expected to be able to canvass past loans were requested to select the first loan in their files of active mortgage loans and every n^{th} loan thereafter, and to trace successor loans back through their closed files in order to obtain the complete history of the transaction.

Transcription cards on which to enter data for individual loans were supplied to each institution. A copy of the card used by insurance companies and commercial banks is reproduced here as Exhibit 4. The card for savings and loan associations was slightly different. A farm property category was added to Item C. For two of the categories in Item D (fully amortized and partially amortized conventional loans) the following were substituted: amortized, share accumulation plan; amortized, cancel and endorse; and amortized, direct reduction. Item E, calling for the original schedule of payments, was replaced by a question on the purpose of the original loan (for example, construction, home purchase, and refinancing of debt owed to another mortgagee).

EXHIBIT 1

Preliminary Data for Study of Mortgage Lending Experience

Bank Identification Number ____________

____

1. What is the approximate number of new urban mortgage loans made since January 1, 1920 (or thereabouts) by your bank? ____________
2. Have mortgage loans made since January 1, 1920 had numbers assigned to them? Yes ( ) No ( )
3. Indicate the manner in which you file ledger cards on active urban mortgage loans and on inactive loans (i.e., those that have been paid in full, sold, or assigned to other mortgagees, or on which property was acquired):

(a) Are they filed separately from all other loans, or are they merged with all types of loans?

	Active Loans	*Inactive Loans*
Filed separately	( )	( )
Merged with others	( )	( )

(b) Are they filed in numerical order, in alphabetical sequence, or otherwise?

Filed numerically ( ) ( )
Filed alphabetically ( ) ( )

If filed by some other method, please explain briefly:

____

____

EXHIBIT 2

Preliminary Data for Study of Mortgage Lending Experience

Name of Association ______________________________
City ______________________________ State ______________

I. Has your association been in continuous operation since 1920, uninterrupted by merger or segregation of assets? (Conversion to federal charter or change in corporate name should *not* be considered an interruption unless accompanied by segregation of assets.)

( ) Yes ( ) No

II. If "yes," please answer the following:

A. Number (an estimate will do) of mortgage loans made since January 1, 1920 ______________

B. Are these loans numbered consecutively? ( ) Yes ( ) No

C. Number of mortgage loans now on books ______________

D. How are ledger cards filed (i.e., alphabetically, numerically, etc.)?

1. For loans now on books ______________
2. For loans paid off, foreclosed, etc. ______________

III. If "no," please answer the following:

A. From what date has your association been in continuous operation? Since ______________ (year)

B. Was this the year your association first began operations? ( ) Yes ( ) No

C. If not, what change occurred on that date? ______________

____

____

D. Number of mortgage loans now on books ______________

E. How are ledger cards filed (i.e., alphabetically, numerically, etc.) for loans now on books? ______________

IV. Name and address of person to receive instructions and forms for reporting mortgage experience:

____

____

EXHIBIT 3

Mortgage Loan Experience Card—Instructions

Section I—Sampling Instructions

In selecting the individual ledger or mortgage cards from your file, use Method A or Method B depending on the way in which your ledger cards on mortgage loans are filed.

USE METHOD A IF YOUR LEDGER CARDS ARE FILED NUMERICALLY

(1) Find the number of the first loan made after January 1, 1920.

(2) The number of *the first loan selected for the sample* should be the first number, *after* the number noted in (1), that ends in two zeros—i.e., the first number that is a multiple of 100. Select that ledger card and the ledger card on *every hundredth loan* thereafter.

Examples: Suppose that the first loan made after January 1, 1920 carries the number 1623. Then the numbers of the loans in your sample would be 1700, 1800, 1900, 2000, and so on.

Suppose that the first loan made after January 1, 1920 carries the number 1104. Then the first loan in the sample would be number 1200, and the following loans would be 1300, 1400, 1500, and so on.

(If you wish, you can prepare a written list of these loan numbers before drawing the actual cards from the files.)

(3) *Omit all farm loans.* That is, if the ledger card bearing any of the numbers determined by step (2) happens to refer to a farm loan, omit that loan and proceed to the next number in the series.

Examples: If loan number 2200 turns out to be a farm loan, omit it from the sample and proceed to loan number 2300—*not to loan number 2201.*

If loan number 2300 is a farm loan also, disregard that loan as well and proceed to loan number 2400, continuing until the next city loan is reached.

(This situation will occur only when city loans and farm loans are numbered in a single sequence.)

(4) *Omit all "successor loans."* If the ledger card bearing any of the numbers determined by step (2) refers to a loan that was a successor to an earlier loan—that is, if the ledger card selected refers to a recast loan that was assigned *a new number*—omit the selected loan and proceed to the next number in the series.

Examples: Loan number 5600 is a "successor loan" because it represents an advance of additional funds on an earlier loan. When the loan was recast it was given a new number, 5600. Omit loan number 5600 and proceed to loan number 5700.

Loan number 9100 is a "successor loan" because it represents an extension of maturity on an earlier loan, with the recast loan given the new loan number 9100. Omit loan number 9100 and proceed to loan number 9200.

(5) Continue step (2) until you have gone through all your mortgage card files. With the exception noted in (4), *do not exclude any urban mortgage loan, even though it may seem extremely untypical of the mortgage experience of your company.*

* * *

USE METHOD B IF YOUR LEDGER CARDS ARE NOT FILED NUMERICALLY

(or if loans cannot be located conveniently by number in the file)

(1) Beginning with any file cabinet you choose, take the first loan card and every hundredth loan card thereafter throughout all your files. That is, the *first six* loans in your sample will be the 1st, 101st, 201st, 301st, 401st, and the 501st from your files.

Caution: Be sure to actually *count* the loans, so that you select every hundredth loan exactly. Do not guess or use short-cut methods in selecting the hundredth loan.

Also, be sure to count *loans,* not cards. If the same loan is represented by more than one card, count all the cards pertaining to that loan as *one* item.

(If inactive loans are filed according to the year in which they were made or paid off, it will of course be unnecessary to sample cabinets containing loans made before 1920.)

(2) *Omit all farm loans.* If urban loans and farm loans made by your company are filed together, some of the loans drawn in counting by the above system will be farm loans. In each such case, disregard the farm loan and proceed to the next hundredth loan until a city loan appears.

(3) *Omit all loans made before January 1, 1920.*

Example: If the 701st loan was made before that date, omit it, continue counting, and proceed to the 801st loan.

If the 801st loan was also made before January 1, 1920, omit it also, continue counting, and proceed to the 901st loan; and so on until a loan appears which was made after January 1, 1920.

(4) *Omit all "successor loans."* By "successor loan" is meant a loan which is a recast of an earlier loan—that is, additional funds were advanced, or the maturity was extended, and a new loan was written. If a card drawn in counting by the above system refers to such a loan, omit it and proceed to the next hundredth loan.

Examples: The 5601st loan from your files is a "successor loan" because it represents an advance of additional funds on an *earlier* loan. Omit the 5601st loan and proceed to the 5701st loan.

The 1101st loan from your files is a "successor loan" because it represents an extension of maturity on an *earlier* loan. Omit the 1101st loan and proceed to the 1201st loan.

(5) Continue in the same way through all your mortgage files. With the exceptions noted in (3) and (4), *do not exclude any urban mortgage loan, either on residential or income-producing properties, even though it may seem extremely untypical of the mortgage experience of your company.*

(6) If there are several files, be sure to sample all of them (except cabinets containing *only* loans made before 1920). For example, sample both active and inactive files; if there is a separate file of FHA loans, or a separate real estate contract file, sample these also, and so forth.

The order in which the file drawers are sampled does not matter. In going from one file drawer to another, or from one file to another, carry over the number of loans remaining in the last file drawer to those in the next file drawer, until the next hundredth loan is reached.

Example: If the last loan in a file cabinet is the 562nd, count the first loan in the next cabinet as the 563rd, and continue counting until you reach the 601st loan, which you take for the sample.

In other words, treat the files as if they were combined in one continuous and consecutive file.

* * *

Complete the Loan Histories

Whether you have used Method A or Method B, you have now assembled a group of ledger cards that represent a 1% sample of the loans made by your company.

The record must now be completed by adding a few more cards which will give the *full history* of each loan selected. This should be done as follows: Go through the sample, card by card. If a card shows that the loan was later recast and given a new loan number, and that another card was prepared, find the later card in your files and attach it to the card representing the original loan.

If the loan was recast more than once, you may have to attach two or more cards to the original card. In other words, you follow the loan forward, through its several modifications, until it was extinguished.

Example: (The numbers used here are those that might appear if cards were selected by Method A, but the principle is the same for cards selected by Method B.)

If loan number 1700 was selected in your original drawing of cards, and you see from the card that it was recast and a new loan written with a new number—say number 2276—then pull the card on loan 2276 and attach it to card 1700 as part of the same loan transaction.

Perhaps loan 2276 itself was subsequently recast, and another new loan written with a new number—say number 3402. Pull the card on loan 3402 and attach it to cards 1700 and 2276.

If card 3402 shows that the loan was not modified again, the three cards give the complete history of that loan.

In a very few cases you may find that the card representing a recasting of a loan is one that you *omitted* in your first drawing of cards because it was recognized as a "successor loan" (see paragraph 4 under Method A or B above). For example, you now find that card 6200 (which you correctly omitted in your first drawing) represents a modification of original loan number 400, which you included in the sample. In this case, card 6200 *does* belong in the sample; you therefore attach it to card number 400.

Exception: There is one type of loan alteration that is considered to be a termination rather than a modification of the original loan. If a loan was recast *because of a substantial increase in the value of the underlying property resulting from improvements*, consider the recast loan a *new* loan, not a modification. Do not attach the card representing the recast loan to the old loan card. Regard this loan as having been terminated at the date of the recasting.

For purposes of this rule, "substantial increase" means an increase of 25% or more in the value of the underlying property.

* * *

With the addition of these cards, which complete the loan histories, the sample is ready to be used for transcribing information to the "Mortgage Loan Experience Cards."

Each loan will use a separate card. We have sent you _____ cards, which allows a margin for wastage. If you need more, please ask us for them.

Instructions for filling out the Mortgage Loan Experience Card will be found in Section II, following.

Section II—Instructions for Filling out the Mortgage Loan Experience Card

These instructions should be read through and compared with the Mortgage Loan Experience Card before any transcriptions are made from the ledger cards that you have drawn from your files by the sampling methods described in Section I.

* * *

Schedules A to H inclusive, and Schedule J, are to be filled in completely (so far as possible) for each loan in the sample.

Schedule I will be filled in for only a part of the loans selected.

Schedule K (reverse of card) will be filled in for only a few of the loans selected.

If data are not available, write "n.a." for the question involved.

If you feel that any special comments should be made on a particular loan, enter them on a separate sheet. Mark this sheet with the same identification number as the card it applies to, and attach it to the card.

* * *

In this analysis, a mortgage loan is defined as an obligation secured by a specific piece of *property*. Therefore, in filling out the Mortgage Loan Experience Card, the information recorded about each loan should carry the history of the loan forward, from its origination, through any modifications, to extinguishment, regardless of the fact that the original obligor may have been succeeded by one or more other obligors.

* * *

Schedule A. Loan Identification Number. A space is provided in which to give a number that will permit identification by your company of the loan on which information is transcribed. Whether this is the loan's actual file number, or a new number assigned so as not to disclose the loan's file number, does not matter for purposes of the National Bureau's analysis. In either case you should keep a record so that you can refer back to a particular loan if necessary; it is especially important to keep such a record if the number given in Schedule A is not the actual file number of the loan.

Schedule B. Location of Property. Enter here the state where the *property* is located, also the city or town. Do not indicate street address.

Schedule C. Type of Property. From among the listed types of property, check the one which best describes the *principal characteristic* of the property mortgaged. If the property is not adequately described by any one of the listed types, indicate its character under Item 13.

Schedule D. Type of Loan at Time of Making. Check the appropriate type of loan. If it is not possible to distinguish between a fully amortized and a partially amortized conventional (i.e., uninsured) loan, bracket types 2 and 3 and check the bracket.

Schedule E. Original Schedule of Payments. Check the type of principal and interest payment schedules which were set up *at the time the loan was made.*

Schedule F. Purchase Money Mortgage. Indicate here by a check mark whether the loan selected was a purchase money mortgage *when first put on the books.* A "purchase money mortgage" means a mortgage taken as part of the consideration received on the sale of property owned by the mortgagee.

Schedule G. Real Estate Sales Contract. Indicate here whether the transaction was initiated as a real estate sales contract.

Schedule H. Original Loan.

(1) Year loan was made: Give the last two figures of the year during which the loan was made; for example, a loan made at any time in 1927 would be indicated 27.

(2) Amount: Indicate the original amount in dollars, omitting cents.

(3) Appraised value: Give the original appraisal of land and buildings combined, in dollars, omitting cents.

(4) Contract term: Give the original term of the contract to the nearest year. If the original loan was written on a demand basis, write in "demand," or "demand after ______ years," whatever the case may be.

(5) Contract rate of interest: This refers to the *gross* rate of interest—that is, the rate charged to the borrower. It should be reported gross of any participations in interest by the company's correspondent or other agent.

Schedule I. Subsequent Modifications in Loan or Sales Contract. This schedule asks for information on such modifications of the original contract as may have been made; for example, an advance of additional funds, or forgiveness of part of the principal through compromise, or the extension of contract term (including cases in which the principal was reduced by payment and the loan term was extended), or changes in the contract rate of interest or loan type.

Such changes should be indicated in the appropriate columns of Schedule I. If several of the loan's features were changed in the same modification, make all the necessary entries on the same line. Leave those columns blank that refer to loan features that were not modified. Give amounts in dollars, omitting cents.

If additional space is needed to record contract modifications, use additional cards and staple or clip together. (Please mark all cards applying to a given loan with the same identification number.)

Unpaid balance at time of modification (column 2) and *unpaid balance after modification* (column 10) should be filled in every case.

In reporting *advance of additional funds* (column 3) ignore changes which resulted from periodic increases in the balance because of tax payment, etc. However, an increase in the balance because of payments of accumulated taxes on which the debtor was delinquent should be considered an "advance of additional funds." Also, if the loan was rewritten and the unpaid balance of the old loan reduced to zero, then the unpaid balance at the time the loan was rewritten should be given in column 2 and the amount of additional funds over and above the former balance entered in column 3; the resulting new unpaid balance should be reported in column 10.

Reduction by compromise (column 4) refers to the forgiveness of part of the unpaid principal balance by compromise, i.e., by agreement between mortgagor and mortgagee.

Under column 6 indicate the additional number of years for which the contract was extended. Thus, a contract having two years to run which was modified to mature in six years would be considered as having been extended for four years. For purposes of this calculation consider as a full year any part of a year which is six months or more.

Under column 7 indicate only the *new rate of interest.*

Column 8, *changes in loan type,* is provided to record such modifications or changes in the loan as alter its original type as shown in D above.

Under column 9 indicate the amount in dollars, omitting cents, of any *new appraisal* made in connection with a modification of the loan contract.

This will be the combined appraisal of land and buildings.

Schedule J. Loan Status. Indicate by year, or by giving the unpaid balance in the case of active loans, the status of the loan.

* * *

If the loan resulted in the acquisition of property *and if this property has been sold,* fill out Schedule K, which is on the reverse side of the mortgage card. In all other cases Schedule K is to be ignored.

Schedule K. Data on Property Acquired and Sold.

The primary purpose of Schedule K is to get a final figure of loss or gain on properties acquired and sold. This is reported in Item 16. Schedule K has been designed to enable respondents to build up a figure of loss or gain which will be comparable from company to company. However, the records of individual companies may provide a direct figure of loss or gain that is comparable to the one that would be derived under Schedule K, although it might be built up in a different way. In this case, it will be sufficient to report the company's available figure directly, but Items 7 and 14 should also be given, wherever possible.

If the figure of loss or gain on property which can be taken directly from a company's records is not comparable to Item 16 in Schedule K, but can readily be adjusted to achieve this comparability, such an adjusted figure will fulfill the needs of this study.

Individual items under Schedule K are defined as follows:

Item (4) This refers to the amount owed by the mortgagor, without giving effect to any write-downs in the book value of the loan made at any time prior to, or at the time of, foreclosure.

Item (5) This refers only to amounts paid out *prior* to foreclosure. Since the purpose is to measure the amount that the mortgagee has invested in a particular item of property, reports should exclude all payments of taxes and insurance for which the mortgagee acted merely as a transmitting agency. Further, amounts paid out prior to foreclosure should not be reported if they were included elsewhere in this schedule (e.g., if they were capitalized and shown in the loan balance given in Item 4).

Item (6) Give the amount of any delinquent interest which was due on the loan at the time it was transferred to real estate, provided this was not added to the loan balance and reported under Item 4. Note that it will be necessary to check under Item 6 if delinquent interest is calculated on a compound interest basis. Do not check if your calculation of delinquent interest is made on the basis of simple interest.

Item (8) Report all foreclosure costs, including legal, court, and advertising costs, incurred in connection with the foreclosure. Whether foreclosure costs are capitalized into the book value of the property or are charged currently against income does not matter for purposes of this schedule. You are asked merely to report the *amount* of the incurred costs.

Item (10) Any recoveries made through deficiency judgments or other settlements should be reported here.

Items (11), (12), and *(13)* If the income earned from property while held as real estate, and the expenses incurred on it (including expenditures for repairs and permanent improvements, and expenses incurred in connection with the sale of the property), are available separately, these should be recorded as indicated on the schedule. However, if there is available only a figure of net income or loss, this can be reported as such under Item 13 with a plus or minus sign to indicate its character.

Item (14) Report only the sale price of the property. Any expenses in connection with the sale (e.g., commissions) should be reported under Item 12.

Item (16) This summarizes the foregoing items in a figure of final loss or gain. As indicated above, you may build up this figure of loss or gain according to the sequence of items indicated in Schedule K; but if your records provide a direct single figure of loss or gain on the property, this figure may be substituted for Item 16 with a general statement, in a note accompanying the group of returned cards, explaining the difference between the process by which this figure was arrived at and the type of calculation indicated in Schedule K. In any case we would like to have a separate reporting of Items 7 and 14.

It will be noted that this schedule ignores changes by adjustment in the book value of real estate. We are doing this because increases in the book value of property, representing a capitalization of costs such as those incurred under Items 5, 6, 8, and 12, will have been provided for by these items; while decreases in the book value of acquired real estate can be ignored in this analysis of sold properties.

* * *

EXHIBIT 4

National Bureau of Economic Research — MORTGAGE LOAN EXPERIENCE CARD — Financial Research Program

A. [ ]

B. Location of property: State__________ City or town__________

C. Type of property (check one)
- 1 ( ) One-family, no business
- 2 ( ) Two-family, no business
- 3 ( ) Three-family, no business
- 4 ( ) Four-family, no business
- 5 ( ) Business and 1- to 4-family
- 6 ( ) Apartments, no business
- 7 ( ) Apartments and business
- 8 ( ) Office building
- 9 ( ) Store only
- 10 ( ) Store and office
- 11 ( ) Manufacturing and industrial
- 12 ( ) Vacant lot or land
- 13 ( ) Other (please specify) ______

D. Type of loan at time of making (check one)
- 1 ( ) FHA
- 2 ( ) Conventional, fully amortized
- 3 ( ) Conventional, partially amortized
- 4 ( ) Conventional, nonamortized
- 5 ( ) Veterans Adm. guar. or ins. loan

E. Original schedule of payments (check)

	Prin.	Int.
1. Monthly	( )	( )
2. Quarterly	( )	( )
3. Semi-annual	( )	( )
4. Annual	( )	( )
5. None	( )	

F. Is this a purchase money mortgage? Yes ( ) No ( )

G. Is this a real estate sales contract? Yes ( ) No ( )

H. Original loan: (1) Year loan was made __________
(2) Amt. $__________ (3) Appraised value $__________
(4) Contract term (in years) __________
(5) Contract rate of interest __________%

I. Subsequent modifications in loan or sales contract:

	Unpaid Balance at Time of Modification (2)	Changes in Outstanding Balance			Extension of Contract Term (in yrs.) (6)	Change in Contract Rate of Interest (7)	Changes in Loan Type (see D above) (8)	New Appraisal (9)	Unpaid Balance after Modifications (10)
		Advance of Additional Funds (3)	Reduction of Principal						
Month and Year of Modification (1)			By Compromise (4)	By Payment (5)					
First	$	$	$	$		to____%		$	$
Second						to____%			
Third						to____%			

J. Loan status: (1) Still on books (state unpaid balance) $__________ (2) Paid off (year) __________
(3) Transferred to HOLC (year) __________ (4) Loan sold or assigned (year) __________
(5) Title acquired (year) __________; by foreclosure ( ); by voluntary deed ( )

(If property was acquired and sold fill in Schedule K on reverse side of this card)

(continued on next page)

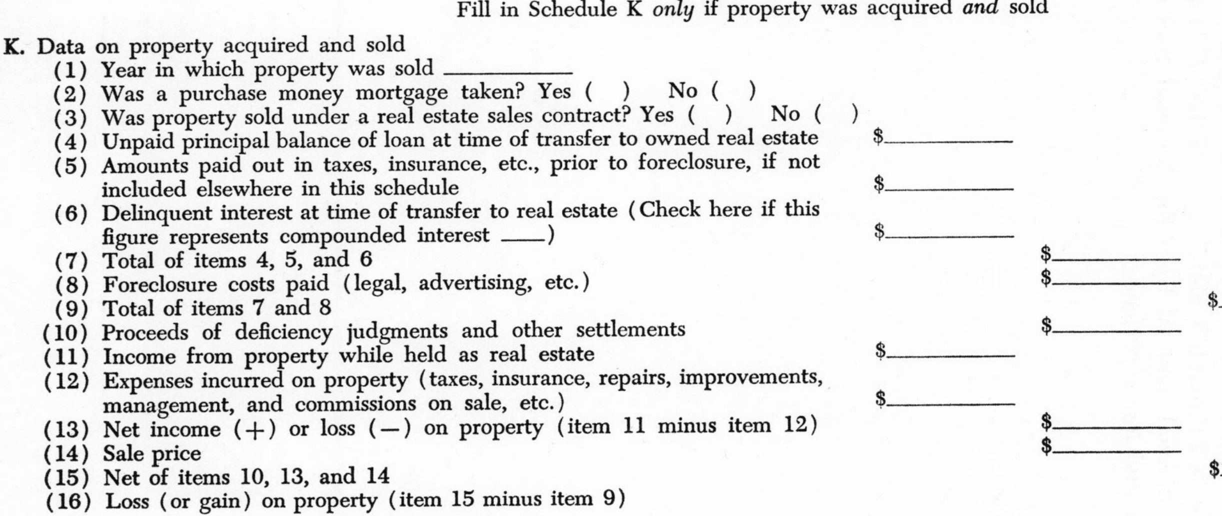

EXHIBIT 4 (continued)

Fill in Schedule K *only* if property was acquired *and* sold

K. Data on property acquired and sold

(1) Year in which property was sold ________			
(2) Was a purchase money mortgage taken? Yes ( ) No ( )			
(3) Was property sold under a real estate sales contract? Yes ( ) No ( )			
(4) Unpaid principal balance of loan at time of transfer to owned real estate	$________		
(5) Amounts paid out in taxes, insurance, etc., prior to foreclosure, if not included elsewhere in this schedule	$________		
(6) Delinquent interest at time of transfer to real estate (Check here if this figure represents compounded interest ____)	$________		
(7) Total of items 4, 5, and 6		$________	
(8) Foreclosure costs paid (legal, advertising, etc.)		$________	
(9) Total of items 7 and 8			$________
(10) Proceeds of deficiency judgments and other settlements		$________	
(11) Income from property while held as real estate	$________		
(12) Expenses incurred on property (taxes, insurance, repairs, improvements, management, and commissions on sale, etc.)	$________		
(13) Net income (+) or loss (−) on property (item 11 minus item 12)		$________	
(14) Sale price		$________	
(15) Net of items 10, 13, and 14			$________
(16) Loss (or gain) on property (item 15 minus item 9)			

APPENDIX C

PERIODIC DATA OF INSTITUTIONALLY HELD NONFARM MORTGAGE DEBT, LOAN CHARACTERISTICS, AND CREDIT EXPERIENCE

Tables C-1 through C-10 present the data that are shown graphically in Charts 2 through 5, and 7 and 8. Tables C-11 through C-13 provide additional material from the National Bureau survey on foreclosure and loss experience.

TABLE C-1

Nonfarm Mortgage Debt Held by Institutional Lenders, 1920-53

(dollar figures in millions)

	AMOUNT OUTSTANDING					PERCENTAGE DISTRIBUTION			
END OF YEAR	*Mutual Savings Banks*	*Commercial Banks*	*Life Ins. Cos.*	*Savings & Loan Assocs.*	*Total*	*Mutual Savings Banks*	*Commercial Banks*	*Life Ins. Cos.*	*Savings & Loan Assocs.*
1920	$ 2,615	$ 2,236	$ 1,172	$ 1,873	$ 7,896	33%	28%	15%	24%
1921	2,780	2,183	1,349	2,137	8,449	33	26	16	25
1922	3,011	2,370	1,524	2,468	9,373	32	25	16	26
1923	3,358	2,874	1,857	2,917	11,006	31	26	17	26
1924	3,748	3,442	2,292	3,519	13,001	29	26	18	27
1925	4,148	4,080	2,768	4,204	15,200	27	27	18	28
1926	4,553	4,352	3,484	4,810	17,199	27	25	20	28
1927	4,986	4,636	3,991	5,488	19,101	26	24	21	29
1928	5,387	4,953	4,663	6,060	21,063	26	23	22	29
1929	5,777	5,074	5,215	6,507	22,573	26	22	23	29
1930	5,898	4,893	5,541	6,402	22,734	26	22	24	28
1931	6,046	4,593	5,689	5,890	22,218	27	21	26	26
1932	5,907	4,030	5,480	5,148	20,565	29	20	27	25
1933	5,692	2,951	5,068	4,437	18,148	31	16	28	24
1934	5,342	2,769	4,611	3,710	16,432	32	17	28	23
1935	5,079	2,885	4,284	3,292	15,540	33	19	28	21
1936	4,901	3,003	4,175	3,286	15,365	32	20	27	21
1937	4,866	3,173	4,327	3,464	15,830	31	20	27	22
1938	4,803	3,445	4,556	3,614	16,418	29	21	28	22
1939	4,807	3,697	4,794	3,806	17,104	28	22	28	22
1940	4,829	4,003	5,073	4,125	18,030	27	22	28	23
1941	4,784	4,340	5,529	4,578	19,231	25	22	29	24
1942	4,601	4,256	5,830	4,583	19,270	24	22	30	24
1943	4,395	4,058	5,873	4,584	18,910	23	22	31	24
1944	4,281	3,966	5,886	4,800	18,933	23	21	31	25
1945	4,184	4,251	5,860	5,376	19,671	21	22	30	27
1946	4,415	6,533	6,360	7,141	24,449	18	27	26	29
1947	4,828	8,623	7,780	8,856	30,087	16	29	26	29
1948	5,773	10,023	9,843	10,305	35,944	16	28	27	29
1949	6,668	10,736	11,768	11,616	40,788	16	26	29	29
1950	8,218	12,695	14,775	13,622	49,310	17	26	30	28
1951	9,869	13,728	17,787	15,520	56,904	17	24	31	27
1952	11,327	14,809	19,546	18,336	64,018	18	23	30	29
1953[a]	12,890	15,768	21,436	21,929	72,023	18	22	30	30

Data for mutual savings banks for 1929-38 and 1945-53, and for commercial banks from 1938 on, are from *Survey of Current Business* (Department of Commerce), September 1953, Table 6, p. 18, and October 1954, Table 6, p. 19. Revised estimates for mutuals for 1939-44 and for commercial banks for 1940 were supplied by the Board of Governors of the Federal Reserve System. Data for savings and loan associations from 1922 on are from *Trends in the Savings and Loan Field, 1953* (Home Loan Bank Board), Table 1, p. 4. Data for life insurance companies for all years are from *Life Insurance Fact Book, 1954* (Institute of Life Insurance), p. 74. Data for years not covered by the given sources are estimates of the National Bureau of Economic Research.

[a] Preliminary.

TABLE C-2

Institutionally Held Mortgage Debt on Nonfarm Homes, 1925-53
(*dollar figures in millions*)

	AMOUNT OUTSTANDING					PERCENTAGE DISTRIBUTION			
END OF YEAR	*Mutual Savings Banks*	*Commercial Banks*	*Life Ins. Cos.*	*Savings & Loan Assocs.*	*Total*	*Mutual Savings Banks*	*Commercial Banks*	*Life Ins. Cos.*	*Savings & Loan Assocs.*
1925	$1,547	$ 1,376	$ 837	$ 3,994	$ 7,754	20%	18%	11%	51%
1926	1,713	1,796	1,062	4,570	9,141	19	20	12	50
1927	1,922	1,927	1,254	5,214	10,317	19	19	12	50
1928	2,139	2,145	1,445	5,757	11,486	19	19	13	50
1929	2,286	2,207	1,626	6,182	12,301	19	18	13	50
1930	2,341	2,199	1,732	6,082	12,354	19	18	14	49
1931	2,436	2,085	1,775	5,596	11,892	20	18	15	47
1932	2,446	1,887	1,724	4,891	10,948	22	17	16	45
1933	2,354	1,707	1,599	4,215	9,875	24	17	16	43
1934	2,190	1,450	1,379	3,525	8,544	26	17	16	41
1935	2,089	1,541	1,281	3,127	8,038	26	19	16	39
1936	2,082	1,634	1,245	3,122	8,083	26	20	15	39
1937	2,111	1,786	1,246	3,291	8,434	25	21	15	39
1938	2,119	1,910	1,320	3,433	8,782	24	22	15	39
1939	2,128	2,096	1,490	3,616	9,330	23	22	16	39
1940	2,162	2,363	1,758	3,919	10,202	21	23	17	38
1941	2,189	2,672	1,976	4,349	11,186	20	24	18	39
1942	2,128	2,752	2,255	4,349	11,484	18	24	20	38
1943	2,033	2,706	2,410	4,355	11,504	18	23	21	38
1944	1,937	2,703	2,458	4,617	11,715	17	23	21	39
1945	1,894	2,875	2,258	5,156	12,183	16	24	18	42
1946	2,033	4,576	2,570	6,840	16,019	13	29	16	43
1947	2,283	6,303	3,459	8,475	20,520	11	31	17	41
1948	2,835	7,396	4,925	9,841	24,997	11	30	20	39
1949	3,364	7,956	5,970	11,117	28,407	12	28	21	39
1950	4,312	9,481	8,392	13,104	35,289	12	27	24	37
1951	5,331	10,275	10,814	14,801	41,221	13	25	26	36
1952	6,194	11,250	11,996	17,590	47,030	13	24	26	37
1953[a]	7,373	12,025	13,000	21,042	53,440	14	23	24	39

From *Housing Statistics* (Housing and Home Finance Agency), January 1954, p. 20, and *Survey of Current Business* (Department of Commerce), October 1954, Table 6, p. 19.

[a] Preliminary.

TABLE C-3
Institutionally Held Mortgage Debt on Nonfarm Income-Producing Properties, 1925-53
(*dollar figures in millions*)

END OF YEAR	AMOUNT OUTSTANDING					PERCENTAGE DISTRIBUTION			
	Mutual Savings Banks	*Commercial Banks*	*Life Ins. Cos.*	*Savings & Loan Assocs.*	*Total*	*Mutual Savings Banks*	*Commercial Banks*	*Life Ins. Cos.*	*Savings & Loan Assocs.*
1925	$2,601	$2,704	$1,931	$210	$ 7,446	35%	36%	26%	3%
1926	2,840	2,556	2,422	240	8,058	35	32	30	3
1927	3,064	2,709	2,737	274	8,784	35	31	31	3
1928	3,248	2,808	3,218	303	9,577	34	29	34	3
1929	3,491	2,867	3,589	325	10,272	34	28	35	3
1930	3,557	2,694	3,809	320	10,380	34	26	37	3
1931	3,610	2,508	3,914	294	10,326	35	24	38	3
1932	3,461	2,143	3,756	257	9,617	36	22	39	3
1933	3,338	1,244	3,469	222	8,273	40	15	42	3
1934	3,152	1,319	3,232	185	7,888	40	17	41	2
1935	2,990	1,344	3,003	165	7,502	40	18	40	2
1936	2,819	1,369	2,930	164	7,282	39	19	40	2
1937	2,755	1,387	3,081	173	7,396	37	19	42	2
1938	2,684	1,535	3,236	181	7,636	35	20	42	2
1939	2,679	1,601	3,304	190	7,774	35	21	42	2
1940	2,667	1,634	3,315	206	7,822	34	21	42	3
1941	2,595	1,668	3,553	229	8,045	32	21	44	3
1942	2,473	1,504	3,575	234	7,786	32	19	46	3
1943	2,362	1,352	3,463	229	7,406	32	18	47	3
1944	2,344	1,263	3,428	183	7,218	33	17	47	3
1945	2,290	1,376	3,602	220	7,488	31	18	48	3
1946	2,382	1,957	3,790	301	8,430	28	23	45	4
1947	2,545	2,320	4,321	381	9,567	27	24	45	4
1948	2,938	2,627	4,918	464	10,947	27	24	45	4
1949	3,304	2,780	5,798	499	12,381	27	22	47	4
1950	3,906	3,214	6,383	518	14,021	28	23	45	4
1951	4,538	3,453	6,973	719	15,683	29	22	44	5
1952	5,133	3,559	7,550	746	16,988	30	21	44	4
1953[a]	5,517	3,743	8,436	887	18,583	30	20	45	5

Computed from Tables C-1 and C-2.
[a] Preliminary.

TABLE C-4

Institutional Lenders Classified by Size of Nonfarm Mortgage Portfolio, 1946:
Number of Institutions and Amount Outstanding
(*dollar figures in millions*)

NONFARM MORTGAGE LOAN PORTFOLIO	MUTUAL SAVINGS BANKS[a]		INSURED COMMERCIAL BANKS[b]		LIFE INSURANCE COMPANIES[c]		SAVINGS AND LOAN ASSOCIATIONS[d]	
	No.	*Amt.*	*No.*	*Amt.*	*No.*	*Amt.*	*No.*	*Amt.*
None	..	..	506	..	36	..	..	..
$1,000 - 99,999	8	e	7,215	$ 229	57	$ 2	693	$ 27
100,000 - 249,999	11	$ 2	2,408	388	35	6	1,098	129
250,000 - 499,999	28	10	1,403	495	21	7	1,175	299
500,000 - 0.9 million	69	54	937	662	35	25	1,031	520
1 - 1.9 million	87	127	488	676	44	65	1,042 (1 - 2.49 million)	1,240 (1 - 2.49 million)
2 - 2.49 million	43	95	99	224	7	16		
2.5 - 4.9 million	109	379	170	580	30	111	624	1,606
5 - 9.9 million	80	556	65	417	28	201	269	1,346
10 - 24.9 million	54	832	29	442	30	475	132	1,341
25 - 49.9 million	25	864	5	148	12	391	29 (25 million and over)	768 (25 million and over)
50 - 99.9 million	11	723	3	236	13	896		
100 million and over	6	801	2	623	17	4,148		
Total	531	$4,443	13,330	$5,120	365	$6,343	6,093	$7,276

Compiled from records of the National Association of Mutual Savings Banks and the Federal Deposit Insurance Corporation, and from *Compendium of Official Life Insurance Reports, 1947* (Spectator Company); data for savings and loan associations prepared by the Operating Analysis Division of the Home Loan Bank Board.

[a] Distributions refer to total mortgage loan portfolios as of December 31.

[b] Covers all banks in continental United States, as of June 30.

[c] Distributions as of December 31, excluding five companies for which data were not available.

[d] Covers all operating associations, as of December 31, classified by asset size. Amounts refer to gross mortgage debt, inclusive of mortgage pledged shares.

[e] Less than $500,000.

TABLE C-5

Contract Interest Rates of Sampled Nonfarm Home Mortgage Loans, 1920-47, by Year Loan Made

	LIFE INSURANCE COS.			COMMERCIAL BANKS			SAVINGS & LOAN ASSOCS.		
		Cont. Int. Rate			*Cont. Int. Rate*			*Cont. Int. Rate*	
YEAR MADE	*No. of Loans*	*Annual Average*	*3-Year Moving Average*	*No. of Loans*	*Annual Average*	*3-Year Moving Average*	*No. of Loans*	*Annual Average*	*3-Year Moving Average*
1920	73	6.1%	..	69	6.2%	..	69	7.0%	..
1921	119	6.2	6.1%	58	6.2	6.2%	58	7.3	7.1%
1922	170	6.1	6.0	113	6.2	6.2	79	7.0	7.1
1923	209	5.9	5.9	147	6.2	6.1	84	7.0	7.0
1924	279	5.9	5.9	182	6.1	6.1	85	7.0	7.0
1925	358	5.9	5.9	200	6.1	6.0	129	6.9	6.9
1926	478	5.8	5.9	182	5.9	6.0	114	6.9	6.9
1927	414	5.9	5.9	188	6.1	6.0	129	6.8	6.8
1928	411	5.9	5.9	186	6.1	6.1	134	6.7	6.8
1929	396	6.0	6.0	134	6.1	6.1	129	6.8	6.8
1930	347	6.0	6.0	114	6.2	6.0	107	6.9	6.8
1931	299	6.0	6.0	114	5.8	6.0	50	6.6	6.8
1932	98	6.0	6.0	41	6.1	5.9	26	7.0	6.7
1933	15	5.9	6.0	32	6.3	6.2	24	6.5	6.6
1934	26	5.8	5.6	32	6.1	5.8	38	6.4	6.3
1935	64	5.5	5.3	87	5.6	5.5	63	6.2	6.3
1936	163	5.2	5.2	106	5.3	5.4	79	6.4	6.2
1937	192	5.1	5.1	136	5.3	5.2	111	6.0	6.1
1938	255	5.1	5.0	151	5.1	5.1	115	6.0	6.0
1939	285	4.9	4.9	198	5.0	4.9	146	6.0	5.9
1940	404	4.6	4.7	220	4.7	4.8	130	5.7	5.7
1941	584	4.6	4.6	194	4.7	4.7	168	5.6	5.6
1942	613	4.5	4.5	160	4.6	4.6	105	5.5	5.6
1943	459	4.5	4.5	152	4.7	4.6	135	5.6	5.4
1944	286	4.5	4.5	152	4.6	4.5	165	5.3	5.3
1945	235	4.4	4.3	164	4.5	4.4	195	5.1	4.9
1946	311	4.2	4.3	380	4.3	4.4	268	4.7	4.8
1947	72	4.0	..	81	4.4	..	184	4.7	4.7

Based on National Bureau of Economic Research survey of urban mortgage lending. Refers to straight loans (i.e. exclusive of purchase money mortgages and real estate sales contracts) that were secured by one- to four-family homes; excludes loans for which year made or interest rate was lacking. Averages are weighted by the original amounts of the included loans.

TABLE C-6

Contract Lengths of Sampled Nonfarm Home Mortgage Loans, 1920-47, by Year Loan Made

	LIFE INSURANCE COS.			COMMERCIAL BANKS			SAVINGS & LOAN ASSOCS.		
		Cont. Length			*Cont. Length*			*Cont. Length*	
YEAR MADE	*No. of Loans*	*Annual Average*	*3-Year Moving Average*	*No. of Loans*	*Annual Average*	*3-Year Moving Average*	*No. of Loans*	*Annual Average*	*3-Year Moving Average*
1920	73	6.0 yrs.	..	68	2.9 yrs.	..	65	11.3 yrs.	..
1921	119	7.9	6.9 yrs.	58	1.8	2.7 yrs.	54	10.6	11.2 yrs.
1922	170	6.6	6.5	113	2.9	2.7	72	11.5	11.2
1923	209	5.9	5.9	147	2.9	3.2	80	11.2	11.1
1924	280	5.7	5.8	182	3.5	3.2	82	11.1	11.0
1925	358	6.0	5.8	200	3.1	3.4	124	10.9	11.0
1926	477	5.9	6.2	182	3.6	3.1	104	11.2	11.1
1927	412	6.7	6.4	188	2.5	3.1	119	11.4	11.3
1928	410	6.6	6.7	186	3.2	3.0	124	11.4	11.3
1929	396	6.8	6.9	134	3.7	3.4	118	11.2	11.2
1930	347	7.5	7.3	114	3.6	3.4	99	10.8	11.0
1931	295	7.8	7.7	114	3.0	3.2	42	10.8	10.8
1932	96	7.9	7.8	41	3.0	2.9	24	11.3	11.0
1933	14	6.3	7.7	32	2.1	2.8	18	11.1	11.4
1934	26	7.9	11.0	32	2.9	7.1	33	11.7	11.7
1935	64	13.0	14.7	87	9.8	8.9	59	11.9	11.6
1936	164	16.2	16.0	106	9.7	9.6	78	11.4	12.2
1937	192	16.7	17.0	136	9.6	11.0	107	12.8	12.8
1938	254	17.7	17.6	151	13.2	12.9	112	13.7	13.1
1939	285	18.3	18.8	198	14.8	14.9	143	12.9	13.8
1940	403	19.9	19.8	220	16.0	15.1	124	14.6	13.8
1941	582	20.6	20.6	194	14.4	14.6	163	13.9	14.0
1942	611	21.1	21.1	160	12.7	13.3	103	13.5	13.6
1943	459	21.7	21.4	152	12.4	10.4	132	13.4	13.5
1944	286	22.1	21.4	152	10.0	10.4	162	13.6	13.8
1945	231	20.0	20.2	164	9.3	11.5	191	14.3	14.5
1946	311	18.8	19.3	380	12.7	12.2	262	15.0	14.9
1947	72	19.5	..	81	14.8	..	181	15.2	15.1

Based on National Bureau of Economic Research survey of urban mortgage lending. Refers to straight loans (i.e. exclusive of purchase money mortgages and real estate sales contracts) that were secured by one- to four-family homes; excludes loans for which year made or contract length was lacking. Averages are weighted by the original amounts of the included loans.

TABLE C-7

Loan-to-Value Ratios of Sampled Nonfarm Home Mortgage Loans, 1920-47, by Year Loan Made

	LIFE INSURANCE COS.			COMMERCIAL BANKS			SAVINGS & LOAN ASSOCS.		
		Loan/Val. Ratio			*Loan/Val. Ratio*			*Loan/Val. Ratio*	
YEAR MADE	*No. of Loans*	*Annual Average*	*3-Year Moving Average*	*No. of Loans*	*Annual Average*	*3-Year Moving Average*	*No. of Loans*	*Annual Average*	*3-Year Moving Average*
1920	49	46%	..	64	48%	..	49	59%	..
1921	61	44	46%	57	49	50%	46	56	57%
1922	117	47	47	108	51	50	59	58	57
1923	182	48	49	144	50	51	61	57	57
1924	260	50	49	176	52	51	62	58	58
1925	333	49	50	195	50	51	98	60	58
1926	448	51	51	178	51	52	83	57	58
1927	383	51	51	187	54	53	98	56	58
1928	354	53	52	180	53	53	104	60	59
1929	312	52	52	127	53	52	107	61	60
1930	248	53	52	113	50	51	89	59	60
1931	226	52	52	111	50	50	43	59	60
1932	70	49	52	41	51	51	21	63	60
1933	14	46	50	31	57	52	17	56	61
1934	24	53	52	32	50	57	34	61	60
1935	62	53	58	84	60	59	50	60	61
1936	163	61	61	104	61	60	69	62	62
1937	191	64	64	130	60	62	104	62	63
1938	255	67	67	143	63	65	105	64	64
1939	284	69	70	192	69	69	131	64	66
1940	402	73	73	210	72	70	123	68	67
1941	586	76	77	191	68	69	158	68	68
1942	609	80	78	155	67	67	101	68	69
1943	459	81	81	150	66	65	127	70	71
1944	286	82	80	150	61	63	159	73	72
1945	235	76	78	164	61	66	195	73	75
1946	311	75	75	379	70	68	265	77	75
1947	72	69	..	80	69	..	183	74	76

Based on National Bureau of Economic Research survey of urban mortgage lending. Refers to straight loans (i.e. exclusive of purchase money mortgages and real estate sales contracts) that were secured by one- to four-family homes; excludes loans for which year made or other necessary data were lacking. Averages are weighted by the original amounts of the included loans.

TABLE C-8

Contract Interest Rates of Sampled Mortgage Loans on Nonfarm Income-Producing Properties, 1920-47, by Year Loan Made

YEAR MADE	LIFE INSURANCE COMPANIES			COMMERCIAL BANKS		
		Cont. Int. Rate			Cont. Int. Rate	
	No. of Loans	*Annual Average*	*3-Year Moving Average*	*No. of Loans*	*Annual Average*	*3-Year Moving Average*
1920	13	5.8%	..	8	6.0%	..
1921	16	6.5	6.0%	5	6.1	6.2%
1922	22	5.9	5.9	12	6.6	6.2
1923	29	5.7	5.8	11	6.0	5.3
1924	38	5.8	5.6	30	5.2	5.5
1925	42	5.4	5.6	29	6.0	5.4
1926	49	5.6	5.5	25	5.6	5.9
1927	44	5.5	5.5	28	6.1	5.9
1928	47	5.3	5.5	37	6.0	6.0
1929	56	5.7	5.5	24	6.1	6.0
1930	27	5.9	5.7	24	6.1	5.2
1931	16	5.4	5.6	9	4.4	5.2
1932	7	5.3	5.3	14	5.6	5.1
1933	..	..	5.2	8	5.9	5.6
1934	3	4.5	5.2	7	5.8	4.3
1935	14	5.3	4.9	9	3.7	4.3
1936	21	4.6	5.0	17	5.0	4.1
1937	22	5.1	4.9	13	5.0	5.1
1938	26	4.7	4.9	13	5.4	5.1
1939	33	4.6	4.5	20	5.0	4.2
1940	26	4.4	4.4	24	3.5	4.1
1941	38	4.3	4.4	24	4.4	3.9
1942	22	4.5	4.3	12	4.5	4.3
1943	14	4.2	4.2	17	3.9	4.2
1944	14	3.9	4.0	23	4.2	4.2
1945	18	4.2	4.1	27	4.2	4.0
1946	22	4.2	4.2	52	3.9	4.0
1947	1	4.0	..	12	4.4	..

Based on National Bureau of Economic Research survey of urban mortgage lending. Refers to straight loans (i.e. exclusive of purchase money mortgages and real estate sales contracts) that were secured by properties other than one- to four-family homes; excludes loans for which year made or interest rate was lacking. Averages are weighted by the original amounts of the included loans.

TABLE C-9

Contract Lengths of Sampled Mortgage Loans on Nonfarm Income-Producing Properties, 1920-47, by Year Loan Made

	LIFE INSURANCE COMPANIES			COMMERCIAL BANKS		
		Cont. Length			*Cont. Length*	
YEAR MADE	*No. of Loans*	*Annual Average*	*3-Year Moving Average*	*No. of Loans*	*Annual Average*	*3-Year Moving Average*
1920	13	4.2 yrs.	..	8	4.1 yrs.	..
1921	15	5.4	5.5 yrs.	5	5.0	4.2 yrs.
1922	22	6.3	5.9	12	4.1	2.9
1923	28	5.8	6.4	11	2.1	8.4
1924	38	7.0	6.7	30	9.1	7.1
1925	42	6.9	7.2	29	2.7	7.0
1926	49	7.6	7.7	25	4.4	3.3
1927	43	8.3	7.9	28	3.3	4.2
1928	47	7.9	7.8	37	4.5	4.3
1929	56	7.1	7.4	24	4.9	4.9
1930	27	7.0	7.2	24	6.1	7.1
1931	16	8.0	6.4	9	8.5	5.6
1932	7	3.9	5.9	14	2.9	5.3
1933	..	..	4.1	8	3.5	3.0
1934	3	5.6	9.4	7	3.3	3.2
1935	14	9.7	10.1	9	3.2	3.8
1936	21	10.6	11.3	17	6.2	4.0
1937	22	12.2	14.3	13	4.6	5.7
1938	26	22.0	15.5	13	5.6	6.5
1939	33	15.3	16.1	20	7.7	7.8
1940	26	13.9	15.2	24	8.5	7.8
1941	39	17.5	14.8	24	6.2	7.8
1942	22	13.2	15.3	12	8.0	6.6
1943	14	13.6	12.8	17	6.6	5.8
1944	14	12.1	12.4	23	5.3	6.9
1945	18	12.0	16.2	27	8.9	5.6
1946	23	20.2	18.1	52	4.8	5.6
1947	1	21.0	..	12	4.3	..

Based on National Bureau of Economic Research survey of urban mortgage lending. Refers to straight loans (i.e. exclusive of purchase money mortgages and real estate sales contracts) that were secured by properties other than one- to four-family homes; excludes loans for which year made or contract length was lacking. Averages are weighted by the original amounts of the included loans.

TABLE C-10
Loan-to-Value Ratios of Sampled Mortgage Loans on Nonfarm Income-Producing Properties, 1920-47, by Year Loan Made

YEAR MADE	LIFE INSURANCE COMPANIES			COMMERCIAL BANKS		
		Loan/Value Ratio			*Loan/Value Ratio*	
	No. of Loans	*Annual Average*	*3-Year Moving Average*	*No. of Loans*	*Annual Average*	*3-Year Moving Average*
1920	13	49%	..	8	41%	..
1921	16	39	45%	5	45	43%
1922	22	47	46	12	46	47
1923	29	50	45	9	48	43
1924	38	40	43	28	43	40
1925	42	42	46	27	28	41
1926	49	52	49	25	52	40
1927	44	52	52	26	49	51
1928	47	53	50	36	51	50
1929	56	44	48	24	47	50
1930	27	45	42	23	52	41
1931	15	33	40	9	34	41
1932	7	40	37	13	54	37
1933	..	..	41	7	44	49
1934	3	48	51	7	50	30
1935	14	51	48	9	24	33
1936	21	46	52	16	52	31
1937	22	56	55	13	35	45
1938	25	64	57	13	39	40
1939	33	54	58	19	43	46
1940	26	57	57	23	55	48
1941	39	61	58	24	47	50
1942	22	57	58	12	51	49
1943	14	53	54	17	51	54
1944	14	53	56	23	56	53
1945	18	61	56	25	50	59
1946	23	57	58	50	63	59
1947	1	60	..	12	43	..

Based on National Bureau of Economic Research survey of urban mortgage lending. Refers to straight loans (i.e. exclusive of purchase money mortgages and real estate sales contracts) that were secured by properties other than one- to four-family homes; excludes loans for which year made or other necessary data were lacking. Averages are weighted by the original amounts of the included loans.

TABLE C-11

Foreclosure Rates for Sampled Nonfarm Mortgage Loans, 1920-47, by Period Loan Made and by Amortization or Insurance Provision

PERIOD MADE AND TYPE OF LOAN	1- TO 4-FAMILY HOMES						ALL OTHER PROPERTY			
	Life Insurance Companies		*Commercial Banks*		*Savings and Loan Assocs.*[a]		*Life Insurance Companies*		*Commercial Banks*	
	No.	*Amt.*	*No.*	*Amt.*	*No.*	*Amt.*	*No.*	*Amt.*	*No.*	*Amt.*
1920-29										
Fully amortized	7.9%	9.0%	6.6%	6.0%	8.7%[b]	9.2%[b]	11.7%	6.6%	13.6%	8.6%
Partially amortized	17.4	20.3	7.6	8.4	..	..	22.6	29.9	12.5	20.7
Nonamortized	22.2	23.2	7.4	9.7	4.5	5.4	18.9	27.0	10.9	7.1
1930-34										
Fully amortized	15.9	17.8	2.9	3.7	9.6[b]	12.8[b]	18.0 (fully and partially amortized)	14.8 (fully and partially amortized)	8.8	3.1
Partially amortized	16.0	19.0	5.8	5.4	..	..				
Nonamortized	24.4	28.1	5.5	8.0	12.5	11.4	7.1	1.6	5.9	1.3
1935-39										
Fully amortized	0.9	1.6	0.4	0.7	0.9[b]	1.5[b]	0	0	11.4	12.3
Partially amortized	5.3	4.8	1.9	4.2	..	..	0	0	6.7	17.7
Nonamortized	0	0	0.8	0.9	0	0	d	d	0	0
Insured[c]	0.8	0.9	0	0	0	0	d	d	0	0
1940-47										
Fully amortized	0.3	0.2	0	0	0	0	0.9	0.2	0	0
Partially amortized	0	0	0	0	..	..	1.1	0.1	0.9	e
Nonamortized	0	0	0	0	0	0	d	d	0	0
Insured[c]	0.2	0.2	0	0	0.4	0.2	d	d	0	0

Based on National Bureau of Economic Research survey of urban mortgage lending. For number and original amount of sampled loans, see Table A-11. Foreclosure rate is the number or original amount of loans made in a given period and foreclosed before date of report (1947) as a percentage of all loans made in that period.

[a] Includes loans secured by all types of property (95 percent representing loans on one- to four-family homes) classified by the following periods: 1920-29, 1930-34, 1935-41, and 1942-47.

[b] Includes the following types of loan: direct reduction, cancel and endorse, and share accumulation plan.

[c] Includes FHA-insured and VA-guaranteed loans.

[d] Not shown because less than ten loans included.

[e] Less than 0.05 percent.

TABLE C-12

Foreclosure Rates for Sampled Nonfarm Home Mortgage Loans Made 1920-29 and Outstanding January 1, 1930, by Year Loan Made and Other Characteristics

LOAN CHARACTERISTICS	LIFE INSURANCE COMPANIES		COMMERCIAL BANKS		SAVINGS AND LOAN ASSOCS.	
	No.	*Amt.*	*No.*	*Amt.*	*No.*	*Amt.*
YEAR LOAN MADE						
1920-22	8.5%	15.5%	8.3%	7.1%	4.4%	3.6%
1923	14.1	20.3	3.2	5.1	6.3[a]	7.9[a]
1924	18.5	23.7	9.3	12.5	10.9	13.2
1925	16.5	16.7	14.4	15.7	16.3	12.8
1926	22.1	25.1	16.2	12.2	15.6	15.3
1927	23.1	22.2	11.9	13.7	11.9	11.1
1928	24.4	28.8	13.3	15.2	14.6	14.9
1929	26.1	29.3	12.9	15.5	12.1	19.4
TYPE OF LOAN						
Fully amortized	11.4	13.0	10.2	9.1	12.3[b]	13.4[b]
Partially amortized	23.0	25.8	12.2	12.9	..	..
Nonamortized	26.8	27.3	12.8	14.3	9.7[a]	10.0[a]
CONTRACT INTEREST RATE						
5.0 - 5.9%	16.6	16.0	6.8	1.9	3.2[a]	3.9[a]
6.0 - 6.9	23.0	27.0	13.0	14.5	10.1	10.8
7.0 - 9.9	21.9[a]	38.3[a]	8.1	12.7	14.0	16.0
CONTRACT LENGTH						
0 - 4 years	25.9	26.1	12.4	16.3	7.1[a]	10.2[a]
5 - 9	23.0	26.8	9.1	6.0	18.6	20.5
10 - 14	14.3	17.0	17.9	15.0	11.4	13.0
15 and over	26.7	23.6	c	c	c	c
LOAN-TO-VALUE RATIO						
0 - 39%	15.4	21.8	5.6	6.3	6.4	11.2
40 - 49	14.2	15.5	12.6	11.3	12.5	13.9
50 - 59	27.1	29.6	12.6	12.6	12.1	14.7
60 - 79	36.3	38.5	15.2	19.1	12.8	10.4
80 and over	..	..	c	c	12.0[a]	17.9[a]
All loans	21.6%	24.4%	12.1%	13.1%	12.3%	13.5%

Based on National Bureau of Economic Research survey of urban mortgage lending; refers to loans made in the twenties that were secured by one- to four-family homes. Foreclosure rate is the number or original amount of loans foreclosed during 1930-47 as a percentage of all loans outstanding at the beginning of 1930.

[a] Based on less than fifty loans.

[b] Includes the following types of loan: direct reduction, cancel and endorse, and share accumulation plan.

[c] Not shown because less than ten loans included.

TABLE C-13

Number and Original Amount of Foreclosed Loans, and Lender's Investment at Foreclosure: Sample Loans Classified by Period of Property Disposal within Period Loan Made, 1920-47

(*dollar figures in thousands*)

PERIOD LOAN MADE	PERIOD OF PROPERTY DISPOSAL	LIFE INSURANCE COMPANIES			COMMERCIAL BANKS			SAVINGS & LOAN ASSOCS.		
		No. of Loans	*Orig. Amt.*	*Lender's Invest.*[a]	*No. of Loans*	*Orig. Amt.*	*Lender's Invest.*[a]	*No. of Loans*	*Orig. Amt.*	*Lender's Invest.*[a]
						One- to Four-Family Homes				
1920-24	*1925-47*	*45*	*$ 301*	*$ 269*	*19*	*$ 96*	*$101*	*16*	*$ 54*	*$ 65*
	1925-29	..	..	..	..	..	..	..	..	..
	1930-34	6	23	24	..	..	..	4	8	12
	1935-39	21	153	117	11	48	56	10	37	42
	1940-47	18	125	128	8	48	45	2	9	11
1925-29	*1925-47*	*419*	*2,457*	*2,642*	*113*	*580*	*672*	*91*	*297*	*317*
	1925-29	1	7	8	1	1	1	1	5	7
	1930-34	37	202	207	24	126	131	20	59	56
	1935-39	189	973	1,034	64	327	395	43	139	142
	1940-47	192	1,275	1,393	24	126	145	27	94	112
1930-34	*1930-47*	*138*[b]	*925*[b]	*1,041*[b]	*21*	*112*	*137*	*37*	*148*	*160*
	1930-34	5	43	44	2	16	18	11	40	43
	1935-39	70	463	528	15	58	70	19	75	82
	1940-47	62	416	466	4	38	49	7	33	35
1935-39	*1935-47*	*19*	*119*	*123*	*6*	*42*	*38*	*5*	*31*	*33*
	1935-39	2	11	11	..	..	..	1	7	7
	1940-47	17	108	112	6	42	38	4	24	26
1940-47	*1940-47*	8	*33*	*33*	..	..	..	*1*	*6*	*7*
	Total	629	$3,835	$4,108	159	$830	$948	150	$536	$582

(continued on next page)

TABLE C-13 (continued)
(dollar figures in thousands)

PERIOD LOAN MADE	PERIOD OF PROPERTY DISPOSAL	LIFE INSURANCE COMPANIES			COMMERCIAL BANKS			SAVINGS & LOAN ASSOCS.		
		No. of Loans	*Orig. Amt.*	*Lender's Invest.*[a]	*No. of Loans*	*Orig. Amt.*	*Lender's Invest.*[a]	*No. of Loans*	*Orig. Amt.*	*Lender's Invest.*[a]
						All Other Property				
1920-24	*1925-47*	*11*	*$ 428*	*$ 606*	*2*	*$ 6*	*$ 8*	*1*	*$ 3*	*$ 5*
	1925-29	..	..	..	1	1	2	..	..	..
	1930-34	..	..	..	..	..	..	..	..	..
	1935-39	4	214	331	1	5	6	1	3	5
	1940-47	7	214	275	..	..	..	..	..	..
1925-29	*1925-47*	*62*	*5,764*	*6,093*	*27*	*645*	*710*	*12*	*38*	*39*
	1925-29	..	..	..	..	..	..	1	4	4
	1930-34	3	67	66	1	5	31	2	7	6
	1935-39	18	1,335	1,362	15	326	326	9	27	29
	1940-47	41	4,362	4,665	11	314	353	..	..	..
1930-34	*1930-47*	*8*	*236*	*281*	*5*	*57*	*119*	..	..	..
	1930-34	..	..	..	1	5	5	..	..	..
	1935-39	3	71	90	2	16	85	..	..	..
	1940-47	5	165	191	2	36	29	..	..	..
1935-39	*1935-47*	*1*	*40*	*32*	*8*	*201*	*173*	..	..	..
	1935-39	..	..	..	1	45	71	..	..	..
	1940-47	1	40	32	7	156	102	..	..	..
1940-47	*1940-47*	*2*	*22*	*22*	*1*	*1*	*1*	..	..	..
	Total	84	$6,490	$7,034	43	$910	$1,011	13	$41	$44

Based on National Bureau of Economic Research survey of urban mortgage lending. Excludes loans for which data on gain or loss were not available.

[a] Includes unpaid loan balances; delinquent interest; advances for taxes, insurance, etc. prior to foreclosure; and foreclosure costs.

[b] Includes one loan for which period of property disposal was not available.

APPENDIX D

COMPARISON OF THE NATIONAL BUREAU SURVEY WITH THE CENSUS SURVEY OF RESIDENTIAL FINANCING

Now that the Census Bureau's tabulations of the Survey of Residential Financing have become available, it is possible to compare the National Bureau's survey with the much larger, later census survey, at least in broad outlines. In making such a comparison it should be kept in mind that there are important differences between the two surveys.

First, there is a difference of about five years between the populations surveyed—years of significant changes in lending patterns, hence in the composition of the outstanding mortgage debt.

Second, there is a conceptual difference between the populations surveyed; the data taken from the Survey of Residential Financing refer to owner-occupied homes only, while those from the National Bureau sample are unrestricted as to tenure. For life insurance companies the population sampled in the National Bureau's survey was limited to large companies; no such limitation characterizes the Survey of Residential Financing.

Many other differences between the two surveys might be mentioned: for example, one is an area, the other an establishment, sample; one uses as sampling unit a mortgaged property, the other a mortgage transaction as defined on page 128; last but not least, there is a substantial difference in the size of the loan samples.

Yet for three outstanding characteristics—type of insurance or amortization provision, type of property, and contract life expectancy of the outstanding loans—a comparison of the respective national estimates reveals no disturbing inconsistencies (Chart D-1).[1] Some of the observable discrepancies, especially with respect to insurance company portfolios and in the distributions of contract maturities, can be explained by the well-known fact that during the intervening period, there was a considerable expansion of lending activity in the market of government-insured and -guaranteed loans.

Our estimates for small groups of loans in tabulations with many breakdowns and many class intervals are bound to be considerably more doubtful—even apart from the nonresponse bias—than the results of a large-scale undertaking such as the Survey of Residential Financing.

[1] For a fourth important characteristic, interest rates, no comparison was possible because of differences in the class intervals used by the two surveys.

CHART D-1

Comparison of National Bureau of Economic Research Survey and Census Survey of Residential Financing by Selected Loan Characteristics

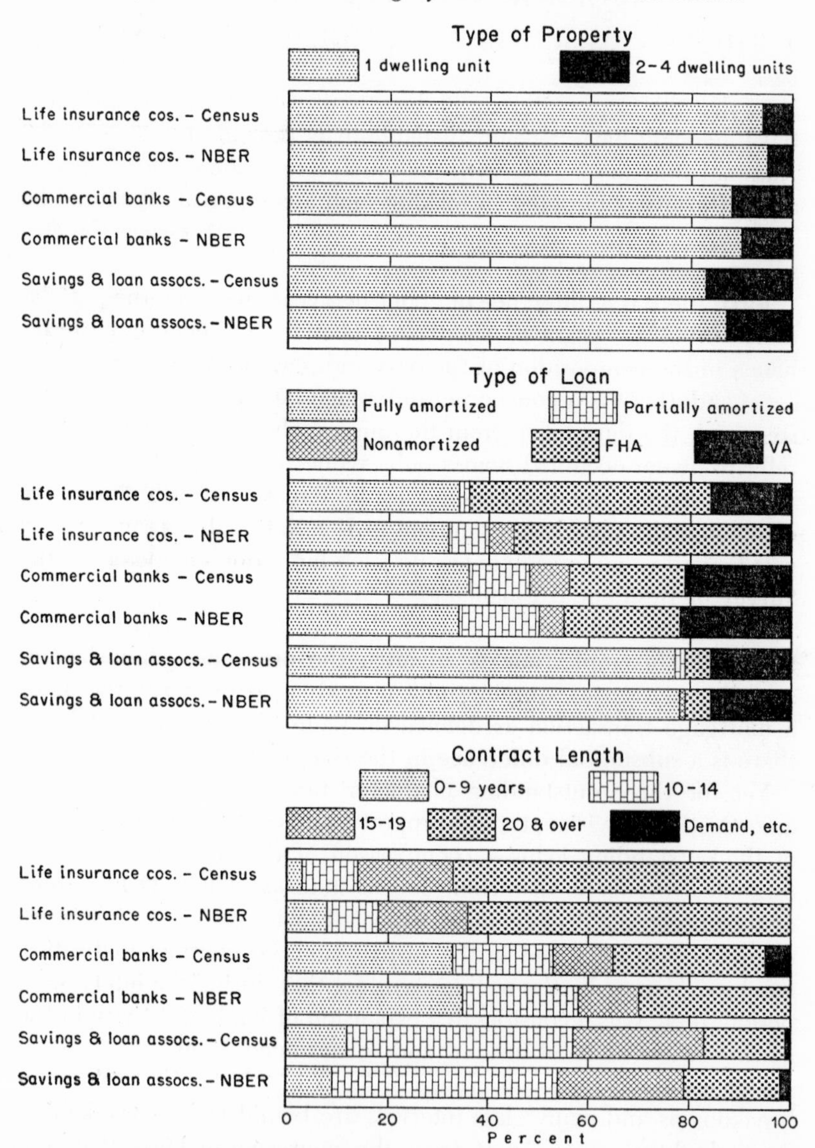

National Bureau of Economic Research survey data are based on distribution of number of loans outstanding in 1947 that were secured by one- to four-family nonfarm homes as shown in Tables 27, 28, and 29. Census data are based on number of first mortgages outstanding in April 1950 on one- to four-family nonfarm homes resided in by their owners, from *1950 Census of Housing*, Vol. 4, Residential Financing, Part 1, pp. 41, 76 f., 79, 159, and 319.

INDEX

RECENT AND FORTHCOMING PUBLICATIONS OF THE NATIONAL BUREAU OF ECONOMIC RESEARCH

NATIONAL BUREAU BOOKS *are available from bookstores or Princeton University Press, Princeton, New Jersey, except that contributors and subscribers to the National Bureau should order directly from the Bureau.* OCCASIONAL PAPERS, TECHNICAL PAPERS, *and* ANNUAL REPORTS *are available from the National Bureau of Economic Research, 261 Madison Avenue, New York 16, New York.*

BOOKS

Personal Income during Business Cycles (1956) Daniel Creamer	208 pp.	$4.00
Input-Output Analysis: An Appraisal (1955) Studies in Income and Wealth, Volume Eighteen	383 pp.	7.50
Short-Term Economic Forecasting (1955) Studies in Income and Wealth, Volume Seventeen	520 pp.	7.50
Minimum Price Fixing in the Bituminous Coal Industry (1955) Waldo E. Fisher and Charles M. James	554 pp.	10.00
Capital Formation and Economic Growth (1955) Special Conference Series No. 6	691 pp.	12.00
Business Concentration and Price Policy (1955) Special Conference Series No. 5	524 pp.	9.00
Long-Range Economic Projection (1954) Studies in Income and Wealth, Volume Sixteen	488 pp.	9.00
Mortgage Lending Experience in Agriculture (1954) Lawrence A. Jones and David Durand	257 pp.	5.00
The Frontiers of Economic Knowledge (1954) Arthur F. Burns	376 pp.	5.00
Regularization of Business Investment (1954) Special Conference Series No. 4	539 pp.	8.00
Shares of Upper Income Groups in Income and Savings (1953) Simon Kuznets	768 pp.	9.00
The Volume of Corporate Bond Financing since 1900 (1953) W. Braddock Hickman	464 pp.	7.50
Wesley Clair Mitchell: The Economic Scientist (1952) Arthur F. Burns (ed.)	398 pp.	4.00
A Study of Moneyflows in the United States (1952) Morris A. Copeland	620 pp.	7.50
The Trend of Government Activity in the United States since 1900 (1952) Solomon Fabricant	288 pp.	4.00
Federal Grants and the Business Cycle (1952) James A. Maxwell	136 pp.	2.00
Studies in Income and Wealth, Volume Fifteen (1952) Eight papers on size distribution of income	240 pp.	3.50
Conference on Research in Business Finance (1952) Special Conference Series No. 3	360 pp.	5.00
Deterioration in the Quality of Foreign Bonds Issued in the United States, 1920-1930 (1951) Ilse Mintz	112 pp.	2.00
The Transportation Industries, 1889-1946: A Study of Output, Employment, and Productivity (1951) Harold Barger	304 pp.	4.00

What Happens during Business Cycles: A Progress Report (1951) Wesley C. Mitchell	422 pp.	$5.00
The Nature and Tax Treatment of Capital Gains and Losses (1951) Lawrence H. Seltzer	576 pp.	7.50
Corporate Income Retention, 1915-43 (1951) Sergei P. Dobrovolsky	142 pp.	2.50

OCCASIONAL PAPERS

50.	*Agricultural Equipment Financing* (1955) Howard G. Diesslin	$1.25
49.	*The Korean War and United States Economic Activity, 1950-1952* (1955) Bert G. Hickman	.75
48.	*A Century and a Half of Federal Expenditures* (1955) M. Slade Kendrick	1.25
47.	*The Ownership of Tax-Exempt Securities, 1913-1953* (1955) George E. Lent	1.50
46.	*Immigration and the Foreign Born* (1954) Simon Kuznets and Ernest Rubin	1.50
45.	*Capital and Output Trends in Mining Industries, 1870-1948* (1954) Israel Borenstein	1.00
44.	*The Growth of Physical Capital in Agriculture, 1870-1950* (1954) Alvin S. Tostlebe	1.25
43.	*Trends and Cycles in Capital Formation by United States Railroads, 1870-1950* (1954) Melville J. Ulmer	1.50
42.	*The Share of Financial Intermediaries in National Wealth and National Assets, 1900-1949* (1954) Raymond W. Goldsmith	1.50
41.	*Capital and Output Trends in Manufacturing Industries, 1880-1948* (1954) Daniel Creamer	1.50

TECHNICAL PAPERS

10.	*Factors Influencing Consumption: An Experimental Analysis of Shoe Buying* (1954) Ruth P. Mack	$2.00
9.	*The Volume of Residential Construction, 1889-1950* (1954) David M. Blank	1.50

ANNUAL REPORTS (GRATIS)

By Solomon Fabricant

35th. *Government in Economic Life* (May 1955)

34th. *Economic Progress and Economic Change* (May 1954)